JOBS IN JAPAN

John Wharton

illustrations by Liz Wharton

Address orders and correspondence to:

The Global Press
1510 York St., Suite 204
Denver, Colorado 80206 USA

Edited by Teresa Falagrady
Cover Design by Marcia McEvoy

Library of Congress Cataloging in Publication Data:

Wharton, John 1951-
    Jobs in Japan.
        1. Job hunting--Japan
        2. English language--study and teaching
        3. Japan--description and travel--1945-
        4. Japan--social life and customs--1945-
I Title. HF5382.7.W46   1986
650.1'4'0952

Library of Congress Catalog Number: 82-84053

ISBN 0-911285-00-8

Printed in the United States of America

Second Edition

For the many people on both sides of the Pacific who helped to make it all possible: Sumie Uno, Kieko Ushijima, Katsu Saito, Mike Obata, Prof. Douglas Gordon, Kyle Davis, JNTO, the Japanese Ministry of Foreign Affairs, "The Vets" and especially my step-mother, Kimino Wharton, "iro iro domo arigato gozaimashita."

The Master said, "To learn and at due times to repeat what one has learned: is that not after all a pleasure? That friends should come to one from afar, is this not after all delightful?"

Confucius (551-478 B.C.)

To the Reader:

In 1979, two restless Americans headed west, *far* west-- to the very Far East. The woman of the duo, a French Lit graduate by training, was to teach English in Japan. The man, a long-time teacher of English to all manner of foreign students in America and step-son of a Japanese woman (with whom he lived in Japan as a schoolboy), was to serve as Director of Education at the same school as his spouse.

But this isn't just "our story." Instead, this guidebook is a cut-and-dried, nuts-and-bolts, meat-and-potatoes, no-nonsense (well, maybe just a *little* nonsense) explanation of how almost anyone can have the same adventure.

If you admire Japan and if you find yourself in or approaching a period of transition in your life when you could afford to spend some time overseas, don't miss this rare opportunity for an infinitely rewarding experience. The real "barriers" you face are not those of the Japanese language or culture but only those of your own uncertainty and procrastination. And while this book may be just the first of your preparations for your grand adventure, as the Master also said, "Even the journey of a thousand miles begins with a single step."

We hope it gets you off on the right foot.

Contents

一 1. Introduction....................................9
Japan: Hit Or Myth?

二 2. Where The Jobs Are....................................18
Is This Really Something Grown-Ups Do?

三 3. Voices Of The Vets....................................26
Comments Of Those Who've Done It

四 4. Of Shoguns And Showdowns....................50
A Not-Brief-Enough History

五 5. Getting There...62
Preparations For The Adventure

六

6. **The Necessary Nihongo**............73
   The Japanese You Really Need

七

7. **The Papers Chase**............81
   Getting The Right Visa

八

8. **Lessons To Be Learned**............97
   Study Opportunities

九

9. **Japan For Kids**............102
   Bringing Your Children

十

10. **Welcome To Wonderland**............106
    Your First Day In Japan

十一

11. **Masterful Transit**............116
    Using Public Transportation

十二

12. **The Nipponese Nest**............125
    Setting Up House

十三   13. **A Stroll Through Anytown**...................142
A Typical Neighborhood

十四   14. **The Class Act**...148
Teaching English In Japan

十五   15. **Arbeit Delight**.......................................160
Part-Time Work Opportunities

十六   16. **Minding Your Millions**..........................167
Where To Keep Your Savings

十七   17. **After Hours Antics**................................178
Recreation And Rehabilitation

十八   18. **Edo Alternatives**...................................192
Living And Working Outside Tokyo

十九   19. **Gambate! (Go For It!)**...........................199
In Summary

Appendix...205

Introduction

So you're interested in working in Japan. Great! I may be somewhat biased in my opinion of the idea, but I think it's one of the best things any adventurous soul could ever consider doing. And I hope you'll stick with me through the next few hundred pages so I can tell you just why it's so very "do-able."

But let me warn you, despite the first edition of this book finding its way into the hands of several thousand Japan-fans, this updated version still may not satisfy everyone. Alas, no tips here on how to retire for life after an hour on Tokyo's Wall Street. Not a single exotic Eastern exercise to make you lose twenty pounds in three minutes. Why, I can't even offer you the inside scoop on how some famous Japanese film star noodle-whipped her tell-all offspring! What I *can* do for you is show you precisely how to accomplish something you may previously have only dreamed of: living and *prospering* in Japan.

The chances are good that you already know or have heard of someone who has worked in Japan. Business people, teachers, artists and technicians--more and more English-speakers are finding out about the once well-kept secret of jobs in Japan. And, to answer the many inquiries I've gotten from concerned readers since this book first appeared in 1983, yes, there *are* still far more job offers than takers. Although there's somewhat more competition today than three years ago, the need for English-speakers still far exceeds the tiny number of people who actually act on their dream of living there.

Writing a how-to book like this one involves tremendous responsibility which I take very seriously, especially since I'm urging you to trot halfway 'round the globe. What if I advise wrong? What if you take me at my word, go to Japan and things don't work out? Although I did my best to ensure the accuracy of the first edition, believe me, visions of hundreds of disgruntled readers burning my book (or an effigy of me!) in front of the American embassy in Tokyo worried my sleep plenty just prior to press time.

But I *was* right and my mail shows it. In the three years the book has been available in America, Canada, England and Australia, I have *never* heard from a single person who followed my advice and regretted the decision. That doesn't mean that life in Japan is a bed of roses for the foreign worker; it's a major challenge. But, evidently, no one thought the "bad" of adjusting to a very different world outweighed the "good" of experiencing it. And, most importantly, everyone I have heard from and of *has* been able to find jobs and enjoyment in "the land of rising opportunity."

So, what makes us foreigners so desireable in Nippon? Primarily the needs of Japanese trade and a tradition of unceasing education. The demand for our services continues to grow along with the Japanese economy and the country's export phenomenon. To interact effectively with the world beyond their islands, the Japanese must know our business practices, our technology and our language. Now more than ever, as the Japanese finally attempt to take their rightful place as world-class citizens and seek to "internationalize" (a favorite buzzword there), Japan needs you!

Sure the thought of living in Japan is a frightening one--the unknown always is. But living and working in "Nippon" probably was also a fairly daunting idea for the more than 35,000 native English speakers living there today. They made it--most without any special background in Japan--and you can too, but *only* if you decide it's a realistic possibility at this point in your life.

Now hold on. Don't start thinking of all the reasons why you couldn't possibly do it. Try thinking instead of all the reasons why it might be a great idea. Don't worry about not knowing the Japanese language; don't fret about being so far from home; don't trouble yourself about a possible lack of experience. All these *can* and have been worked out completely by the thousands of foreigners who've actually done what you're now only considering.

About the only thing that *can't* be worked out is an unreasonable reluctance or fear of the unknown--the idea that Japan is just "so far away." Don't let yourself get into that mind-set, please! In this age of cheap jet travel, nowhere in the world is really "far" any more if you see travel for what it is: a function of time. Try instead to think of it this way: for most readers, the flight to Japan is no "farther" than driving less than 1,000 miles on a major highway. The travel time's about the same.

And don't let your current lack of information about Japan dissuade you from trying it--the Japanese aren't going to expect you to know everything about their incredibly rich culture. Most would love to teach you whatever you'd like to learn. At this point, it's most important that you examine yourself and your desires closely. And, if you think you're at a time in your life when you could afford to take some time to explore a fascinating (and in all ways enriching) alternative, *do it!* With this book, you'll learn how.

Who should consider going? Well, certainly anyone *could* but perhaps especially: a) people who are fed up with local employers requiring experience before hiring but refusing to hire first to give that experience; b) veterans (victims?) of one career who are ready to see some of the world before beginning a new one; c) burned out teachers who are somewhat weary of confiscating switchblades instead of contemplating Swinburne; c) long-time lovers of the grace, delicacy and wisdom of the Japanese culture; d) foot-loose adventurers; and e) basically anyone who believes that there's a whole world of excitement and wonder lying just beyond their city limits.

But is traipsing off to Japan a responsible thing for grown-ups like us to do? Well, your humble scribe (me) believes most fervently that especially in this age of silicon chip-quick change, the future belongs to those who are able to recognize trends and act decisively, learning from the success of others and using shifting circumstances to best advantage.

Circumstances (and opportunity) *are* shifting today as the Western world looks to Japan--a land long known for its stability and refinement--to provide insight to global problems. It seems to me that those few Westerners who are willing and able to accept the Japanese invitation to be a part of that dynamic culture should certainly benefit in terms of both overall cultural awareness and possibly career development.

"But," you cry, "what do I know about Japan? Their language sounds like a telegraph gone haywire; they all live in shoeboxes and their idea of cuisine is what I feed my cat just before pay day! How could I live in a place like that?" Very comfortably, actually, as you'll learn after we first debunk a few popular myths about Japan to make sure you have an accurate picture of what awaits you.

Myth 1: "You've got to know Japanese to work there." Not at all. The foreigner's value to the Japanese company is usually his or her knowledge of the native language--especially English--not Japanese. Very few foreigners are hired because of their professional talents alone--there are too many native Japanese professionals who could do the job more efficiently and for a fraction of what the company must pay a foreigner. Companies (especially private English schools) hire "gaijin" (foreigners) largely for their *language* ability; there must be some aspect of the company operation that would be improved by having on the staff someone who speaks native English.

You honestly do not need to know *any* Japanese to live, work and develop friendships with people in the larger cities. Of course, it *helps* to know the language (and it is essential in many rural areas) but there are thousands of foreigners who've lived in Japan for decades who still have difficulty counting to ten in "Nihongo."

Why? Because the Japanese (unlike, say, the French) don't *expect* you to know their language. They realize that Japanese is spoken only in Japan and, considering its awesome complexity, they acknowledge that it really doesn't pay to learn it well unless, of course, you intend to put down roots there.

Those foreigners who work by teaching English (the most common occupation) aren't expected to know any Japanese whatsoever because their classes are almost always conducted *only* in English. After having had a minimum of six years of English just to graduate from high school, students generally have a good grasp of English grammar and astonishingly good vocabulary. They often need a native-speaker merely to practice what they've already learned and help them with the difficult pronunciation of our language.

Myth 2: "Japan is a terribly expensive place to live." If you insist on maintaining your exact present lifestyle there then yes, Japan is expensive, but only because you are not living like the average person. The situation's certainly not unique to Japan. Imagine for a moment how much it would cost the average Japanese to maintain *his* native lifestyle in the West. How much is "sushi" in Omaha? What might sea weed cost in London? How many "tatami" makers does Vancouver have? Foreign lifestyles are always expensive simply because they are not the norm. Westerners trying to maintain their "normal" way of life, of course, *will* pay a fortune to do so in Japan.

Erik Kuehnelt-Leddihn, a leading commentator on the Japanese scene, rather indelicately affirms in an article in *The National Review* that Tokyo *can* be very expensive but "only if you are a Western simpleton who heads for the most luxurious hotels, or if you insist on eating the Western way, especially fancy 'yottsu-ashi' or 'four-legged food.'

"Beef costs a fortune, as do milk and butter, for Buddhist tradition is averse to raising animals for food. But if you eat the Japanese way, you can get a good meal for $4 to $6. The subway is, on the whole, cheaper than in New York (and vastly superior), and so are taxis. Clothes and shoes cost no more than they do in Europe..."

According to the Japanese Ministry of Foreign Affairs, in 1983, the average Japanese family of four lived quite well with home, car, and most other amenities of First World life while spending approximately $1,080 per month. And if they can do it, so can you. Consider this:

* The Japanese diet of rice, vegetables, "tofu" (bean curd) and fish is exceptionally healthy--the life-expectancy of the people is the highest in the world.

* Their living accommodations, although small by Western (especially North American) standards are comfortably efficient and promote personal relationships and a healthy respect for the rights of others.

* Transportation costs and efficiency are far superior to those in countries which expect citizens to drive their own vehicles instead of relying on a superb mass transit system.

* Their National Health Insurance program pays 75% of ordinary medical expenses, more in the case of catastrophic liability. Most foreigners living in the country are eligible to participate upon payment of a small monthly premium.

Despite its undeserved reputation for sky-high prices, you can get along quite well even in Tokyo on about $700 a month if you're willing to adapt to life as the Japanese live it. The Ministry of Education even suggests that foreign college students shouldn't need more than $450 a month. That particular amount may be somewhat understated, but there are instances where it's close to true. One Japanophile I knew spent his spare time mastering the Japanese flute and studying Zen philosophy, living simply (but well) on the $600 a month his ten hours of teaching English per week paid him.

Myth 3: "The Japanese are such perfectionists that someone without top credentials and years of experience wouldn't have a chance of getting hired." Of course, as anywhere, the more formal experience and related training you have, the better the position and pay you can get. But the gap between the pay of a seasoned career professional and that of an inexperienced novice is not as great as it would be in the West where the novice might not be hired at all. The Japanese are great believers in the value of on-the-job-training and there seems to exist a feeling that experience and training not provided by the company itself is somehow less significant.

In a study on US-Japan education systems, the New York Stock Exchange noted that "the Japanese company generally hires young men right out of college who have had little or no classroom training that directly prepares them for their vocation." Thus corporations, for example, pay little attention to the college degree of the freshman executive. They expect him or her to have one but realize that extensive training in the "company way" is always necessary, regardless of the person's background. The term "college graduate" is used to indicate *potential* for performance, not current worth in the land where attitude, not credentials, is the key criterion for success.

As a foreigner, though, it is not even essential that you have a college degree to work. Many non-graduates support themselves well by, for example, teaching English part-time while attending classes on their "cultural" (student) visa to learn some aspect of the culture.

For full-time teaching sponsorship (i.e., a "work" visa), however, the government and most private schools do require that the teacher be a graduate of a four-year college program but not necessarily have any teaching experience. As for what *kind* of degree you need, the Japan-US Educational Commission (which administers the well-respected Fulbright Program) says, "the major field of study is not a primary factor in hiring English language teachers. The attitude still prevails that any native speaker can teach his own language, and what matters is that the foreign teacher be reliable and sincere."

Myth 4: "If I did get a job over there, I'd wind up working like a dog." OK, the Japanese *are* workaholics and managers expect all their minions to slave away, every day. But you're different. As a foreign worker in short supply, you would probably not be subject to the same grueling work schedules as the Japanese. Even though Japanese employees work 300-500 more hours per year than their foreign counterparts, you, as a "transient" employee, would have much fewer demands made on your time--maybe even fewer than you're used to at home.

The Japanese understand that, although a survey in 1985 showed that only 3.1% of the Japanese prefer leisure to work, most of us Westerners just aren't as keen on the idea of "senyu koraku" ("struggle first, enjoy later") as they are. And that's alright by them. To most Japanese companies, foreign workers are like contract laborers to be used to accomplish a specific task. As such, most foreigners receive hourly wages of anywhere from $14 to $45 an hour. And at those prices (much higher than

Japanese labor), our services are generally used sparingly and well.

In turn, the price Westerners pay for not being honest-to-gosh members of the corporate team is a lack of such amenities as fringe benefits and retirement programs. But forsaking a room in the company dorm is a small price for a short-time visitor to pay when, in exchange, he or she gets good compensation and the time off and freedom to enjoy it.

Myth 5: "Women are treated like second-class citizens in Japan." Like almost all Asian cultures, Japan's is essentially patriarchal. But, looming large in the Japanese conscience is the fact that past Japanese societies were matriarchal and that, according to their eons-old mythology, the imperial line was started by the sun-goddess, "Amaterasu." In tradition-oriented Japan, such ladies are not taken lightly.

It's true that Japanese women are pretty much apart from the work world. (It was only in May, 1985 that the parliament allowed women to work past 10 p.m.) But a great deal of it has to do with their own inclinations. The huge majority of women seem absolutely content to do menial secretarial work (as "office flowers") until they meet "Mr. Right" and can start raising their 2.3 kids. It's astonishing for a lot of Western women to learn that the main reason the women's movement is not a powerful force in Japan is not because of masculine opposition but because of a lack of interest--on the women's part.

Frankly, compared to Japanese men, the women have it made. Which would *you* rather do: work 10 hours a day, six days a week in a fairly bleak office with a tyrannical boss barking at you or stay home, keep house, care for the kiddies and give the occasional backrub to your exhausted spouse (after, of course, you have relieved him of his paycheck)?

Japanese women seem somewhat mystified that Western women want to be a part of the man's workaday rat race. They see their contribution to the family as every bit as significant as their husband's and generally aren't afraid to let their husbands know it--but never in public. In the home, wives are usually very vocal in expressing their opinions on family matters and carry considerable weight in the decision process.

Although they may secretly "tut-tut" her work-oriented lifestyle, the Japanese generally don't criticize the foreign woman. They just see her as unlike themselves. They know all about the developments Western women have experienced in the last few years and Japanese men and women alike pretty much respect them.

Knowing that the visiting foreign woman has different values from their own, the Japanese treat them with the same courtesy they extend to all visitors, regardless of sex. There may be superficial differences between the treatment of Japanese men and women but foreign men and women are almost always treated with identical respect. Fret not, there are no foreign "office flowers."

Myth 6: "Japan is too crowded for Westerners." The big cities of Japan *are* crowded but no more so than major cities all over the world. Most of Japan, in fact, is mountainous and very sparsely populated. Japan is not the most crowded country. Hong Kong and, surprisingly enough, the Netherlands and Belgium have higher population densities than Japan.

Despite (or perhaps because of) having 121 million people in an area the size of California, the Japanese have learned how to be exceptionally inoffensive and tolerant of each other. People waiting almost always form a queue; there's rarely any jostling; a voice is hardly ever raised in anger. The result? Japan's homicide rate (per capita) is less than one-fifth that of America's; there are less than 10% as many rapes per capita; and the rate for robberies is about 1% of America's. Clearly, the Japanese understand the value of getting along with each other better than any other "civilized" nation.

In short, the person living and working in Japan: 1) doesn't need to know a word of the language or have extensive credentials (*most* people who go over don't); 2) can make an excellent income, while living very comfortably and well on little more than he spent at home (an estimate of approximately $700 per month for one person, $1000 for a couple is fair); 3) probably is being treated better and feels safer than ever before in her life. In other words, Japan is, for most foreign visitors, a truly wise, welcoming and tremendously generous land.

Where The Jobs Are

Admittedly, a short stint in Japan may not be right for everyone. Nevertheless, assuming an ability and willingness to learn from the culture there is, in my opinion, almost no native English-speaking young adult who could not benefit from spending at least one year in Japan.

At the same time, it's important to notice that, although I strongly endorse the place, the people, and the work possibilities, I'm *not* advocating moving there permanently. I suggest you plan initially on staying a year, then extend if it seems appropriate. As a dyed-in-the-wool flag-waving citizen of my own US of A, I think it's essential that we never lose our own cultural identity, no matter how we may come to admire another culture. In the long run, there really should be no place like home, be it Europe, North America or Down Under. And the Japanese, while welcoming you as a visitor, will never let you forget that their home is not yours; nor should it be.

Some foreigners, of course, do stay forever (a few get on the next flight home) but most veterans of the experience (myself included) would probably recommend a year's stay at least to allow you to peel even the most superficial layers of mystery from the culture. Peeling them all (as with learning the language completely) takes a lifetime.

Committing yourself to one year also helps overcome the temporary disorientation and homesickness almost everyone experiences in trying to live in a foreign culture. Furthermore, a year gives you a chance to pick up a fair amount of the language, make some excellent (and often lifelong) friends, *and* save a tidy sum of money for the next phase of your life.

Those who decide to live abroad (as opposed to tourists) do so for myriad reasons: some are disillusioned with their own culture, some believe other cultures know how to live life in a superior manner, some are just curious and want an intimate glimpse into other modes of life. Recently, however, a new kind of voyager has ventured abroad: the person seeking foreign economic opportunity.

Such people have been rare, of course, because up until the '80s, opportunity was always best in the West-- ours was the culture all others flocked *to*. Today, though, many Westerners are beginning to question the fortuitousness of their native citizenship. Times are tough in many English-speaking nations in the world today--but, of course, they have been before. What makes this wide-spread slump unique, however, is that, for the first time, conditions are worse in many Western countries than in some non-Western countries. And some people are beginning to look beyond their borders for the opportunities their own land seems to deny them.

"But is it really necessary," you ask, "to go to the other side of the world to get a decent job? Surely there are jobs here for people who really look for them!" Well, some people do have connections, some get lucky, but too many of us find mostly closed doors when we go looking for satisfying and rewarding employment.

So where in the world, then, is today's intelligent and adventurous job-seeker reasonably sure of finding plentiful and rewarding work? In Japan, where the unemployment rate hovers around 2 or 3% and there's a constant need for enterprising English-speakers.

But if Japan has so much to offer, why aren't the opportunities more widely known outside the country? Possibly because the foreign media have focused almost exclusively on Japan's international economic affairs and have virtually ignored more personal aspects of the society.

An example: quick, who's the current Japanese Prime Minister? Stumped? Most Westerners would be. On the other hand, how many of Yasuhiro Nakasone's countrymen do you suppose know who's at the helm of the major English-speaking countries? The Japanese long ago recognized the value of international awareness, but we (especially Americans) seem reluctant even to try to understand the world's second most successful free nation. Here's why it's important that we *do* try:

Japan has what is probably the most organized, goal-oriented and consistent economic policies in the world, making the whole society function as smooth as, well, silk. This, together with a work ethic which shows little weakening despite great material success, makes many economists think Japan has a fair chance of overtaking even the USA. Consider that from 1977 to 1984, Japan's productivity increased 67.4% while labor costs increased only 46.9%. America's productivity, on the other hand, grew by a scant 15.6% and labor costs zoomed up 69.4%. Japan's GNP is already 40% that of America's while it works with only 4% of what the US has in land area. No one disagrees that the Japanese are doing something right and the West had better learn what if it hopes to compete.

From a personal perspective, the stability of the Japanese society as well is, of course, legendary and laudable. Compared to the West's, Japan's crime rate is insignificant, most marriages last decades (despite the added pressure of small living spaces), Japanese longevity is the highest in the world and they have successfully avoided joining the world's "nuclear club" despite having many times the resources necessary to construct a huge nuclear stockpile.

A utopia? Well, there *is* another side to the story. In fact, there's definitely plenty to dislike as well as admire about Japan. For example, one aspect of the culture that is frequently criticized by long-term foreign residents is its predictability. Genuine change comes very slowly in conservative Japan--although entertaining fads regularly sweep the nation. The Japanese know they've got a winning formula and are generally reluctant to tamper with the smooth functioning of their purring social engine. In terms of reliability, constancy and design, theirs is the Volkswagen of world cultures (although visitors with "Alfa

Romeo" lifestyles certainly will not be disappointed, especially in the larger cities.)

It is difficult to get to know the Japanese people on a personal level. So often they prefer to maintain relationships (even among themselves) on a somewhat formal plane, at least until time and trust have assured them that their confidences will be respected. Ironically enough, one occasional annoyance to foreigners in Japan is that renowned "politeness" which, although a delightful relief from the arrogant rudeness now commonplace in the West, at times takes the form of perceived insincerity and superficiality. As might be expected, Japanese young people are at the forefront of the recent trend toward greater candor and forthrightness, qualities which up to now, have not been encouraged.

But these are, quite honestly, really not the concerns of the first-time visitor. You'll have your hands full just dealing with the world you find yourself in, working in your chosen field or teaching your native language to those for whom the ability to speak it is almost a necessity for their economic survival.

And survival is at the heart of the Japanese craving for English. To survive as a nation with far more people than its land was ever meant to support, Japan must export; to export, Japan must be able to communicate with the rest of the world; to communicate, Japan must know English. And that's where you come in.

At the risk of disappointing some readers, I must warn you that the emphasis of this book is definitely on teaching English. This is simply because teaching offers vastly more jobs for the average English-speaker than any other occupation in Japan. It's also well-paying work that can be done quite well (sometimes outstandingly) even by those lacking credentials and experience.

But don't think of teaching necessarily as an end in itself. Many people going over use it as a "foot in the door" to enter their chosen field, be it writing, art or business. Teaching English is the great entre into Japan and frankly, you'd have a tough time working full-time (i.e., getting a visa) in any other capacity, including business.

The problem for business-types wanting to work overseas is that more and more companies are hiring natives. One 1985 survey reported in *Newsday* found that half of the 126 US corporations interviewed had reduced the number of American managers working overseas during the past decade while only 23 percent had experienced an increase.

Why? "Among the major reasons: foreign nationals were considered more efficient, with better political connections in their own countries, and were also cheaper to hire. And foreign nationals are often hired at the insistence, or at least the prodding, of the foreign governments themselves."

The good news for "gaijin," though, is that Japanese companies (which historically have almost never had full-time foreign staff) are actually increasing their foreign contingents as part of their global wheeling and dealing efforts. Foreigners are finally beginning to be admitted as regular employees into Japanese companies, allowing the "gai-jin" or "outside-person" to work his way inside the Japanese social, political and business system after decades of arm's-length treatment.

Jean Pearce, the well-respected and long-time columnist for *The Japan Times* (Tokyo's largest English newspaper), says "Japanese firms are hiring foreigners, including women, and using their abilities, not just putting them at a desk where they can be seen to demonstrate internationalization." Still, Pearce, points out, "certain areas of employment predominate: teaching English, writing, entertainment." The number of foreigners in business is still miniscule compared to people teaching English and for the person not fluent in Japanese, teaching may be the only way to work there.

But why not use teaching English as a way to get the job you may ultimately want? After all, the *Newsday* article points out, "Business opportunities do exist for internationally inclined students, experts say, but mostly within the United States...There is a widespread assumption that American firms increasingly need domestic managers well-versed in foreign affairs."

So for the aspiring world trader, it's a "Catch-22": companies won't send you overseas but they want to hire people who have been overseas. Now, I realize that teaching English may not be your life's calling but it will get you jobs (and, most importantly, a visa) in Japan. And, if you do it right, many of those jobs can be in the international business world or wherever else your interests might truly lie.

. Although the need for English-speakers is particularly acute in Japan, it is a global phenomenon. As *Newsweek* magazine explains, "English has replaced French in the world of diplomacy and German in the world of science. It is the dominant language of medicine, electronics and space technology, of aviation, international business and advertising, of radio, television and film."

That is to say, according to Robert Birchfield, editor of the <u>Oxford English Dictionary</u>, "Any literate, educated person on the face of the globe is deprived if he does not know English." Only a slight exaggeration considering that the number of people speaking English in the world has increased 40% in the last two decades to 700,000,000--a full 10% of the world's population.

The Japanese are at the forefront of the "English boom" since most Japanese consider knowledge of English absolutely vital to the country's economic well-being. In a study conducted in 1983, an incredible 74.7% of the executives in a major Japanese oil company said they believed English was "essential" to their careers.

That may explain why Teaching English as a Foreign (or Second) Language (TEFL/TESL) is booming in business, but it doesn't really explain why in Japan, according to *The Wall Street Journal*, fully 11% of all adults (more than 9 1/2 million people) are now attending English "conversation classes"--best taught by native speakers.

It almost seems to be an attempt by the average citizen to actively search for his or her place in the world community. In its December 8, 1980 article, the *Journal* adds, "The current English resurgence reflects a growing tendency among the Japanese to look beyond their own insular borders. Polls suggest that interest in foreign travel, both for business and for pleasure, is the most important motive." And because almost all adult "conversation" students have had at least six years of formal grammar instruction, they look to native speakers of English to provide them a chance to actually communicate using the "textbook English" they learned years earlier.

And despite the large number of Japanese already quite proficient with English, there seems to be no slacking in the demand for classes. As *The Wall Street Journal* itself admits, there is such a demand for people who merely speak English that, "many of the private schools will hire almost any native English speaker, regardless of teaching ability."

Due to the high demand for native speakers, teaching pay ranges from good to excellent, depending on fluctuating yen exchange rates. The Japan National Tourist Organization's standard exchange rate is 220 yen to each US dollar which we will also use throughout the book even though it undervalues the pay you'll earn in Japan. Actually, on November 22, 1985, the yen hit 200 to the dollar which means that at that time, dollar figures (including your potential income) cited in this book could have been increased about 10%.

At 220 yen to the dollar, even a person with no experience in the classroom can expect to earn a starting salary of about $14 per hour. More experienced teachers and those with teacher-training can usually command upwards of $20 an hour while special tutoring sessions with well-to-do professionals earn those diligent enough to organize them $45 an hour and often much more. Income potential can be remarkable for those who make it a priority, especially when Japanese income taxes average less than 10% and there's rarely a sales tax.

One young couple I know went over with the expressed intention of making all they could in as short a time as possible. Their feeling was that if they saw the country, fine, but if not, well, they could always come back for a real vacation in a few years. They worked six days a week and took advantage of almost every good teaching offer that came their way. In less than a year, their workaholic pace took its toll; they burned out, but not before they had accumulated together over $20,000 which they brought home with them to America.

Although at least a modicum of experience may be expected of others wanting to work in Japan, English teachers are often hired even if they've never taught a day in their lives. The reason, of course, is that most "instruction" consists primarily of familiarizing the Japanese students with how English is used in ordinary conversation--something most educated foreigners can do without special training as long as they do have sensitivity and compassion for the needs of their students. Complete knowledge of the structure of English, while certainly desirable in an instructor, is rarely required of English teachers in Japan.

To support this contention, one day in mid-May, I contacted at random ten schools in the Tokyo area, pretending to be a 22 year-old American college graduate with a four-year degree in (variously) Economics, Art, English and Sociology. I explained that I did not have a working visa but was eager to teach English, despite having no teaching experience whatsoever.

Of the ten, eight invited me for an interview saying that they were looking for instructors who could start immediately; five said the pay would range from 3,000 to 3,500 yen ($13.60 to $16) per hour, two said the pay could be as high as 5,000 yen ($22.70) per hour for certain classes and the others refused to disclose pay rates except in person.

All schools agreed to pay local transportation costs between the teacher's home and the class location (often in a meeting room of the client's). All said most classes were held weeknights.

Regarding my lack of professional experience, the administrators told me such things as, "Don't worry about the experience; that's no problem...we prefer teachers with experience, of course, but we are willing to train...you would have no trouble teaching for us if you attended our training course...no experience is all right, depending on other factors...the most important point in teaching is character and personality...[and my favorite, told to me by the delightful Miss Komine of the English Telephone Club] you must speak beautiful English and teach English conversation in a kindly way."

Only two of the schools said they weren't currently hiring but they *did* urge me to call back in September.

Voices Of The Vets

Obviously, before you embark on this grand adventure, you'll probably want to discuss the idea with your more open-minded friends--ideally those who've lived in Japan or at least overseas. But beware of those "friends" who may try to dissuade you simply because they are afraid to try it themselves or don't want to lose your company for a year.

Be especially sure to take with several grains of salt the soporific yarns of such old-timers as your Uncle Harry--especially if his only contacts with the culture consisted of weekend cavortings with "them cute little geesha gals" while he was stationed there with the Army. You'll be seeing a whole different and much more authentic world than he ever did while living on a military base.

For an excellent first-hand account of what's in store for you, try to get in touch with someone who's actually worked in Japan, preferably doing what you'd like to do there. One good source of such people would be an English as a Foreign Language (EFL) school, private or university-affiliated. You should be able to find several in the yellow pages under "language schools" if you live in a fairly large city or by contacting your nearest large community college or university. Teachers in Japan commonly do various other language-related jobs as well--such as writing, editing or research--and can also give advice on the opportunities in those areas.

When you call the school, ask the secretary if anyone there has taught EFL in Japan. Odds are, there will be several; it's a fairly common destination for globe-trotting teachers. EFLers are a friendly and gregarious bunch for the most part and the teachers you talk to will probably be more than happy to give you the inside scoop.

But if for some reason you're unable to personally contact people who've actually taught in Japan, you may be especially interested in what the following veterans have to say. These first-hand accounts were gathered mostly by calling local ESL schools and asking for comments from those who had taught professionally in Japan. No "veteran" I spoke to regretted the experience; all said they would do it again; a few plan to. Should you have questions or comments for any of them, they may be contacted through the publisher, whose address is in the front of the book.

Melinda Wood, a native of Denver, Colorado, quite reasonably went to Nagoya, Japan after getting her degree because, "it was the only job I was offered." And despite a Japanese friend's warning that the city was "hot, horrible and disgusting," Melinda wound up staying a full two years and eight months.

"My friend was right about the weather--it *was* the pits. But, wherever I've travelled, I've always found the people to be the most important thing and Nagoya was no different.

"I knew a little Japanese before I went over but it wasn't really enough because Nagoya just doesn't have as many English speakers as some of the larger cities. I was really shocked when I visited Tokyo and Osaka and saw the number of people there who spoke good English. I'd definitely suggest that people who don't know Japanese stick to the big cities until they feel comfortable with using the language fairly extensively.

"I had originally wanted to stay only a year, but after about eight months, I decided that wouldn't be nearly long enough, so I signed another six month contract with my school. Then, at the end of that contract, I signed another one for a year. Finally, I decided I'd done enough teaching so I changed my work visa to a cultural visa and tried to study Japanese seriously, something I'd been wanting to do since I got there.

"I guess I didn't make nearly as much money as I could have while I was in Japan. The pay at my school was not the greatest, but they did take good care of their teachers.

"I usually made between $14 and $23 an hour, but I knew people who were making $45 an hour and more. But then again, I didn't want to kill myself working as much as possible just to make money, as I saw a lot of people doing.

"My first impression of Nagoya was that it was a neon fantasy. I felt it was going to be a lot of fun right from the start. It was, except for some initial problems I had with the trains and the writing. I forced myself to learn the katakana alphabet in the first week I was there. If I hadn't, I think I might have starved; without knowing it, you can't even read the menus at the western restaurants.

"I think the cost of living problem in Japan is really exaggerated. Except for some entertainment, I was able to live a lot cheaper in Nagoya than I could in Colorado. In Japan, I paid about $150 a month for a very nice two-room apartment with kitchen and bath.

"As for food costs, I ate out for almost every meal and almost never paid more than $5 for good food in unglamourous surroundings. I learned pretty quickly where to find the bargains, I guess. All in all, I'd say it's easier to live cheaply but nicely in Japan than in the US.

"In my school, we had Japanese English teachers and 'native speaker' English teachers. Generally, the Japanese took care of teaching the grammar to the lower level students and the gaijin taught conversation to help the students practice what they'd learned. I thought it was good rewarding work that really helped people who needed to know the language.

"I'd certainly suggest trying to get a work visa before you go. But if you do, it may be with a school that doesn't pay nearly as well as others you could find on your own, once you're over there. On the other hand, the schools that pay less usually offer more fringe benefits like housing and sometimes air transportation back home and to Korea if you need to change your visa.

"One of the most difficult things for me during my stay was coming home to visit. I went back for my sister's wedding and felt a little...different. The reverse culture shock of coming home to America from Japan was, for me, actually worse than the shock of going over in the first place. I really couldn't understand the way my American friends acted; they seemed so uninterested in learning about the rest of the world. They really couldn't understand why I'd gone over at all. Of course, I couldn't imagine why they hadn't!

"One thing that made my stay especially nice is that I really like Oriental men. I know some people would disagree with me but I think Japanese guys may be more honest in some ways than American men. I always felt while I was there that if a Japanese guy does something nice, it's sincere--they're genuinely motivated. I think American men do a lot of things just because they think they have to in order to impress a woman.

"My Japanese women friends have told me that younger men, especially those under 30, are a lot more open and sensitive than their fathers ever were. Just from talking to my friends here, I know that a lot of people who've never been there have the wrong idea about relationships in Japan.

"My mother told me when I got back that Japan had changed me a lot--I assume for the good. I think I developed a sense of community and family there, for the first time in my life. It was really wonderful actually belonging to a tightly-knit group, a neighborhood, a close circle of friends. Of course, the other side of that is that sometimes the Japanese do get a little nosy. They don't seem to have bad intentions, but when I was there, I did get a little tired of people prying into my personal affairs. But all that did help me develop a great deal of Japanese-style patience!"

George Bilgere, of Riverside, California, had heard a lot of rumors about the opportunities in Japan but didn't actually know anyone who had made the trip. Attempting to do the research himself, he found that there was practically no information available for the person interested in teaching English in Japan.

"I think I checked all the right sources, but I couldn't find a thing, except at the Japanese Consulate in San Francisco, which sent me a list of about 25 schools in Tokyo. I wrote to them asking if they had any openings but got only a few replies and only one which sounded like they *might* be interested in hiring me. The message that I got from all the schools was a very clear, 'Come over first, then we'll talk.'

"I had some serious doubts about making it in Japan. I really knew no Japanese at all, and was worried about living on the Japanese economy, especially when I wasn't sure I could find a job. But, I had heard enough stories about people who had gone, to just say to myself, 'Do it and see what happens.' The way I rationalized it, of course, was to tell myself that if it *didn't* work out, I'd just consider it a nice vacation. It *was* nice and things certainly worked out.

"The first mistake I made was coming in to Narita Airport in Tokyo. When I went over, I hadn't known that Haneda even existed or that China Air Lines flies into it from the West Coast. When I went back to California for Christmas, there was never any doubt in my mind about where I wanted to leave from. Avoid Narita whenever possible; it's an incredible headache!

"I did have an acquaintance in Tokyo and was able to stay with him a few days while I scouted around for work and a place to live. When I started looking for a job, I was amazed at how many were available, just in the classifieds alone. The day after I arrived, I had a sponsor and a full-time teaching job.

"I had taken a short Japanese course before I left the States, but couldn't say much more than 'How much?' and 'Where am I?' (I found the second phrase particularly useful in Tokyo.) But I really had no problems not knowing more--almost everyone I met there spoke at least enough English to let us communicate. I guess I feel a little guilty about having come back to the States not knowing much more Japanese than when I went over, but the Japanese people just make it so easy for a foreigner *not* to learn. There's just not much incentive to other than as an academic exercise.

"My sponsor found me an apartment and arranged for me to fly to Korea to change my tourist visa to a working one. After I got back from Seoul, I began teaching, even though technically, I was working illegally because my new visa hadn't been approved yet. That was definitely what the school expected me to do, though. And once I got my work visa, I started working far more than I'd ever expected to. I'm not sure why exactly; I was just always meeting people who needed another teacher. Eventually, my schedule got very insane.

"Let me give you an idea of what a typical day was like. I'd get up at 7, take my morning bath, then ride my bicycle 10 minutes to the nearest train station, where I'd catch the express into Shinjuku. I'd get to class with a few minutes to spare so I'd grab a roll and a cup of coffee before I went in to teach. I'd teach four hours, then race down to the basement of the building where the subway stopped.

"I'd make it to Ikebukuro with about two minutes to spare before my super-express left so I'd pick up a box lunch to eat on the way. Then, after a one-hour ride that took me about 80 miles outside Tokyo, I'd be greeted by a company limousine and chauffeur who would take me to my class of upper-lever executives. My class with them lasted two hours and I would then be taken back to the station and get another express back to town. That particular class was unusually far from the city so my school paid me not only for the time I was actually teaching but for my time on the train as well--in addition to the ticket, of course. At $25 an hour, I learned to love that train ride.

"That was about the average as far as what I earned teaching. I discovered fairly soon that the big difference in pay wasn't because of the teacher's qualifications; it had more to do with how much the school was willing to pay. It caused problems sometimes and a little bit of resentment too. I remember we had a guy with a Ph.D. in Linguistics from Yale at one school where I worked who was pretty upset about receiving the same pay as the other teachers, some of whom just had BAs and no teaching experience at all.

"I really didn't make as much as I could have because I got involved with television work there, something I always wanted to do, but couldn't in America because I didn't have the experience or training.

"I hadn't had any acting classes at all but I'd heard of other gaijin just walking in to an acting job so I thought I'd give it a try. I went to NHK, the public broadcasting network to see if I could get on a show. Sure enough, I had lunch with the director of NHK's English program for students, 'English for Today' and after our conversation, he told me he'd like to have me join the cast- -as a regular.

"I also did shows for NHK radio that year, basically just performing in skits and having fun with the other people on the show. By the end of the season, I was getting dozens of fan letters from all over Japan. I was a semi-celebrity!

"Sometimes, though, I did feel a little alienated in Japan. It wasn't that the people were cold or aloof, but I always felt a little isolated, as though the people liked my being there but didn't want me to get too close to them or the culture. But they were certainly always warm and friendly to me and I never doubted their sincerity about it.

"I had some Japanese friends but most of the people I knew were other foreigners, mostly teachers. I especially liked the other gaijin I met in Japan. They all seemed to be interesting, well-travelled people who had come to Japan because they really liked the country and the people. Unfortunately, I did meet a few foreigners who had come to Japan, apparently just to exploit the Japanese- -something that's not too hard to do if you're willing to act overbearing enough.

"I think what I loved most about Japan was the constant sense of newness and adventure. Even walking down a little back street was exhilarating because I knew I would find something exciting, even if it was just a little shrine or kimono shop. And it was especially nice not having to worry about any threat of danger, just to be able to relax and enjoy the sights.

"In a way, I feel a little guilty that I was so blinded by all the work opportunities. I really did turn into a workaholic and, although I was making very good money - -except in my TV work which took up some of my most valuable teaching time--I wish I had taken more time to get to know the culture.

"Japan gave me a lot more than some money to take home, though. Most important to me, I think, was the tremendous confidence it gave me--confidence to deal with even the most extraordinary situations. It also made me fairly intolerant of all the crime and rudeness that seem to have become so common in America.

"If you're thinking of going over, I'd suggest you learn at least something about the country and the people-- it makes the adjustment much easier. And be prepared to get homesick and even depressed at times. Everybody does, but just remember that it's only a phase and in a few days you'll probably be back to loving the place again. I know I certainly did!"

One 35-year-old native of upstate New York went to Japan first in 1976 and has since made it her home. With so many years in the country, she has been able to advance to an excellent position with a prestigious girl's college in the fashionable Roppongi district of Tokyo, a position which has resulted in her requesting anonymity for her comments here.

Although she enjoys her students and the instruction she gives them, she cautions newcomers that they may have to "suffer at first until you learn the system. It takes time to make the connections but that is definitely how you get ahead in Japan.

"Sony offered me a job in Fukuoka and, once I got there, I was lucky enough to make a good American friend almost as soon as I arrived. We met at the local McDonalds--not exactly the kind of place I usually go to but it had the only sign I could read. My friend had gone there for the same reason: a little bit of home, however tacky.

"Since she spoke some Japanese, she helped me enormously. It would've been much more difficult without her, actually. Things were just a little too foreign and different at first.

"I think my first impression with the place was that everything seemed so 'cute'--the shops, the roads, the people, everything. And that's fine, but then, when you learn that there's a tremendously complicated society behind the cuteness, things change and you learn to be a little cautious.

"Fortunately, Sony treated me well. It's the only school I know of that has been unionized and the teachers are now protected by the largest union in Japan. But a lot of little fly-by-night schools will really take advantage of the naive teacher. Teaching English is definitely a business over there and you've got to make sure you're treated fairly.

"Some schools will require you to work a 40-hour week which usually means you wind up doing a lot of 'busy work' in their office. Still, even if you do get stuck with a less-than-perfect sponsor, you can always change jobs in six months when your visa expires. It's a good idea, though, to stay on good terms with your employer, even if you're planning to leave. Your old boss could make things sticky for you by delaying the signing of your 'release' papers that let you transfer elsewhere.

"In 1980, Sony asked me to transfer to Tokyo where I found good extra part-time jobs, always by word of mouth, never in the newspaper. That's how I got my rewriting/proofreading job with J. Walter Thompson, the international advertising agency. My job there had me editing the translations of Japanese ads and news releases for Thompson's accounts. These English versions are then sent to the client's home office so they can know what's being said about them and what advertising is being done in the Japanese media. The pay is very good and I would think anyone with editing experience could find similar work without too much trouble.

"I make 5-6,000 yen per classroom hour for my teaching but jobs vary from 2,500 to 10,000 per hour. I like my job but sometimes I get the feeling that English is just a hobby for my students and they could as easily be studying the tea ceremony. But English classes always look good on a girl's "resume" which is shown to prospective husbands.

"I think there are a lot of companies out there hiring a lot more gaijin now, especially anyone with some knowledge of Japanese. I've got one friend who is working for a securities company with 12 other gaijin and is making good money and getting great experience. I think that sort of thing is becoming more common.

"Still, there are many, many jobs in teaching and they range in prestige and pay from Language Institute of Japan (which requires teachers to have an MA in TESL) to 'Joe's' English School which'll basically hire anyone who speaks English. There really are lots of English schools and they're always looking for teachers. I do think there is some competition as there are more qualified English teachers like those who used to be in the Middle East. Still, there seem to be more schools than ever and English is still the 'in' thing to study. Everybody wants to speak English, especially with native speakers, so long as they are neat and well-groomed.

"It's more difficult to get a teaching job without a BA or BS degree. Some people get a cultural visa under which you're supposed to study some aspect of the culture. With that, I think you can still work up to 15 hours per week, which should be enough to support yourself if you're careful and getting paid decently.

"Even if a school sponsors you, you must also have a private person (usually the school's president) sign a statement of financial stability and personal responsibility, agreeing to pay for you to leave Japan if necessary and assume all your debts in Japan. Another gaijin can also sponsor you if they've established themselves for several years in their community but, as you can imagine, it usually has to be someone who knows you *very* well to be willing to take that kind of responsibility for your actions.

"Try to arrive about one month before the start of the terms in January, July, April and September (the last two being best) to make sure you have a good choice of jobs. I don't think new people have much room to negotiate their first salary. Just accept what's offered and learn the ropes.

"Unfortunately what works and what doesn't for visas is still decided pretty much 'case-by-case.' It's amazing how much power immigration has! You definitely want to be on your best behavior when you talk to immigration officials.

"You almost have to have a Japanese person with you when you go to rent an apartment. A lot of realtors just don't want to deal with gaijin: too risky. Some realtors, though, are pretty open-minded and will give you a chance, especially if there's a Japanese with you to assure him you're all right. Also in terms of living comfortably, you might think twice about going if you're physically large. Despite what they say about the young generation growing taller, Japan really is still made for smallish people.

"I would recommend that anyone going to Japan look at her motivation. You've got to like Japan and the Japanese if you expect to do well. I know that sounds simplistic but it's something I think a lot of people don't consider. You'll *never* change the Japanese so you'd better accept the way they are. Also, remember patience and humility above all else. You've got to go with the flow to a certain extent. If you enjoy being aggressive or intimidating, try somewhere else.

"If you're sensitive and patient, however, you'll have few problems. Japan is clean, safe and fun--fun because you have a kind of 'license to be different'--but not in a 'trampy' way. You just don't have to play by all the rules that the Japanese have to. In some ways, it's very liberating, but in others, it's restrictive because the Japanese limit themselves to such a great extent with all their unwritten rules of behavior.

"Make friends and make connections. It can be hard to make close Japanese friends because they lead such different lives from ours. The women tend to stay home and the men work overtime with only a few hours after work for drinking with their friends.

"If you do want to socialize with some foreigners, go to a place like Roppongi in Tokyo. You'll meet a lot of gaijin and Japanese who like gaijin at places like 'Maggie's Revenge' and 'Charleston'. Subscribe to the *Tokyo Journal* if you're living there. In a city like Tokyo, there's always going to be plenty to do if you know what's on.

"All in all, obviously I recommend the experience. I live there and I enjoy it a lot. I have a lot of respect for the Japanese and their general willingness to help foreigners. You'll always find someone who remembers their college English who'll help you out of a tight spot and not expect anything but your thanks in return. Even though they do tend to see us gaijin in stereotypical terms and refuse to believe that after eight years of eating their food, yes, in fact I *can* use chopsticks, I like my life in Japan a great deal. Not everyone is going to want to stay as long as I have but I certainly think anyone going for any length of time will get a lot out of the experience."

Ron Spinks, former Director of Courses at a major private American English school, had no experience with

Japan whatsoever before he decided to take the plunge and see what awaited him across the Pacific.

The 35-year-old native of Dallas had been intrigued by the few Japanese students he'd had in his two years of teaching English and wanted to learn about their background first hand. Having hired many teachers for the school he worked for in Osaka, Ron is a valuable source of information as to what school administrators look for in a teacher when hiring.

"I sensed in the Japanese students I'd had in America a sense of purpose and serenity which I envied. I especially appreciated their politeness and sense of order and just had to find out where in their upbringing those things had come from.

"For the first year I was in Japan, I basically just 'sat in the corner' and watched everything that was going on around me, trying to learn the Japanese way of doing things. I think careful observation is especially important for a newcomer unfamiliar with the culture. The bull-headed person who walks into the country and the classroom thinking he has all the answers is going to have

a hard time getting along. It's *their* country and you've got to be extremely sensitive to *their* way of being.

"Getting sponsored outside of Japan is difficult because the schools like to meet who they're sponsoring before they take them on. Sometimes, the more reputable schools will send recruiters over to interview prospective teachers but many times the salaries offered are less than what a teacher could earn by finding a sponsor on his or her own in Japan.

"In some ways, it's to the teacher's advantage as well as the sponsor's to meet face-to-face before the commitment is made. It is possible for a teacher to change sponsors after a work visa has been issued but if the old sponsor won't sign a letter of release, you have to plead your case before the Immigration Bureau and explain why you want to leave that school and why the school doesn't want to let you go. You also have to have another sponsor lined up and ready to hire you immediately, of course. All in all, it's far better just to get yourself a good sponsor right at the start and stick with him the whole time you're in Japan.

"I'm just amazed at what a huge business teaching English is in Japan; it must be a billion dollars a year, maybe more. I was never really sure how it got to be that size either but part of the reason, I suppose, is the Japanese love of self-improvement, whatever the subject, be it flower arranging or English conversation.

"But also, of course, knowledge of English can open some important career doors for the Japanese. Having English ability is for them like having, say, word-processing skills is for us: even if your employer doesn't have a computer at the moment, you never know when that talent's going to come in handy.

"For people interested in going into international trade or commerce, of course, it's almost an essential skill because English is the international language of business. And for students hoping to enter almost any good university, it's necessary to pass a very rigorous test of English, both written and spoken.

"After two years of teaching, I was made Director of Personnel and Curriculum so I did quite a bit of hiring for the school. I very quickly learned to look for the same things in a prospective teacher that the Japanese did. And probably the single most important thing was 'image.'

"You see, Japan is at the end of the 'hippie trail'-- the route that a lot of the counter-culture types took through Europe, the mid-East, India and Southeast Asia. So Japan was at one time flooded with unkempt gaijin whom the Japanese didn't really understand and certainly didn't care for. We sure didn't at my school!

"The very first thing that my Japanese boss and I looked for in an applicant was good grooming, which for a man meant wearing a tie and for a woman meant wearing a nice skirt or other 'professional' outfit. You really must dress well in Japan if you hope to do well.

"We had many cases of bright and really talented teachers insisting on wearing blue jeans in class and getting a whole rash of complaints from the students while teachers of only average ability would get nothing but praise simply by dressing well. It's essential to realize that the Japanese *do* tend to judge things by their appearance.

"Another part of 'image' is always looking like you know what you're doing in the classroom. It's fine to ask the supervisor for teaching tips--that was most of what I did as Director--but a teacher should never ask the students, for example, what they'd like to do. The teacher is always supposed to know what comes next in a class, and if the students don't see some kind of direction, they might lose respect.

"We also paid a lot of attention to what we thought the person's potential as a teacher might be. I think it's safe to say that in many ways experience and credentials are secondary to the right *attitude* in Japan. Our school looked for people who genuinely cared for their students, were willing to be trained and could understand that teaching English does not involve simply pouring a bunch of grammar data into the students' heads. 'Classroom manner' is extremely important to the Japanese.

"I think because of that famous Japanese 'reserve,' a lot of Westerners misunderstand the culture. One of the first comments I would hear from new teachers was how the Japanese had no will--that they didn't mind riding crowded trains and living in small homes. Well, of course the Japanese don't like the lack of space any more than Westerners do but they've accepted it as the price they have to pay for the conveniences of living in a large city. They'd all love to have a big house but they've made a conscious choice to accept less for other considerations. And I like that about them very much; they've always made the very most of what little they've had.

"I especially appreciated the sense of community and of people working together toward a shared goal. I think the biggest difference between them and us is that they regularly pull together, while we Americans only seem to come together in the face of some shared crisis. The Japanese think it's nothing short of miraculous that a culture like ours can even exist when we all seem to be pulling in about twelve dozen different directions at once. Sometimes it amazes me, too!"

Cec Jacobs, 35, from Wichita, Kansas, was one of those brave souls who dared to go to Japan with neither job nor visa nor the assurance she'd ever get either. She found a sponsor the second day she was in the country.

"I stayed in Tokyo about ten months and mostly just wanted to get as much money together as possible. I usually taught about six hours a day but sometimes did as many as nine hours of teaching, which meant a 14-hour day including time spent commuting on the trains.

"I worked for three schools regularly but picked up additional work wherever I could. My pay averaged about $16 an hour but I knew some people who worked a lot more by concentrating on private tutoring instead of the classroom teaching I mostly did.

"I definitely think that my personality got me most of my jobs. I'm convinced that if you make the school administration like you, you can get anything you want: more hours, better classes, better pay. If the school likes you, they'll do almost anything to keep you. There's such a need for teachers over there that they can't afford to lose a good one.

"I remember one interview (if you can call it that) where I met the director of the school at the train station and all he said to me was, 'Hello, I'm Mr. Saito. Can you start Wednesday?' That was it. No questions about my background, my qualifications, nothing. I spoke native American English and that was enough to get me teaching jobs that paid better than any job I'd had in America.

"I was always on the lookout for more or better work and never had any trouble finding enough. In fact, I was so used to being in demand as a teacher that the one time a school told me they *weren't* looking for teachers, I was absolutely flabbergasted. I had never before heard of *any* school that wasn't looking for more teachers!

"One school I worked for liked me so well that they were actually willing to create a class just for me, whenever I had some extra time and wanted to fill those hours in my schedule. Apparently, they were always able to find students who wanted to have a class just when I wanted to teach it. It sure made me feel wanted!

"Another thing that I particularly liked were the trips and parties involved with the work. One time, I was flown all the way north to Sapporo just to teach one class of businessmen. Another time, I went to a resort with a class, just so they'd have someone to practice their English with--all expenses paid plus my usual teaching fee.

"And then there were the regular get-togethers with my students. At least two or three times a week, I'd be invited to go out with the whole class for dinner and drinking downtown, just so we could all get to know each other socially. Needless to say, I thought it was a great idea and I loved always being the guest of honor.

"Despite all this, I guess I found the culture a little alienating, but that partly may have been because I couldn't really socialize with other Westerners very easily. Most of us were teachers and evenings were always our busiest time of the day. And the thought of getting back on the train to get together with someone on the weekend was never too appealing. After spending four hours a day on trains during the week, I really just wanted to relax and walk around my neighborhood.

"I think you have to be persistent, adventurous and maybe a little aggressive to be successful at teaching in Japan. I sent out about 50 letters to schools asking for sponsorship and a job and didn't get a single job offer. But, even so, I decided to go and figured that, at the very worst, I'd see a place in person that I'd only seen in travel books before. I just took a chance and it paid off."

Armed only with her BA in English, a one-way ticket and a well-thumbed copy of the first edition of

<u>JOBS IN JAPAN</u>, Teresa Falagrady of Denver, decided at 25 to see if the living and working situation for gaijin in Japan was all that your humble author cracked it up to be. In my opinion, she is the ideal person to work in Japan: open-minded, outgoing, adventurous, and curious. Her verdict after a year's visit: "What you said in the book was all true, everything but the price of vegetables. You said food wasn't all that expensive but fresh fruit and vegetables are steep!

"I'm not a gambler by nature," she continued, "but after reading <u>JOBS IN JAPAN</u> and a few other books, my girlfriend and I decided to just do it. We had a friend over there teaching in the Osaka area but he hadn't really promised us a job. He just said he didn't think there would be any problem with our finding work there. Hearing it from a friend actually on the scene definitely helped reduce our anxiety.

"We flew from Seattle to Narita in Tokyo in March of 1984. After a long bus ride into the city, we picked out a place from the book's list of accommodations and found a room at the Okubo House. I have never in my life slept in a smaller room; it was just barely the length of our bodies and we crammed ourselves and 11 suitcases into it. But it was clean and cheap. We loved it!

"We had heard about a program whereby you work for the summer on a dairy farm without pay but with free room and board and plenty of clean air. That sounded like our kind of adventure but we never made it--got sidetracked, I guess. Instead, we took the 'bullet train' to Osaka after five days of exploring Tokyo mainly because we wanted to get a little settled down.

"Actually, if we hadn't known someone in Osaka, I think we would've stayed in Tokyo. It felt exciting and liveable. But our friend had called a company and asked if they needed teachers and sure enough, they did. We probably could've started work the day we got there. And, in a way, we did because we decided to try living in a place with Japanese students called the Osaka English House.

"The deal at the English House was that you (the gaijin) live and/or teach in a dormitory style 'house.' Rent includes breakfast and dinner Monday through Friday. Unfortunately, I think we were ripped off because the owner, Mrs. Watanabe, wasn't very scrupulous. Luckily, two of my friend's students were a couple who had just had a new house built.

"They were going to rent the old house in Kyoto but when they found out that my roommate and I weren't happy where we were, she offered to rent it to us--an entire house for about $175 a month! Incredibly enough, my students thought that was too much to pay because the house was 40 minutes by foot from the train station. My friend and I didn't care; it was only a 12 minute bike ride and we still thought it was 'yasui' (cheap).

"We met a Canadian guy in Osaka who started us at 4,000 yen an hour to teach classes through his company. We knew that was pretty good pay for us because we didn't have any teaching experience (I'd taught racquetball) and our degrees weren't technical (mine is English and my girlfriend's is in Business Recreation). On the other hand, he couldn't give us sponsorship so we had to get legal some other way to work.

"We thought 'ikebana' (flower arranging) might be fun so we got cultural visas to study it at the Kyoto YMCA. Of course, we had to leave the country to change from our tourist visas but we just thought of it as a vacation. Unfortunately, we picked the wrong spot to visit: Seoul, Korea. It was awful! The people weren't very friendly; it was dirty, grey and generally uncomfortable. We originally planned to sightsee for three days but instead we just stayed in the hotel room the extra two days after we got the visa until we could leave. Even though it is more expensive to go to another country, if you have to leave Japan for your visa, definitely don't go to Seoul!

"But Japan really was great. Most people were nice and accommodating and I've never felt safer in a big city. However, we still had to watch our step sometimes-- especially on the trains when the 'ruthies' were in action. That was the name my girlfriend and I gave the 'ruthless' women (some as old as my grandmother!) who take on anyone regardless of size to get that last seat on the train. They're deadly!

"I noticed that the Japanese are tremendously polite if they're dealing with you personally but en masse, it's a real free-for-all. If there's a line for something, people will use it and wait their turn. But if there isn't a queue, it's just a mad scramble to get to the front.

"All in all though, the Japanese are incredibly helpful to foreigners. They sure were to us! We were constantly invited to dinner and sightseeing trips by our students/friends. I think the Japanese are kind to just about all 'gaijin.' Still, I can't help but wonder if they were so very helpful to us because we were American and women also. I think those probably helped somewhat.

"However, too much kindness can develop into a kind of problem too if you're not careful. Gift-giving is a very important part of their lives and you really should bring something (cookies, cake, fruit--always gift-wrapped!) if you visit a Japanese home for lunch or dinner. No one will say anything to you if you don't but it's considered an important courtesy.

"Gift-giving is a very big custom and if you are given gifts frequently (as we were), it becomes a little overwhelming. It's almost as if you must 'keep score' on who's given what to whom. But if you just reciprocate the nice things they do for you by being kind and generous yourself, you'll get along fine.

"Even though most of my students were men and would frequently take me out after class as a group, I never got any feelings of anything but friendship (and curiosity) from them. Partly, I think, it was due to my position as 'teacher' which is pretty honorable. Also, of course, as a 'gaijin,' I think I was just too different for them to be interested in me as anything but a teacher. However, I think it was precisely because I was a gaijin woman that they enjoyed being seen in my company. At any rate, it was great not being hassled and just being able to go out and have a great time without any more expectations from the men. I've never felt as safe as I felt in Japan. And that safety is one of the biggest things I miss about the place.

"The Japanese seemed to me to be very bright people. I was lucky in that I knew my English grammar so I didn't have much trouble answering their questions. Other teachers I knew did. I'd definitely recommend anyone planning to teach over there to bone up on grammar just so you know somewhat how our language works and what the various parts are called. I think that's

especially important to the Japanese because that's the way
they learn their own language, which, by the way, English
teachers are not expected to know. In fact, even though it's
obviously a good idea to learn some Japanese before you
go, it's very easy to function well in the country without
knowing much Japanese at all.

"As a teacher, it's not at all necessary to know
English grammar inside and out or to even have a lot of
teaching experience. The students mostly just want to learn
'conversational English' which basically involves just
talking with them. The fact is, of all the gaijin I met in
Osaka and Kyoto teaching English, none had had any real
teaching training and a lot didn't even have as much
experience as I did.

"I looked into a few other kinds of jobs and did
some free-lance editing for 4,000 yen an hour but decided
I wouldn't be comfortable with a lot of the other
alternatives. Modeling jobs are available, as are 'hostess'
ones which I interviewed. Even for up to 5,000 yen an
hour, though, I wasn't very interested in lighting the men's
cigarettes (they *all* smoke!), laughing at their jokes and
generally looking pretty at their side. I guess the tips
would've been good and I was assured there was nothing
else expected of me but it just wouldn't have been worth
it.

"By the time I left in April of 1985, I had a pretty
good set-up. I was working about 17 hours a week for
4,000 yen an hour and had my cultural visa for ikebana
which I only studied about one hour a week (but had to
tell immigration it was six). I had my own furnished house
with garden for under $200 a month (which I split with
my friend) and I had met a woman on the train who
turned out to be a good friend and even agreed to sponsor
me.

"But I just got tired of Japan. Even though I loved
having all that time to read, I spent too many hours on the
trains, too many hours just waiting for trains, busses and
classes to start. And although I liked the anonymity, I felt
a little too isolated from my own culture and maybe just a
little overwhelmed by the place. It's nice to feel special
but, after awhile, you get tired of people looking at you
like you're Michael Jackson. Although I certainly don't

regret going and I'd do it again, after a year in Japan, I knew it was time to come home.

"The key to really getting the most out of the experience is to be flexible at all times. You play by their rules or not at all. It's difficult sometimes for an American especially to deal with the Japanese because they're never straightforward about anything. Instead, you must be *very* sensitive to non-verbal cues and sometimes that gets very tiring.

"In the long run, I definitely prefer being able to speak out but then, that's my cultural background. Although I am fascinated by the two cultures and appreciate their differences, ultimately I prefer the American lifestyle. I still love Japan and the people I met there but it definitely felt good to get home and sink my teeth into a real pizza!"

Our last veteran of teaching English in Japan asked that she not be identified because she, like many short-term (and some not-so-short-term) foreign residents of the country, worked illegally. She is now afraid it might be difficult for her to return to Japan (as she would like to do someday) if the Japanese government learned she had violated the terms of her visa.

Having graduated from a four-year program of Japanese studies, of course she wanted to visit the country and see if what she'd learned had any relevancy to contemporary Japan. Originally planning to go on a tourist visa, she was asked by a former professor of hers to go instead on a research visa and help the professor gather information for an upcoming series of articles on the role of women in Japanese society. With research visa in hand, she headed off for adventure.

"I'm just the kind of person who likes to do things impulsively. I had been warned by friends and teachers not to just go over until I had a job and a place to live but I wanted to go immediately and I knew, deep down, that everything would work out somehow. Luckily, everything eventually did, but for awhile, I wasn't so sure.

"I arrived in Tokyo with $800 in my pocket so I had to find work quickly, despite the warning I'd gotten from the Immigration man at the airport that I was not to work in any way. He really didn't need to worry about it (at least not at first) because I made the mistake of arriving at New Year's when the whole country shuts down. Not only couldn't I find work, I couldn't even find a place open to *apply* for work!

"After the holidays, though, I was able to find jobs with no difficulty at all. After staying at the Asia Center for a week, I moved into one of the places in Tokyo that offered free rent in exchange for English conversation lessons. But I really didn't have enough privacy there, so when I was offered a house to rent for about $300 a month, I jumped at the chance.

"Then I started to get some very good jobs. My first was a part-time research position I got from a friend of a friend which paid about $2,300 a month. A little later, I picked up a job teaching English to a group of skin divers (believe it or not!) for $45 a hour, four hours a week. Finally, I also accepted a class teaching company executives at a chemical company for $60 an hour, also four hours a week.

"For a short time, I also worked at an advertising company, writing ad copy, and at a bar as a hostess, but I took those jobs primarily for my research project to learn how Japanese men treat women under those circumstances.

"All the while, of course, I had been interviewing just about every woman in my neighborhood for my project and had gathered quite a lot of information for my professor back home, almost all of it suggesting that Japanese women are not only *not* oppressed but, in many ways, are the real force within the culture and exercise considerable control over men. I was very much looking forward to sharing all this with the woman in charge back in America.

"After I'd been in Japan for several months, my professor and several of her graduate students came over to do some research of their own with, I think, some preconceived ideas about the project. They felt so strongly that Japanese women were subservient to men and without any significant rights that it didn't seem to me that they took my contrary findings seriously. In my opinion, Japanese women aren't the oppressed and abused people a lot of foreigners seem to think they are.

"I loved Japan even more than I thought I would and I don't think my knowledge of Japanese had that much to do with it. Most of the time, my friends would want me to speak English so they could practice theirs.

"Almost all my friends were Japanese because I tried to stay away from the other foreigners as much as I could. I got the distinct feeling that most gaijin in Japan were walking around with cultural chips on their shoulders, down on all cultures--sometimes including their own.

"One thing that really bothered me was the culture shock, not going but coming home. I think it was at least twice as difficult readjusting to the American culture as it was getting used to the Japanese.

"I was really frustrated for a long time at how almost none of my American friends were the least bit interested in what I'd seen, learned and experienced in Japan. The prevailing attitude seemed to be, 'I haven't done it so I'm not interested.' They just seemed to be incapable of relating to what I'd accomplished. That really surprised me because my Japanese friends were *always* interested in learning about America."

Still uncertain about going? Try this: just for fun, I stopped in at Kinokuniya book store in Shinjuku to browse through the city's largest English book selection. Lurking near the language instruction texts, I was able to spot a number of teachers, apparently searching for classroom help. I asked them for their opinions and I believe you'll find their responses typical of the more than 6,000 foreigners now teaching English as a Second Language in Japan.

According to Ruth Hoffman, 27, of York, Pennsylvania, "The money's great and so are the students!"

Val Beadelman, 25, and John Armstrong, 27, both of San Francisco, California, agreed that teaching gives "tremendous contact with the culture." John added, "There's definitely never a lack of jobs here. If you want to work, you can."

Chris Leatherwood, 23, of Sunnyvale, California, had been teaching in Tokyo only three months when interviewed. He urged prospective teachers to "do everything you can to get a work visa." Working for several schools, he estimated his average hourly income as 3,500 yen ($16)--"and there are lots of jobs available."

Twenty-two-year old Chris Witmer of Buffalo, New York, admitted he had no training as a teacher before he began working. "I was just a native-speaker and that seemed to be all they were looking for." As for his wages, he commented, "I get so much money teaching that I feel a real responsibility to do the best job I can."

Toledo, Ohio's David Bloomfield, 23, summed up his feelings about work opportunities by claiming "if you can meet the right people and are willing to pound the pavement and be perseverent, you can easily average $20-$25 an hour teaching."

"Most of the classes are evenings, mornings and weekends," said Michael Smith, 23, of Eugene, Oregon. "The best time of year to find work is probably just before the semesters start or in mid-summer. But really, anytime at all is OK.

"I've had mixed feelings about Japan," he continued, "I'll hate it for awhile and then suddenly I'll love it again. I think the most important thing you can do to get comfortable here is to build your confidence which, I think, happens naturally. Now whenever I get lost somewhere, I just use it as a learning experience."

Of Shoguns And Showdowns

Of course, if you're really (or even semi-) serious about pulling this off, you have to give yourself plenty of lead time--at least three months, preferably four. To help give you some idea of what you should be doing when, a "time line" is provided in the Appendix. Follow it and you should have no problem making preparations in plenty of time.

At some point, you should certainly read a few books on the culture, especially Edwin Reischauer's <u>The Japanese</u>, Robert Christopher's <u>The Japanese Mind</u>, George Fields' wonderful interpretation of contemporary Japan, <u>From Bonsai to Levis</u> and maybe even <u>Japan as Number One</u>, the runaway best-seller in Japan by Ezra Vogel that was scarcely heard of in Vogel's native USA. It will convince you that you'll be joining a winning team in Japan.

Don't forget the literature either. A few of Kawabata's or Mishima's books will give you a real feel for the values of the people and how their minds work. (Expect to be surprised.)

But by far the most important preparation you can make is to start saving your travelling money. You'd probably be wise to bring at least about $1,000 (plus your plane ticket to get over there) which will give you enough to get set up without undue money woes. True, a few easy-going types have been known to drift in with about $100 to their name and somehow survive but not many newcomers to the country will care to deal with that kind of anxiety in addition to learning all the ropes.

Japan, like any place in which you're a stranger, *is* an expensive country until you learn how to live like the natives. Once you've learned how to avoid the tourist traps, your expenses shouldn't be much more than what you're used to spending back home. (Warning: if the help speaks fluent English, you're probably going to pay a small fortune.)

But before we get into the nitty-gritty of how to get over and survive the process, let's get some predictable preliminaries out of the way: history and geography. Try not to doze through this section, though. Being aware of the Japanese past and land-form really is essential to reaching a true understanding of the people. And don't worry, I promise to keep it somewhat short by avoiding mention of all but the most entertaining plagues, revolutions and natural disasters.

Japan comprises 47 prefectures, which are roughly equal in their system of government to American states. These are scattered among four main islands (Hokkaido is northernmost, then, moving south, Honshu--the largest, Shikoku and Kyushu) and hundreds of smaller ones, including Okinawa, about 500 miles south of Kyushu.

The main islands are located in a piece of the Pacific slightly smaller than California but a little bigger than Italy or Britain. In this something-less-than-vast expanse, there live about 121 million reasonably contented Japanese, making it the third most densely populated country in the world (after the Netherlands and Belgium).

Although the country has outstanding natural beauty, the major cities (with the notable exception of culture-rich Kyoto) do not have a lot of greenery. Easily accessible by train, however, are numerous national parks and recreation areas--Tokyo, for example, has 37, some just a few hours away. Parks in the cities proper (land values make them somewhat scarce) are immaculate and very cleverly designed to give the weary visitor that much-needed escape from city pressures--anytime, that is, except Sunday afternoons when thousands of near-forgotten "salaryman" Daddies flock to any patch of green to get briefly reacquainted with their tykes before the next 70-

hour work-week begins. (Don't worry, *you'll* probably be working less than 40.)

It's generally accepted that the Japanese came to the islands from China and Korea (with whom they have been on less than loving terms for centuries--seems the Nipponese have this nasty habit of trying to conquer them every so often...). Anyway, a feudal system much like Europe's in the Middle Ages developed which resulted in almost non-stop fighting until the country was unified in the fourth century.

Two centuries later, there came a very powerful force to the islands, one which still plays a major part in the actions and beliefs of the Japanese people. This force (not really a religion so much as belief system) was Buddhism, which German scholar Kuehnett-Leddihn calls "a mixture of wisdom, morality, and tradition...the driving moral force behind [the Japanese people's] intelligence, energy, their predisposition for hard and systematic work, team spirit, strong sense of personal responsibility, and-- last but not least--loyalty and patriotism."

The Sea of Japan is a rather nasty piece of water with some fairly ferocious storms on it, so early contact between Japan and China was irregular and limited. Thus, somewhat isolated, the Japanese went about developing an Asian culture that, while it does owe a great deal to the Chinese (especially the writing system), it is in many ways totally unlike all other cultures in the region.

This feeling of uniqueness among the Japanese is well-demonstrated by a recent poll taken in Japan which indicates that most people feel more kinship with Western (especially European) cultures than with those in their own geographical back yard. Only recently have Japanese tourists "discovered" the rest of Asia, which they see as being in many ways more "foreign" than the West.

Largely because of the difficulty they have relating to other Asians, the Japanese are sometimes grossly insensitive to those cultures, resulting in the resentment many Asians feel toward "the ugly Japanese." Obviously the Japanese notion of separateness and homogeneity has aided them in their efforts to turn their resource-poor country into a world power, but it's also made them somewhat condescending toward those with values and achievements unlike their own.

Much like our own history, the church (i.e., Buddhist priests) eventually became quite powerful and threatened the sovereignty of the Emperor. The capital was moved from Nara to Kyoto in about 800 A.D. where it remained for 800 years. Eventually, the emperor's powers were compromised and he was reduced to a mere puppet of the real power behind the throne: the shogun.

The shoguns, for the most part, were a good thing for Japan (especially the Tokugawas) because they finally unified the country (after battles too bloody to imagine) and began to open the country to foreign trade. In the 16th Century, some Portuguese merchants and a handful of Christian missionaries were allowed to settle in a tightly restricted area of southern Japan, under close government scrutiny.

In a rather short time, however, the government began to realize that its earlier fears about letting in the foreigners were indeed well-founded. The traders and clergy were sowing seeds of discontent among those around them and so they were summarily booted out. The door to the West was slammed shut behind them and locked tight.

For about 250 years, Japan existed in blissful ignorance of and isolation from the events of the rapidly industrializing Western world. For that period of time, Japan changed very little, sheltered from the technological innovations sweeping other countries.

Stories about what was going on "out there" drifted into Japan, as did a few shipwrecked sailors who were either put to death or sent packing before they could contaminate the populace with their wild Western ways. But, since the penalty for a native's leaving the country was death, interest in things foreign was scant, to say the least. The nation was totally self-sufficient and wanted simply to be left alone. But the samurai age couldn't last, not when all around Japan Western frigates sailed like sharks, eyeing the one last holdout against colonial exploitation...

Much has been written on the ambivalent love/hate feelings the Japanese still hold for Americans. After all, no enemy had wreaked such havoc on their country as did the US forces during World War II; yet no conquerer ever showed such compassion toward the vanquished as did the GIs after the war. The Japanese fully expected to be enslaved; instead they were lavished with aid, which was, in large part, responsible for the success Japan enjoys today. Very inscrutable, these Yankees.

These mixed feelings probably had their origins far earlier than the Second World War, however, for it was in 1853 when Commodore Matthew Perry sailed imperiously into Tokyo Bay, pointed his American cannons at the Royal Palace and politely requested an audience with His Majesty, the Emperor. Thus were the Japanese people *forced* against their will to open their country to the long-nosed barbarians once again.

But a person fond of life's unceasing ironies couldn't help but chuckle at how the Japanese, forced to join in the haggling at the global marketplace, have today proven themselves even more adept at trade than those Western brigands who thought to drain the country dry-- just as they had China. In 1985, America took in about $45 billion more worth of Japanese imports than it sent out in exports.

Could it be the West now regrets Commodore Perry's arm-twisting that day? In view of the current trade imbalance with Japan, it doesn't seem totally implausible that someday *another* fleet of American warships might sail into Tokyo, this time with orders to *close* the country back up again!

So Japan, at the point of a gun, joined the world community. The people knew they couldn't beat the West, so, in true Japanese fashion, the entire society mobilized, reorganized and brought itself roaring full speed into the 20th century.

A strong central government was needed and, in 1867, the Emperor provided it by supplanting the shogun and having his power restored. The Emperor's name was Meiji--and this one is a definite must-remember. His reign is known as the Meiji Restoration and, during it, never was a more feverish game of catch-up played by any backward backwater burg anywhere.

Unbelievably, in just 27 years, Japan went from a country of gentlemen warriors (firearms were outlawed for all, even the Emperor's own guard) to one of the most powerful military forces in the world. In 1895, it won a war with China and then, ten years later, when Russia seized one of Japan's northern ports, Nihon accomplished

what had been thought impossible: defeating a Caucasian nation.

Realizing that they would probably be unable to put the Japanese genie back into the bottle, the Western powers recognized the upstart powerhouse as one of the Big Five nations of the world, but only after it agreed to side with the Allies during World War I.

This was all very heady stuff for the already smug Japanese. Their belief in themselves grew to enormous proportions but who could criticize them after all they'd accomplished? Japan had tasted success; never again would it be content with an insular existence.

Firmly planted in the circles of power, Japan's next step was to see what the other big boys were up to. In the 1930's, it seemed that everyone was up to snatching whatever territories hadn't yet been colonized. Rarely reluctant to exploit weakness (especially when it appears socially correct), the Japanese joined in the fun. In retrospect, though, perhaps no other world power was more justified in participating in that era's global grab-fest than Japan.

The country, you must remember, has never had any real natural resources other than its people. For centuries, Japan was just barely able to feed herself. Then, with the development of international trade, the population exploded, forcing Japan to import more and more. Today, the majority of its energy and foodstuffs comes from abroad, creating a dangerous dependency on the smooth flow of international commodity traffic. It's been estimated that if Japan were totally deprived of her imported food, she would starve in a few months.

Of course, in the mid-1930's Japan was not nearly so dependent on foreign supplies but, still, the pressure to guarantee security was substantial. Why not, the people reasoned, just claim the resources of our neighbors who could never do as much with what they have as we could? The Japanese came to believe that it was their "manifest destiny" to rule Asia as leader of a regional "Co-prosperity Sphere."

Japan took China without much struggle and set up a puppet government. The West was willing to wink at this bit of the prodigy's willfulness but the feeling was growing that the new kid's britches might be getting a bit tight for him. Japan knew that it was being viewed as "uppity" by the West and realized that it probably had to find new friends with similar interests.

Although Japan had little in common with Germany, it saw the war in Europe as a convenient diversion which would allow it at last to take the resources it thought a world power was entitled to. Against the advice of many high government officials, Japan's military-controlled government sided with the Nazi's.

Rightly figuring that the West would not let it continue acquiring countries, Japan attempted to hamstring the US military at Pearl Harbor. Most Japanese today agree that the move was a desperate one, but still, it was their only chance to make a reality of what before existed only in name: the Japanese Empire. But against the huge wealth and might of America, even the Empire could not keep the force with them.

In 1945, with the war already lost for Japan, Little Boy and Fat Man nuked their niches into history along with their targets: Hiroshima and Nagasaki. And, in the face of such awesome power, the already decimated country capitulated totally.

But why, many still wonder, did America, self-proclaimed liberator and lover of humanity, wreak such misery on innocent civilians and become the *only* nation in history to be branded nuclear warrior?

The official explanation was that President Truman thought that the Japanese would fight to the bitter end if an invasion of the main islands were attempted. Estimated casualties were half a million American GI's and countless millions of women and children (about all that was left in Japan at that time) who, like the kamikaze, would give all for their homeland.

They had to be utterly overwhelmed, the story goes, and shown that the US was in possession of a weapon so powerful that resistance would be absolutely hopeless. The two cities were selected as targets because, supposedly, they both had war materials factories in them.

Curiously, however, both cities were "virgin;" neither had ever been bombed before. What a perfect place to judge the full effect of the bomb! Just to make sure, the pilots of the planes were given instructions to bomb their alternate targets if clouds interfered. With what? Does a nuclear bomb care if its cloudy or bright? No, but the scientists, seeing the two cities' residents as their personal guinea pigs, wanted a clear view of the fruits of their nasty labors. Clouds would hamper the observation plane's picture-taking and related blast-measuring activities.

One can't help but wonder why, if the purpose of the bombings was simply to demonstrate the ferocity of the weapon, it was necessary to destroy cities. Wouldn't the Japanese have gotten the message if we had, say, evaporated Mt. Fuji instead of 240,000 civilians, as the Japanese government says died as a result of the two attacks?

In fact, one historian, Gar Alperovitz, claimed in July, 1985 that once-secret documents now indicate that the bombs were detonated for demonstration purposes--for the Russians, just to let them know they could be the next victims of US technological superiority. Gar states that, "President Truman was advised two months before Hiroshima that if he assured Japanese officials they could keep the emperor (as he ultimately did), this was likely to produce surrender."

Alternatively, he was also told that "when the massive Red Army entered the war, Japan was likely to collapse." The Russians declared war against the Japanese

August 8, 1945, two days after Hiroshima and one day before Nagasaki, mainly (say the Japanese) to seize northern territory from the soon-to-be-vanquished empire. What they saw happen in those cities certainly did impress them. They immediately starting developing A-bombs of their own.

Well, right or wrong, it's a moot point now. In any case, the Japanese don't like to talk about the war, and especially not about the atomic bombings. They seem honestly fond of Americans but, unless you're as vehemently opposed to nuclear arms as are almost all Japanese, it's probably a topic of conversation best left alone.

Although Hiroshima and Nagasaki have become synonymous with war's devastation, actually they suffered nowhere near as much total destruction as, say, Tokyo, which was subjected to round-the-clock firebombing. The "City of Paper" (as the allies called the capital) as well as most other major cities was decimated by the war's end. Then the rebuilding began.

Speaking of their remarkable tenacity, an admiring US Secretary of State under Presidents Kennedy and Johnson, George W. Ball, once commented, "The Japanese are a people with a genius for doing anything they set out to do as a matter of national decision." And after the bombing stopped, the decision of the defeated nation was to immediately reestablish order--but this time under the watchful eyes of thousands of American Occupation troops overseeing every aspect of reconstruction. For the first time in its long history, Japan surrendered its autonomy to foreign conquerors, a deep humiliation which they still have not fully recovered from.

After their defeat, the Japanese were strangely submissive to the Americans' desire to restructure the country from top to bottom, forcing that totally alien culture into an American mold. America administered the occupation forces and General MacArthur ruled the country with a delicate but iron hand.

Despite Japan's long history of a strong central government, MacArthur insisted on diffusing power by granting local authority to both the national police force and education system. The Japanese heartily assented but then, in quintessential Japanese style, promptly returned both systems to their pre-war centralized form as soon as the Occupation ended in the mid-1950's and they were once again in control of their own government.

Surprisingly enough, despite the notion of a constitution being totally alien to Asia, Japan's has worked reasonably well, thanks to very broad interpretation of its contents by the country's high courts. The keystone of the document is certainly the anti-war clause which insists that Japan "renounce war as a means of national policy forever." Even today, Japan has no military whatsoever, except the Self-Defense Force, theoretically intended only to help Japan defend herself but still constituting a larger Pacific force in 1985 than those of Canada, Australia or New Zealand.

The 40's and 50's were a time of terrific social chaos for the Japanese, even more than that caused by the massive reorganization of the Meiji Era. This time, foreigners were *everywhere*, the kids were having their heads filled with all kinds of crazy notions about freedom and equality and--who knew for sure?--maybe the long-noses had something there. After all, they *had* won the war.

Whereas under Meiji, the *system* had changed, under the occupation by American forces, *values* changed. Japan quickly adopted many American attitudes--at least superficially. Beneath, there lay the bedrock of ancient Asian civilization and values, as it does today.

Industrially, Japan during reconstruction provided the world with some pretty good chuckles. Their attempts to match US economic might with cheap, shoddy, unsophisticated goods (about all their war-ravaged economy could produce at the time) were ridiculed mercilessly. In sharp contrast to its implied meaning today, "Made In Japan" 25 years ago was synonymous with "second rate."

Today, Japan has bested the West in a dozens of areas. Japan makes more and often better cameras than Germany, watches than Switzerland, cars than America-- and every nation's worried about their computer industry in view of recent Japanese advances in *that* area.

Only in weapons of destruction is the West's manufacturing and export lead still substantial--but not because of any lack of Japanese expertise. Although their anti-war constitution forbids the making of any war materiel, Japanese companies are not even attempting to circumvent the law--they appear to have made a moral decision to leave such industry to those nations with less conscience.

As for Japan's future, it looks bright indeed if world trade continues to flow smoothly without interruptions or trade barriers erected by nervous governments seeking to protect the jobs of their often overpaid and underproductive workers. No country in the world has a greater stake in "free trade" than the country with only 20% of its land arable, making it dependent on foreign imports for even most staple foods.

If you regard wealth as being how much people owe you, Japan is the richest country in the world thanks to its position as top creditor nation. Conversely, America, for the first time ever, became a debtor country (owing more than it is owed) in 1985. If you look at simple Gross National Product (how much is produced), Japan is now the third wealthiest country, with just 13% less gross national product than the number two, Russia, which has 2.25 times as many people, almost 60 times as much land and incalculably greater natural resources.

But the Japanese know how tenuous their success is. They know that if imports of food to Japan were stopped, it would be only a few months before actual starvation would begin. The Japanese liken their country to a bicycle: it must keep moving forward or it will simply fall over. It would certainly be a nasty fall.

In their schools, homes and workplaces, the people are reminded constantly of the value of cooperation, dedication, honesty and productive living. It's apparently not born of any high-minded sense of moral propriety or religious obligation, either; they work together simply because it works. And in Japan, everything and everyone *has* to work--their survival depends on it.

The Japanese are astounded by Americans' propensity for suing one another. Why, they wonder, don't they work together instead of bickering? In Japan, it's considered a major failing if two parties in disagreement can't resolve the matter by personal negotiation. Perhaps that's why in all of Japan there are fewer attorneys than are currently practicing in the city of San Francisco.

In many ways, Japan today may reflect the world civilization of the future--one of cooperation and consideration born of limited space and resources. The Japanese have always known how to live well with little. Consider that they use one-sixth as much energy per capita as Americans, yet, on the average, live more than three years longer--but only recently has the rest of the world begun to appreciate the wisdom of their culture and tried to emulate it.

Getting There

Sound interesting? Well, most people who have made the trip will agree: getting to Japan is simple, living in Japan is first a challenge then a joy, and working in Japan is for the most part fun and rewarding if you like working with people. Probably the greatest obstacle you'll have is money--you'll need some to get set up.

Especially if you go over without a firm job offer (quite likely), you really should allow yourself a generous cushion to fall back on if need be. In an emergency, a bank wire-transfer may be sent to your embassy in Tokyo (the address is in the Appendix) and takes just a few hours to speed to your rescue. Just make sure the money is somewhere, accessible by someone.

Another matter to be taken care of prior to leaving is opening a local checking account. This will allow you to order things from home simply by sending one of your checks to the company, paying in that particular currency and requesting delivery in Japan--a very common and tremendously useful practice. (Conversely, of course, it might also be a good idea upon leaving Japan, to maintain a yen account there, possibly accessible to a trusted friend so he or she can send you things you might want after your return.)

Failure to maintain an account back home will mean you'll have to change currency every time you need something from "the real world." Exchange rate fluctuations and bank commissions make frequent currency exchange a risky, time-consuming and expensive annoyance to be avoided as much as possible.

Be sure to stock up on apparel before you go over, especially shoes if your size is larger than 7 (for women) or 10 (for men). Some larger size shoes are available at special stores but the limited demand causes sky-high prices. It's best to bring your own or arrange for someone to send replacements.

Gaijin-sized clothing is somewhat more available, although it too is more expensive than what you may be used to paying. Again, however, if you're larger than a size 8 for women or a size 38 in men's suits, pack your own.

If you *do* have to buy clothing there, try the department stores, especially those in the outskirts of the city where they don't have to figure their astronomical rent into the prices *you* have to pay. Keep an eye out for "bargain tables," usually to be found only on a single floor of a department store. Although the Japanese are becoming more bargain-conscious of late (it used to be a sign of low breeding to worry about cost), your competition at the sales will be far less than what you're used to at home.

Japanese wall current is 100 volts at 50 cycles in the northern half of the country (including Tokyo) and 60 cycles in the south (including Osaka and Nagoya). This means that most of your small appliances from home (electric razors, curling irons, radios, etc.) *will* work without a transformer.

If you're coming from North America with its 117 volts, your appliances will do quite well with less juice than they're used to; they just won't do their job quite as energetically. Be forewarned, however, that electric clocks will run slow on Japanese current and some people find that certain things with heating elements in them never regain their pre-Japan pep once they're brought home again. European appliances designed to use 220 volts, of course, need converters.

Never use anything designed to accept only Japanese 100 volt current anywhere but Japan unless you also use a transformer to "step down" your local current. Shooting 220 or 117 volts into something expecting only 100 has left many an unsuspecting returnee with nothing but a smouldering mound of melted transistors where once stood a gleaming testament to Japan's electronic wizardry...

You will be far better prepared psychologically for your stint in Nihon if you learn something about the people by making a few Japanese acquaintances in your home town prior to leaving. Besides being generally nice people to be around, Japanese are usually delighted to tell foreigners all about what to expect there--they may even give you some people to look up in whichever city you decide to settle.

The best place to meet Japanese and find material to help you get ready for living in their country is in your local Japanese community. These areas, usually called "little Tokyo" (or some equally "cutesy" term), are almost always found in the downtown area of major cities. Even a few hours of just strolling through the shops and watching the people there can give you a fairly good (albeit Westernized) idea of what life in the Nihon might be like.

Another good way to meet "Nihon-jin" (literally "Japan-people") is at the same ESL schools where you found your veteran Japan EFL teacher. Talk to the school's student advisor or director and tell him or her that you are considering living in Japan for awhile and would like to get to know some of the people. Offer to have one or two Japanese students from the school over to your home for dinner and conversation about Japan. The kids will be delighted and will probably offer to fix a Japanese meal for *you* in return.

If your town is too small for a "little Tokyo" or ESL school, you should also be able to meet and learn from Japanese people working at a Japanese restaurant, something which only the tiniest of cities wouldn't have. Like any of the people you're liable to meet, these folks will probably be truly tickled to tell you anything at all about their homeland.

Although it isn't absolutely necessary, knowing even a bit of Japanese will help make you overcome that brief sinking feeling that you just stepped off the first manned probe to Alpha Centauri instead the plane from home. It's highly recommended that you purchase an extensive phrase book and dictionary which should be available in your town.

If not, any local book store can special-order them for you or you can write to the grand-daddy of the Japanese book store, Kinokuniya. In America, you can get almost any book about the country, people or language from them in Los Angeles at 110 S. Los Angeles St., 90012; in San Francisco at 1581 Webster, 94115; and in New York City at 10 W. 49th St., 10020. In Vancouver, try Sophia Books at 725 Nelson St. V6Z 2A8 and, in London, Books Nippon should have plenty at 64 St. Paul's Churchyard EC4M 8AA.

But of all the pre-trip preparations you perform, probably the biggest favor you could do yourself before going would be to learn--inside and out--the 48 basic letters of "katakana," one of the three Japanese alphabets. What makes katakana so invaluable even to those who can't speak a word of Japanese is that it is used to "spell" a large number of very useful English words for which no translation is necessary. The beauty of katakana for the gaijin (foreigner) is that it's not Japanese; it's usually trying to be English. Figuring out what English word or phrase is being "spelled," however, can be a very vexing experience.

For example, what would you think if you had finally decoded the katakana you saw in an ad on the train, only to be left with the sounds " ai su ku ri mu?" It may be fairly nonsensical now but don't worry, after a few weeks of reading the stuff, you'll be quite adept at sliding all the sounds together and saying them as the Japanese would. In this case, you'd come up with what we all scream for: "ice cream." Not only fun but downright useful if you happen to be searching for a cozy "ho te ru" or a tasty and affordable "re su to ra n."

As for the rest of the language, good luck. The other two alphabets are "hiragana" and "kanji," neither of which will do you much good at all unless you can also *speak* Japanese. Like katakana, hiragana also has 48 basic characters (plus a few variations) but, because it's almost always used as Japanese, it is not especially useful for you, the Nippon novice, to take the time to learn before you go over. Unfortunately, most short-timers living in Japan never get around to learning any of the three alphabets-- unfortunate for them. Without making at least a slight effort to learn the language, the average gaijin will never develop more than a cursory feel for what Japan is really all about.

One thing that many people forget to take care of before they leave is meeting obligations. Rest assured that during your absence, you will not be forgotten: any debts you leave behind will only have worsened by the time you return. This is not to say that you need to close out your life before you go; just let everyone know where you'll be and for how long.

If you maintain your local checking account, it's as easy to make loan payments from Tokyo as from Tottenham, Toronto, Tacoma or Toowoomba (and you'll probably have a lot more in the bank with which to do so). According to all known rules of etiquette, it's quite acceptable to have your Japanese address put on your current checking account checks--the bank will even send your regular statement to you overseas. Just be sure you keep the account well-stocked with regular infusions of transfers from your Japanese account.

Before you can go anywhere, of course, you'll need a valid passport. Make sure yours is still OK and will remain so while you're abroad. It is possible to have your passport renewed by your embassy in Tokyo, but it's a pain and you shouldn't take the chance of something going amiss with such a valuable document. Your town's main post office can give you full details about getting or renewing a passport. Just be sure to allow a least a month for all the red tape.

No vaccinations are necessary to travel to Japan, but if you expect to be going to the more exotic lands in Asia (e.g., the Phillipines, Indonesia, Ho Chi Minh City), you'd do well to check with your doctor or local hospital as to exactly what the requirements are. If you're not sure where you'll be travelling, you could easily wait and get the shots in Japan.

If you apply for a work visa before you go, you'll need to submit a couple of small black and white photos of yourself along with your other papers for the consulate. But even if you go over as a tourist, bring at least half a dozen head-and-shoulders shots which you'll have plenty of occasion to use when you *do* get sponsored. You generally can't use them in passports, but in Japan, pictures from automatic photo machines are quite acceptable.

Japan, and especially Tokyo, is very much a "four season" region with humid summers (thankfully air conditioning is now commonplace) and bone-chilling winters. With the exception of the exceedingly frigid Japan Sea side of the country, though, the temperature rarely drops below freezing south of the capital.

Tokyo temperatures range from 39 to 77 degrees Fahrenheit (4 to 25 degrees Centigrade) with humidity from 57 to 79%. The capital averages about 36 days of precipitation annually. The northernmost city, Sapporo, gets 47 rainy/snowy days with temperatures averaging from 23 to 68 (-5 to 20 Centigrade) and humidity 68 to 80%. Kyoto to the south has 25 days of precipitation, temperatures staying remarkably constant from 67 to 72 degrees (19 to 22 Centigrade) but with 67 to 76% humidity.

Sorry to complicate your wardrobe but this means you'll definitely need a full complement of clothing; all the way from shorts to long-johns--and don't forget your rain gear; it gets rather soggy over there. Since it would certainly make your first few days more pleasant if you didn't have to lug your entire wardrobe with you from home to "ho te ru," you might want to arrange to have the *next* season's clothing mailed to you when needed (usually May and September). There's nothing that'll put you in a bad mood faster than "schlepping" half a dozen suitcases through the streets of Tokyo while you're still wondering if you're even in the right country. Try to travel light and enjoy the view.

Your friends shouldn't mind mailing the bulk of your wardrobe when you need it if you pre-pack everything for them (don't forget anti-mildew packs if you live where this is a problem) so that all they need to do is take the box down to the post office, slap some stamps on it and off it goes--by *sea mail*. (Air mail costs a fortune.) Allow a full month for the clothes to reach you by boat and you'll save money on the mailing and hassles aplenty by not dragging your winter coats around with you in July.

Just so your friends and relations don't think you're sailing off over the edge of the world and into the Great Void of Incommunicado, tell them that, if it's absolutely necessary to contact you before you get a more-or-less permanent address, they can do so either through your embassy (see Appendix for the address) or care of General Delivery, Central Post Office, Tokyo, Japan 100.

Certainly the first thing you should do once you arrive in Japan is to call your embassy in Tokyo and tell them that you have arrived and where you'll be staying. Oftentimes, your embassy will be the only agency in the entire country that will have the means and desire to locate you in case of an emergency back home. It's important to keep in touch with them.

Many Tokyo-based gaijin have their mail first sent to the Central PO when they arrive until they get their own place; some *keep* having mail sent to it and the Japan Times very kindly publishes long lists of gaijin with mail waiting for them at the CPO. Fortunately, the CPO is conveniently located in the heart of Tokyo's financial district in Marunouchi and you'll probably pass near it many times a week, whatever your employment.

If you plan to do extensive travelling before you get down to work, you might want to consider picking up one of the Japan National Railway's Japan National Rail Passes before you leave. The larger travel agencies and all Japan Air Lines offices have them and they allow you to travel anywhere on JNR's 13,000 miles of track all over the country for 7, 14 or 21 days in Deluxe Class or Ordinary. Prices for adult passes range from about $100 for an Ordinary 7-day pass to about $300 for a Deluxe 21-day pass. Like Europe's Eurail Pass, the Japan Rail Pass must be purchased prior to departure; it can't be bought in Japan.

As for health matters, not to worry. There are excellent drug stores in the larger cities which cater specifically to the international community and carry many of the prescriptions and over-the-counter medications you're familiar with; all, unfortunately, costing much more than at home. If a particular brand is near and dear to your heart, you would probably be well-advised to bring a goodly supply with you, especially if it's been formulated just for you. If you do need to buy local medications in Japan, however, there's no need to worry about the purity of the item. The Japanese in

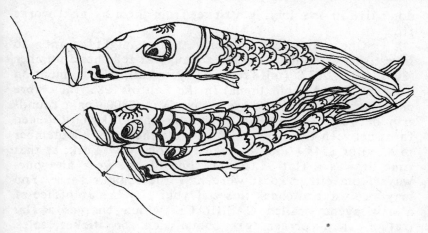

general are *exceedingly* cautious about such matters and the odds are that health standards in Japan meet or exceed those you're used to at home.

Conveniently enough, many drugs which require prescriptions at home are readily bought in Japan. On the other hand, birth control pills are almost impossible to obtain in Japan. People there think they're too dangerous making condoms and abortions the major forms of birth control.

Usually, however, you'll get what you need simply by strolling into any drug store and playing a lively round of charades with the amused pharmacist as you try to act out what ails you. "Indigestion" may be alright for rank amateurs, but masters of the game won't be satisfied until, like one friend, they've demonstrated and been treated for a bladder infection.

A bit of advice about transportation to Japan: don't count on your local travel agency to get you the best fare. The way the travel industry works, agents receive commissions based on the fare you pay. Obviously, they're not going to be too highly motivated to find you the lowest possible fare if it's going to mean less for them in commission and there's little local competition to encourage them to do so. Agents all over the US use the same ticketing computers to find schedules and fares and they can all sell tickets from point A to point B. Usually the best fares are to be found in big cities but even if you don't live in one, buying a ticket from them by mail works fine.

One American agency you might want to investigate is called Travel Exchange at telephone number (800) AIR-GATE (toll-free). (If you call, please mention how you heard about them.) In the Fall of 1985, they were charging a regular fare (year-round) of $800 for a round-trip between LA or San Francisco and Tokyo. Reduced fares between the same points were either $665 (September to May) or $745 (June to August). From New York, at that time, it was a flat $1,085 anytime of the year and one-ways from either coast were half the regular fares. You may also want to check to see if your city has an office of a new agency called CASHBACK which charges a flat (rather than percentage) commission on ticket sales. Especially for an international ticket, you could save a tidy sum with them.

A lot of the best deals in America are advertised in the classified ads or travel section of the newspapers of large coastal cities. Just call the number in the ad, even if its long-distance (the phone call costs nothing compared to what you'll save), and ask what their lowest fare to Japan is for the time of year you want to go (summer and the Christmas holidays are most expensive usually). Then call another agency; then another. Never take the first quote you're given; air fares vary tremendously even for seats in the same section on the same flight! Then, just for fun, call a local agent and ask how much *their* cheapest fare is. You'll feel smug for weeks after.

Since you're planning ahead and probably don't care if there's a lovely linen doily adorning your seat when you board the plane, there's no need for you to use a daily and/or high-priced flight primarily intended for businessfolk and other expense-account passengers. I recommend China Air Lines departing from Los Angeles and San Francisco for the best in cheap, reliable transportation from the West Coast. If you'd rather leave from the East Coast, prepare to pay more for your flight over the north pole, but check New York papers for good bargains--sometimes even the major airlines have them. More likely, China Air, Korean Air Lines, Thai Air, Varig, Phillipine Air and other not-quite-first-world carriers will be the cheapest.

For those coming from Europe, check the possibility of flying first to Hong Kong--it's a very busy route and so fares are good. After a few days of frolicking there, you'll be ready to continue on to Japan. Those from Down Under, unfortunately, will probably wind up paying top dollar for the trip; discounts are rare on that long, relatively lightly-traveled route.

The "off-brand" airlines fly hand-me-down 747's, bought from the major airlines which, although the seats may be a bit threadbare, are subject to the same tough safety standards as the major carriers. They pay less for their airplanes; you pay less for a seat on one. (Just make sure it's not in a plane being piloted by the Korean CIA.)

The service is fine and while the grub is not the greatest (ever tried freeze-dried foo yung?), you might prefer to go steerage class with one of the cheapies, forgo the linen napkin and sirloin, and spend what you saved on a super-nice dinner in downtown Tokyo when you land.

Another bonus if you fly cheap is that you can enjoy such in-flight cinematic masterpieces as "He Never Gives Up," a Taiwanese howler (unintentionally so) which made my last flight on China Air Lines far more enjoyable. Might not be everyone's cup of green tea, but I thought such immortal sub-titles as "He thinks he's happy, but his legs are artificial" were pretty hilarious. Inscrutable or merely warped?

Probably the biggest attraction about China is that it lands at Haneda airport, right in the heart of Tokyo. All other international airlines have to use the New International Airport at Narita about forty miles away. The new airport is impressive but mainly due to the hundreds of police permanently assigned there to discourage displaced farmers from vandalizing the place. (For years, radicals have occasionally chucked the odd rock, block or homemade bomb over the fence too, but so far, no injuries.)

The reason for two international airports in the same city is that they represent a classic Japanese solution to a somewhat sticky wicket: what do you do with two airlines, both claiming to be a country's one and only national carrier? The solution, in the case of Taiwan and the People's Republic was to send the airline of the

current government of the mainland to Narita and
Taiwan's airline, China Air Lines, to Haneda.

It seems to have worked; there have been no
reported incidents of the two rivals playing bumperjets
with their Boeings and CAL has learned to live with its
outcast status--laughing all the way to the "ginko" as the
word gets around that Haneda is *the* place to land in
Tokyo and China's the only international flight landing
there.

About the only nice things that can be said for
Narita by comparison *is* that it is modern and almost
everyone there speaks good English. The bus that takes you
the 40 miles into downtown Tokyo (the driver even loads
your luggage) isn't bad and the train is rather fun too.
Then again, you'll probably be spending so much time
"training" to get to work that you may wish to start
minimizing train time as soon as possible. Haneda really is
tops in the convenience department, but you may have to
pay for it with slightly higher fares on CAL than you'd
find with other "Brand X" carriers.

The Necessary Nihongo

We just couldn't let you traipse on over to the land of milk and tofu without arming you with at least enough "Nihongo" to get you to your hotel, should you be so unlucky as to ask directions from the rare bird who doesn't speak at least a bit of English.

Probably your very first stop after you've gotten settled at the hotel should be one of the excellent English book stores in Tokyo. There you'll find dozens of guide and language books which are far more comprehensive than anything we could provide you with here. Use them and you'll increase your rate of learning about the language and culture tremendously.

Japanese grammar is at the same time unbelievably convoluted and delightfully simple. There are no articles (a, an, the), no plural forms and much conversation takes places in the infinitive, with the verb at the tail end of the sentence. For brain-bending example, "Japan's person own their language difficult sometimes think" is the literal translation of the phrase "Japanese sometimes think their own language is difficult."

It's for reasons like this that one of the finest language schools in the world, the US government's Defense Language Institute in Monterey, California, considers Japanese to be one of the ten most difficult languages in the world, along with Arabic, Korean, Chinese, Russian, Polish, Czechoslovakian, Bulgarian, Turkish and Thai. Still want to learn the stuff?

On the other hand, Michael Strumpen-Darrie, Director of Curriculum for Berlitz School's world headquarters in Princeton, New Jersey, suggests that the average native English-speaker would find Japanese only a bit more difficult to learn than Greek, but much easier than Russian. "At least the Japanese sound system," he asserts, "should pose no problem for the student of the language--it's not inflected like Russian and doesn't have the different tone levels that Chinese does.

"The biggest problems, we've found, have to do with the degrees of politeness. Westerners are just not used to more than about two levels: informal and polite. Japanese has at least half a dozen. But in the early stages, it's really quite an easy language to learn--only when you get to the intermediate level does it start becoming very difficult. To learn the language really well literally takes a lifetime. We've heard from foreigners who've studied Japanese in Japan for 15 years and are still discovering new forms of speech."

The secret to effective communication, it seems, is not adhering absolutely to the mechanics of the language (grammar and vocabulary) but concentrating instead on developing a sensitivity for the rhythms of it, especially pronunciation and intonation.

By keeping your initial communications simple and really listening to the sometimes unspoken messages the Japanese will send, you should find the people altogether scrutable, if you remember to pay attention to the very subtle inferences that will greet you.

It may be something less than totally time and cost-efficient to study Japanese out of Japan. The language is evolving so very quickly that schools abroad can only teach the most formal kind which, if used with your Japanese cronies, might make you sound like a bit of a prig. (Think how stilted some foreigners sound who have studied English overseas and speak it without a trace of slang or colloquialism.)

In addition, the Japanese sometimes are reluctant to teach foreigners the language the layman uses for fear of making a bad impression. By teaching the gaijin only formal Japanese, the teacher feels sure etiquette won't be violated and, although the foreigner may always sound as though he's reciting "haiku" poems to the Emperor, at least he won't grossly offend anyone.

Unfortunately, most schools overseas (and many in Japan itself) insist on teaching a great deal of written Japanese. Now, although the two "kana" alphabets (hiragana and especially katakana) are very useful for all visitors, the main objective for most people who study the stuff is to talk with the people. And it may take upwards of five years of mind-numbing memorization to learn enough "kanji" to even read the morning paper.

Mr. Strumpen-Darrie of Berlitz advises students to minimize study of the writing unless the person's stay in Japan will be lengthy. "We've found," he says, "that if a beginner is made to learn to write everything he's taught in Japanese, he'll learn only about one-half as much as if he had concentrated solely on speaking. Of course, eventually it does become necessary and beneficial to learn the writing as well, but this point is usually not reached until the intermediate level."

As mentioned earlier, there are three "alphabets" in Japanese: "kanji" (the elaborate pictographs), "hiragana" (the curvy "letters" used primarily as grammatical markers and to "spell" certain words) and the gaijin's friend, "katakana" which I'd advise you know inside and out before you arrive. By knowing katakana, not only will you be able to immediately understand all sorts of useful written information but you'll also have learned the whole Japanese sound system.

It's not enough, though, to just learn the individual katakana characters. You've also got to practice reading as much of it as you can to familiarize yourself with how the Japanese transliterate foreign (mostly English) loan words into their own language.

A good place to get katakana reading practice is in one of the dozens of Japanese weekly magazines imported by almost all Oriental markets. Don't just figure you'll get all the practice you need once you're in Japan. Reading practice is almost as essential as knowing the symbols. It takes real familiarity with the stuff to be able to guess what they're trying to say with it.

In fact, recognizing transliterated words will probably be the most difficult part of learning katakana for you, but it's essential. Being able to read the individual

KATAKANA

	A	I	U	E	O	VOWEL SOUNDS				
	ア A	イ I	ウ U	エ E	オ O	AS IN	A cot	I easy	U loot	E say	O flow
K	カ KA	キ KI	ク KU	ケ KE	コ KO	G	ガ GA	ギ GI	グ GU	ゲ GE	ゴ GO
S	サ SA	シ SHI	ス SU	セ SE	ソ SO	Z	ザ ZA	ジ JI	ズ ZU	ゼ ZE	ゾ ZO
T	タ TA	チ CHI	ツ TSU	テ TE	ト TO	D	ダ DA	ヂ JI	ヅ DZU	デ DE	ド DO
N	ナ NA	ニ NI	ヌ NU	ネ NE	ノ NO						
H	ハ HA	ヒ HI	フ FU	ヘ HE	ホ HO	B	バ BA	ビ BI	ブ BU	ベ BE	ボ BO
M	マ MA	ミ MI	ム MU	メ ME	モ MO	P	バ PA	ビ PI	ブ PU	ベ PE	ボ PO
Y	ヤ YA		ユ YU		ヨ YO						
R	ラ RA	リ RI	ル RU	レ RE	ロ RO						
W	ワ WA				ン N						

NOTES:

1) Dots (") or circle (°) in upper right corner alter initial consonant sound as shown.

2) "N" used as terminal consonant only.

3) Dash (—) extends vowel sound.

4) Small "tsu" is *not* pronounced but serves to double the *following* consonant sound (e.g. "kissaten").

Reading Practice

スポーツ   ディベート   スピーチ

トレーニング   ディスカッション

symbols "ha-n-ba-gu-su-te-ki," for example, isn't going to satisfy your hunger pangs unless you're also able to put them all together and realize that you're reading a Japanized version of "hamburger steak." Compared to trying to figure out what they're using katakana to spell, learning the symbols themselves is a real piece of "keki."

Paradoxical to those of us who think of the Japanese as very "rule conscious," they constantly violate the rules of their culture and language--usually totally oblivious to it. They much prefer to operate on a "case-by-case" basis, meaning that everything is subject to extenuating circumstances and practically nothing is hard and fast. (And yes, I am suggesting that that may be true of the whole culture as well.)

For example, the "rule" regarding katakana is that it is used to spell non-Japanese sounds (including onomatopoeic noises like our "bang!"). Usually this means foreign words, with which the average Japanese vocabulary is filled. But lately, more and more advertisers are bending the rules to allow certain foreign words to be spelled in other "alphabets," usually hiragana.

The best example of this probably, is the name of a popular magazine for working women entitled Travail or "work" in French. Strictly speaking, because "travail" is obviously a foreign word, it must be spelled with katakana. But the advertising people decided that since it was a magazine for women, the title should be written in more "feminine" lettering. They used hiragana, which really does look more delicate and sensual than the rather starkly angular katakana but, if the rules are to make any sense at all (which they rarely do in Japan), it's totally incorrect to spell a foreign word with hiragana. (Just for fun, ask a Japanese friend about hiragana and katakana and when they're used. She'll more than likely tell you that hiragana is strictly for Japanese words, never foreign. Happy enlightening!)

Certain common katakana words--for which there are no precise Japanese equivalents--are known by practically all Japanese people, whether or not they "speak" any English. The trick to communicating successfully with someone whose English is weak, is to use as many of these "Japanglish" words as possible. Words like "car," "banana," "theater," "business," and even "school" are almost as much a part of the Japanese language as "sukiyaki." But of course, to make the other person recognize them, you must pronounce them according to the Japanese sound system.

Once the gaijin planted themselves in Japan, it became necessary to invent some way to spell the Japanese language using our alphabet (in contrast to katakana which is used to spell our language in their alphabet). This "fourth alphabet" is called "romaji" and, because the Japanese use it only in their dealings with foreigners, knowledge of it is spotty. It's important, though, to remember that the acquaintance spelling his name for you is not necessarily a dullard just because he mixes up a couple of letters; just try "spelling" your name for him in Japanese!

The rules of spelling and pronunciation for romaji are fairly simple. Some people think the pronunciation is similar to Italian or Spanish but far less rhythmic. The five vowel sounds are pronounced "ah," "ee," "oo," "eh," and "oh." They are spelled "a,i,u,e,o" (respectively) and are about the only things you can mispronounce in the entire language. Just remember that they are always pronounced as above regardless of what other letters they are placed in conjunction with.

Most of the 14 Japanese consonants can precede any of the five vowels and all vowels accept the single terminal consonant "n," with or without an initial consonant. No other consonant but "n" is found at the end of a word, although many times the terminal "u" sound is almost silent; e.g., "desu" often sounds like "des."

The only other tricky bit of pronunciation is the double consonant; e.g., "kissaten," what they call a coffee house. The double consonant is a kind of hesitation or extra holding of the consonant sound, but, like the double vowel sound (which also merely lengthens the sound) really shouldn't complicate efforts at communication. The most critical thing to remember is to always pronounce the vowels as indicated. "Kissaten" may look vaguely familiar to the English speaker well-versed in osculation, but it's pronounced "kees-sa-tayn."

The spoken language really isn't all that difficult for beginners. It's complicated by the complete lack of any words you might recognize from English (with the exception of the many "loan-words" such as "ha-n-ba-ga") but the rules are straightforward and exceptions are few. In a linguistic nutshell, here are the most salient points of language, at least enough to let you limp through a simple request in the unlikely event you're not able to find an English-speaker:

First, speak in a monotone. Unlike Chinese, Japanese has no pitches or "sing-song" effect. The usual word order in a sentence is subject, object, verb with adjectives coming before their nouns and adverbs coming before the verb.

Questions are made simply by adding "-ka" to the end of the sentence and inflecting up as you would an English question. Negatives are usually formed by adding "-sen" to the end of the verb.

So, for example, you could say in very simple but completely comprehensible Japanese, "I eat rice" by saying "Watashi (I) gohan (rice) tabemasu (eat)." To ask "Do I eat rice?" you would say "Watashi gohan tabemasuka?" And to say "I don't eat rice" (don't you dare!), it's "Watashi gohan tabemasen." Grammarians will object to my lack of particles and the like in the above examples but, for simple survival, this pidgin form will serve you well until you have the time to learn the real thing.

It's very important that you know their numbering system well before you go over--it's your money that's being counted. Up to a point, their numbers are identical to ours: 9,999 is expressed as "nine thousands, nine hundreds, nine tens, and nine ones" (in Japanese, of course). No exceptions. The number "10,000," however, is not "ten thousands" but represents another totally discreet unit, just like ones, tens, hundreds and thousands. In Japanese, "10,000" is one "man" (pronounced "mahn").

Thus, a Japanese doesn't say, for example, "hyaku sen" (hundred thousand) for 100,000; he'll say "ju man" (ten ten-thousand). Your rent may be in the neighborhood of "yon (four) man" or 40,000. And if you're exceptionally enterprising and make all the right connections with the Tokyo moneybags, it's not inconceivable that you could eventually pull down a salary of "issen (one thousand) man (ten thousand) en" or 10,000,000 yen a year.

In English, we never allow a unit to repeat itself; ten tens are a "hundred." The Japanese, too, have a larger unit for ten thousand ten-thousands, but it's unlikely that you'd have much call to use "oku" (100,000,000) unless you were discussing, say, the population of Brazil or had decided to make a detailed inventory of rice grains in your neighborhood paddy.

It's a confusing system for foreigners, of course, and even when you know that one million is really one hundred "man," it'll still take time to juggle the decimal point around to where your numbers make sense. Conversely, you'll have great empathy for the average Japanese when he takes a solid minute to express a figure of more than ten thousand to you in English. His English is probably all right; it's converting his numbering system into yours that's so time-consuming. In view of all this, is it any real surprise that the Japanese are the electronic calculator barons of the world? They need to be just to balance their import/export books with those funny-looking foreigners and their odd-ball counting system!

The Papers Chase

As tourists, most people aren't too concerned about visas when they go to a foreign country. They just pick one up a few days before leaving--if the country they're visiting even requires one--and assume their tourist money will make them quite welcome wherever. That's quite true in Japan also *if* you're a real tourist. I'm assuming, however, that you're not since you want not only to spend yen but earn it too. Getting the right visa for *that* may well turn out to be your biggest pain in the whole process.

As anyone who's worked in Japan can testify, you'd be miles ahead if you could arrange for sponsorship (and therefore a working visa) before you go over. To do this, you first must find a company or school willing to assure the Japanese government that it needs you desperately and that no Japanese citizen will fill the bill for the job they're offering. Fortunately, getting a working visa--especially as a teacher--is still a fairly easy matter in Japan even these days as governments everywhere tighten up their immigration laws to keep out competition for their own folk.

The Japanese government very wisely realizes that for Japan to succeed with its export ambitions, (really the heart and soul of their success story), it is absolutely vital that their people learn and be exposed to the English language and Western ways in general. This makes things rather easy for those wanting to teach English because it's a well-known fact that virtually no Japanese teachers of English can teach *conversational* English well, regardless of how many years they've studied the lingo or how many holidays in Brighton they've had--the language/culture chasm is just too wide. (Conversely, of course, it's almost a given that foreigners never come *truly* to know the Japanese culture.)

Unfortunately, there's something of a Catch-22 involved with this visa business: many people interested in working, understandably don't really want to just traipse over to Japan without being dead sure they have a job waiting for them. But, equally understandably, most employers want to personally interview the individual *before* they commit themselves to sponsoring him or her and thereby assume full responsibility for that person's behavior while in the country.

The solution for those wanting to teach says the Japan Association of Language Teachers (JALT), the largest professional organization for ESL teachers in Japan, is to "come to Japan on a tourist visa to find a job. The local English language papers carry a number of ads for teachers daily. Schools tend to hire people in-country rather than to risk a one or two-year contract on someone sight unseen."

(This is in contrast to the Japanese embassy in Washington D.C. which, predictably enough, states that teachers "must have the proper working visa issued by the Japanese government before leaving for Japan." What they mean, of course, is that teachers must have the proper visa to *work*. It's perfectly acceptable--and frequently necessary--to go over on a tourist or cultural (student) visa to *find* that work.)

Even for non-teachers, JALT's advice is sound. Although resumes and letters of inquiry certainly should be sent to the business and professional organizations listed in the Appendix, you may find the response to such letters disappointing. Unfortunately, the need for professionals (other than teachers) is not nearly as great as that for English instructors. Those people wanting to delve into such areas as international trade, law, engineering and the many entrepreneurial activities that exist can expect most of their opportunities to come as from personal contacts made once they're actually in Japan.

Takeshi Hirose, Japanese Consul-General in San Francisco concurs. "The person interested in working in

Japan," the Consul says, "will find it much easier to get the proper work visa as an English teacher than in any other capacity. We have a great need for native-speaking English teachers and probably always will because of our international activities. But in almost every field other than language instruction, we have a great number of qualified Japanese citizens who, of course, almost always must be given preference for hiring." Non-teaching sponsorship is difficult at best and almost impossible without a personal meeting or some other significant connection with a Japanese company. With that connection, however, doors may open with surprising ease.

As a result of this, even non-teachers usually support themselves initially by teaching English until sufficient inroads have been made to allow them to move into their chosen field. Even if you don't plan to make teaching your primary activity, it might be wise to do so just long enough to make some useful business connections in and out of the classroom--they'll come quickly in "network"-rich Nippon. And when a preferred job is proffered, changing sponsors usually can be accomplished with a brief bit of paper work at the local immigration office.

The words of the Japanese embassy notwithstanding, a large number of hopeful gaijin *do* go to Japan first on a tourist visa, changing it later to a proper working visa. The tourist visa is very easily obtained by presenting to the local Japanese consulate a visa application, passport and (sometimes) a round-trip (return) airplane ticket to prove you have the means to get home if need be.

Due to special agreements between their government and Japan's, some foreign tourists don't need visas at all. To wit, if you're British, you may stay in Japan up to 180 days without a visa if you promise not to work, Canadians may stay 90 days and New Zealanders 30 days. Tourist visas for Americans and Australians can usually be issued on the spot at the nearest consulate or by mail.

But before you resign yourself to going over on a non-working visa, try your best to convince the schools, companies or organizations you contact by mail that they would be quite safe in sponsoring you. After all, *they* certainly realize that it would be far more convenient for all concerned if you could come to Japan with your papers all taken care of. But it's up to you to impress this upon them.

For teachers, an alternative to going to the schools yourself is to let them come to you. About the biggest referral and placement service is offered by the granddaddy of organizations for teachers like you (or like you are about to become), Teachers of English to Speakers of Other Languages (TESOL).

TESOL, once a very small organization, has grown right along with the Teaching English as a Second Language (TESL) field. It can now provide those interested with plenty of invaluable information about teaching opportunities, not only in Japan but (if you like the work) around the world.

Also seeking to help the established or aspiring teacher to find work is English Educational Services International in Boston. Along with TESOL, EESI publishes a newsletter which lists job opening around the world, including, of course, Japan. They also offer a resume and dossier referral service for employers looking for just the right teacher (i.e., you). Like all of the teaching organizations listed in the Appendix, both TESOL and EESI are non-profit and work with college graduates, both professional and temporary ESL teachers.

Some of the larger English schools in Japan have ambitious teacher recruiting programs which have representatives regularly travelling to English-speaking countries in search of experienced additions to their teaching staff. In your initial letters of inquiry to the schools listed in the Appendix, be sure to ask if they do overseas recruiting and if so, request an appointment to see the recruiter when he passes through your home town or nearby. Because of the expense to the school of sending a recruiter over, generally only professional teachers are hired this way. Smaller schools in Japan are unlikely to have any kind of advance recruitment program; they generally just wait for the right person to amble through the door.

In view of this unfortunate "Catch 22" where employers won't hire without a personal interview and teachers won't go over without a job, I am working with several schools and placement agencies in Japan in the hopes of helping college graduates get teaching sponsorship before they go over. I can't promise a position, but if you send me a resume, I will try to act as your intermediary and do my best to get you something while you're still at home.

Bear in mind, though, that the few offers to teachers overseas are usually not quite as lucrative as what you may find for yourself in Japan. But you would be relieved of having to leave the country to change from a tourist to a work visa and, of course, you'd have considerably greater peace-of-mind knowing that you were going to a definite job and wouldn't have to knock on doors there to find one.

Just send a resume (nothing fancy) to me care of the publisher, along with a self-addressed stamped post card or envelope so I can notify you of having received your vita. There's no charge for keeping your resume on file but there would be for actually placing you with a school or company, if and when something suitable is found for you. But please don't rely on me alone to find you a position. Write to the organizations and schools in the Appendix yourself, too, and seriously consider going over on a tourist visa if nothing else pans out. There *are* jobs out there.

One question that you'll want to ask when you write to or visit the schools listed in the Appendix is whether they teach primarily "in-company" or "in-house" classes--the two most common types of conversational English class for which teachers are sponsored. Each has advantages but essentially, "in-company" schools offer flexibility, good pay and the freedom to pursue other activities while "in-house" schools offer community, a generally professional environment, and usually more enthusiastic students.

Most large schools concentrate primarily on "in-house" classes held in their own facility; i.e., the school. Unfortunately because their expensive classroom space must be utilized to the fullest possible extent, classes are often packed to capacity--30 or 40 students are not uncommon. Such students, however, because they're paying their own tuition, do tend to be more conscientious in their studies. Because classes are held in a proper school, camaraderie among the faculty and the students is considerable.

The "in-company" school with most classes held at the office of the client (usually a large company), of course, has only a fraction of the overhead of an actual school and so is sometimes willing to pay teachers better wages. What is especially nice for those interested in using teaching as a means to another end is that not only does the "in-company" school tend to make few demands on the instructor outside the classroom but also, by picking and choosing class assignments, the teacher can arrange to teach middle and top-level executives in just the company he or she would like to someday work for--at that very company. And thus are connections made.

The drawback to "in-company" classes, however, is that frequently the students are required to attend as part of their ongoing company training. After they've put in a 10-hour work day, you might find a few snores mixed in with your choral drills. Also, since classes are held miles from each other at various company locations, it's entirely possible to go many months without even catching sight of one's fellow teachers. Esprit de corps is usually nil.

Some professional teachers with at least two years experience teaching their primary subject may have the good fortune to get with one of the "international" schools (see Appendix) which pay quite well. Most such schools are in Tokyo and students are usually the children of foreign diplomats, businessmen and Japanese who want their kids to get a Western education.

Annual salaries for teachers with credentials (the only kind hired) range from about $12,000 at the Nagoya International School to the American School in Japan's $24,000. Most international schools offer excellent benefits often including housing and home leave. Very nice work for the seasoned classroom professional.

In private language schools, your skills should bring you a minimum of 3,000 yen (at time of writing, about $15) an hour. If you're offered a monthly salary, find out what sort of teaching load you could expect, then do some division to figure an hourly rate. But don't be surprised if your offer works out to considerably less than 3,000.

One friend in America was offered a teaching position in Japan, but finally decided not to accept it for the very reason that the pay the school offered did not jibe with all that she'd heard about the excellent teacher salaries in Japan. They expected her to work 25 hours per week and be paid about $8 an hour. She went to Samoa instead.

Now, before you too decide to head for the South Seas, remember the sample salaries shown here are those of large schools recruiting overseas. Some offer benefits in lieu of pay, some just assume the foreign teacher doesn't know the real score with sensei salaries. Although you may have to accept something like one of these temporarily to get your work visa, your free-lance work should easily earn you that $15 an hour and much more. There are plenty of well-paying jobs, but you will have to turn down a lot of chintzy ones to find the plums.

The Japanese-American Conversation Institute (21 Yotsuya 1-chome, Shinjuku-ku, Tokyo) is fairly generous, offering 2,870 yen ($13) per hour to new teachers.

Time-Life Educational Systems (Time-Life Building, 3-6 Otemachi 2-chome, Chiyoda-ku, Tokyo) gives its teachers from 192,000 to 243,000 for a 60 hour month (about $14.50 at the low end).

Tokyo Foreign Language College (7-3-8 Nishi-Shinjuku, Tokyo 160) asks teachers to work 9 to 4 Monday through Friday, teaching 20 hours a week. First year teachers start at 248,000 with a one-month bonus paid after one year.

The largest ESL school in Japan, Kanda Institute of Foreign Languages (2-13-13 Uchikanda, Chiyoda-ku, Tokyo) pays about $9.75 per hour but will advance you a month's salary to cope with moving expenses.

But at the "slave wages" end, there's the Sunshine Language College (Sunshine 60, Toshima-ku, Tokyo 170) which provides a starting monthly salary of about 190,000 yen (about $860) for 30 hours per week or about 1,600 yen ($7) an hour and the notorious Executive Language School (Kowa Bldg. #16, Akasaka 1-chome, Minato-ku, Tokyo 107) whose parsimony is legendary in local ESL circles. Executive is reported to pay new teachers recruited overseas an unbelievably paltry 1,300 yen ($6) per hour. Incredibly, they somehow always seem to find warm foreign bodies to put in front of the students; just make sure yours isn't one of them!

One of your first letters certainly should be to your nearest Japanese consulate or embassy which can send you information as well as the forms you'll need to submit for your visa. (You'll also find a complete list of embassies, consulates and other useful organizations in the Appendix.) In case you later decide to go over on a tourist visa (which would also be issued from the consulate serving your region), it might be wise to use the name of a friend when requesting even general information about teaching visas.

I've never heard of it happening but it's not inconceivable that the consulate would be a little reluctant to grant a tourist visa to someone they knew was trying to go over to teach English. Tourists, by international agreement, are supposed to restrict their activities to heaping piles of foreign money on local merchants--not working.

Japanese embassies are located in most capitals of the world. Consulates are found in most major cities and the Japanese government likes their foreign friends to deal only with the office closest to their home.

Despite the preference of some people to always go straight to the "honcho" or "head man," there's really nothing the embassy can do for you that a consulate can't, even though embassies do have somewhat higher authority. If you approach the embassy with a routine request for forms and information regarding teaching, they will almost certainly refer you to your regional consulate unless your home is within the jurisdiction of the embassy rather than any of their consulates.

Another useful organization mentioned in the Appendix is the Japan National Tourist Organization (JNTO) from which you should try to get all the information you can. It's a government-subsidized (but fairly independent and objective) organization, designed to help those wishing to visit Japan--and not just tourists. JNTO has a true wealth of information on the country (including free maps) which they would love to share with you in exchange for a simple postcard. Be sure to ask if they have any information especially pertinent to living in (rather than visiting) their country. As with the consulates, you should address your request for information to the office nearest you.

After gathering as much general information as you can from these and other sources (e.g. references in the Appendix), you then must decide where in Japan you'd like to live and work. Although I strongly recommend Tokyo for first-timers--especially if you don't speak any Japanese--other areas are discussed later in the book and may be appropriate for the adventurous (as if going to Japan itself wasn't exciting enough!) and the claustrophobic (Tokyo's crowding can get a bit intense).

Your next step will be to start shooting off brief, one-page letters of inquiry (aerograms are a bit cheaper than regular first class air mail) to some of the private English schools and (if teaching is not your primary interest) the trade and professional organizations as well. I strongly recommend this double-edged approach of pursuing teaching as well as your primary profession (should it not be teaching) to increase your chances of getting to Japan any way you can. Always remember, your first priority is to get a job and that work visa in whatever way you can. You can always change jobs (and sponsors) after you're "connected."

Most private schools have three-month terms usually starting in April, July, September and January, with the most hiring done in April and September.

Getting the visa itself usually takes two months but sometimes as long as three. And, just to be on the safe side, you'd probably want to give the potential sponsor at least a month to decide if he wants you. So, to be sure you don't cut things too close, decide when you want to go (September or October are best), count back about four months and send off your barrage of letters. The "Time Line" in the Appendix spells out what you need to do when.

Use a form letter that you can photocopy only if you can make it sound somewhat *un*like a form letter. Cover your education and work experience briefly but thoroughly and state emphatically that you *are* coming to Japan (to set you apart from the many who never actually make it) and would like to work for their school during your stay, which will be for at least a year.

Don't worry if your degree is somewhat esoteric (e.g., Abyssinian Shard Analysis). Many Japanese companies are not too terribly concerned with the person's major in school; they figure they can teach him what he needs to know. What they usually look for is willingness to work dependably and with dedication--something we do not learn in Economics 101.

Those without degrees however, take note: while it is possible for almost any native-speaker to teach English in Japan (either illegally as a tourist or legally as a student), it is almost impossible to get a work visa for teaching without having a degree from a recognized four-year institution.

The government and most schools don't really care which school you graduated from or what your major was, but the diploma is needed if you hope to work full-time legally. If you haven't yet graduated from college, you may have to work part-time while studying full-time on a cultural visa unless, of course, you can develop those magical connections which seem to invalidate all restrictive rules.

To those first letters you send to schools, you may get a few replies, some cautiously requesting more information. In response to these, send your letters of recommendation from former instructors or employers, transcripts, diploma copy. Include a cover letter in which you convey the depth of your commitment to helping students learn your language in a supportive environment as well as your interest in and respect for the Japanese culture. Do all that you can to assure potential employers that, while you can understand their concern about sponsoring a stranger, you will not disappoint them. Sincerity counts for a lot.

Success in Japan depends most of all on personality and for this reason you must do everything you can to *personalize* your application. Make them know you as a person, not a faceless name on a letter or resume. Stand out! To the best prospects, you may want to send a cassette or even video tape of you candidly commenting on your field or, for teachers, demonstrate how you would work with a student (correcting grammar, explaining vocabulary, pronunciation, etc.)--perhaps using as your model student one of the Japanese students you met at your local EFL school. At the very least, include a flattering color photo with your resume. And if you get a distinct nibble from a school, don't hesitate to *call* and reiterate your strong desire to work for them. A three minute direct-dial call from the U.S. to Tokyo can cost as little as about $6 and the gesture genuinely will impress them.

Sadly, many would-be adventurers get discouraged when they don't receive overwhelmingly positive responses to their letters from abroad. They mistakenly interpret this as meaning their services aren't needed. Not so! Most schools in Japan (like most companies world-wide, I suppose) operate with "management by crisis." It's usually not until a few weeks before the start of the new semester that the hundreds of schools let out a collective "Yipes!" when they realize they need teachers--and fast.

If you're there when they need you, you'll get in, not only because of your immediate availability but because just by being there, you've demonstrated to the administrators that you can cope with the culture (and hence, their students). It's just a lot easier and safer for them to hire that gaijin walking through the door than sponsor one to come over only to have him (it?) flake out.

If you come as a teacher-cum-tourist, you should take the first week you're in the country to call as many of the schools we've listed in your area as you can and ask if they need full-time teachers (don't mention sponsorship until you've got your foot in their door).

"Full-time" usually means more than 12 hours per week and if a school has that many hours available, you have a pretty good chance of talking them into sponsoring you. But be delicate with the topic of sponsorship. Make them want you first, then tell the director of the school that you might like very much to work for his school full-time but there is the one oh-so-minor problem of a work visa... If you do it the Japanese way and finesse the issue a bit, chances are good they'll go for it and may even foot your transportation bill to get the visa.

You'll need to leave the country to apply for the work visa when you find a school to sponsor you. Most people go to Korea because it's the closest and therefore cheapest place to fly to. But many savvy sensei's recommend Hong Kong or Taiwan as more pleasant places

to get the new visa. It costs only about $250 for a round
trip (vs. $215 to Korea) when bought through one of the
dozens of discount travel agencies advertised in the
English newspapers in Japan. I do love my "kim chee" but,
in my opinion, there really are nicer destinations than
Seoul (the Korean capital), unless, of course, you're into
heavy industry and garlic.

Technically, you're supposed to sit wherever you
apply for the visa and just wait for it to be approved. But
since it takes about two months to get it digested by the
bureaucracy in Tokyo, most teachers fly back to Japan
(still on their tourist visas) and either take the opportunity
to travel around the country or teach illegally, as many
sponsors expect them to.

Then, when the Japanese consulate in Hong Kong,
Korea or wherever notifies you by mail that your visa is
ready, you can't merely ask them to stamp your passport
with the visa in Japan and thereby save you the expense
of *another* round-trip flight. No, you must return to the
same consulate where you applied for the visa and have
your passport stamped in person.

Needless to say, the pointlessness of this
requirement has caused more than one shouting match
between gaijin and government man but the rule is
absolutely unbendable: IF YOU COME ON A TOURIST
VISA, YOU'LL NEED TO MAKE *TWO* ROUND-TRIPS TO
ANOTHER COUNTRY TO GET A WORK OR
CULTURAL VISA. Once to apply; once to pick up. You
may find a sponsor willing to pay for the trips, but don't
count on it. Plan your finances accordingly!

Now would probably be a good time to offer a
stern warning: never, repeat *never*, lose your temper with a
Japanese government official; never threaten, never even
raise your voice. True, you'd probably feel better after you
did, but there's also an excellent chance that you'd have
your work visa refused or (in extreme cases) revoked.
Reason? You'd simply not be the kind of visitor they want
in their country. Period. No appeal. Remember "case by
case"?

And that kind of cut-and-dried attitude toward
what they consider troublemakers covers scofflaws too.
There are myriad stories about gaijin getting in hot water

over the silliest things: silly Japanese rules, even sillier behavior by the foreigner in reaction to them.

Always remember: the Japanese are *very* law-and-order conscious and because there's so little crime in the country, the odds of your getting nailed for some indiscretion are pretty good, regardless of how minor. And because the laws and their interpretation are so intentionally vague, the authorities can usually be as punishing or forgiving as the transgressor's behavior warrants. Humility pays; crime doesn't.

Perhaps the best example of backfiring bluster is that of the couple who went to Japan on tourist visas, found sponsors, then had to go to Korea to obtain work visas. When the time came to pick up the waiting visas in Seoul, only the man went back, hoping somehow to get his girlfriend's visa at the same time, without her actually being present as the law required.

He managed to pull it off using sheer bravado and triumphantly returned to Tokyo with both passports and visas in hand. All went well until the woman had to have her work visa renewed (they're usually good for only six months) and a sharp-eyed immigration man happened to notice that her passport had exit and entry stamps for only one trip to Korea. It was only thanks to some fast thinking and faster talking that she was able to avoid deportation.

Whether you get your work visa in Japan or at home, the process is the same, as far as the government is concerned (although some items may be waived at the discretion of the consulate). The school that wants you must provide the government with the following papers which are submitted to the government by you when you give the consulate your visa application:

1. School registration ("tohon"), stating when the school was founded.

2. Contract agreement ("keiyakusho") between you and the school (which sometimes needs to be witnessed by another person and notarized).

3. National tax certificate ("nozei shomeisho").

4. Business tax certificate ("tomin-zei").

5. Letter of guarantee ("hoshosho"), in which a school representative (usually the president) promises to

pay for your return if you turn out to be a no-account louse and it becomes necessary to send you packing.

      6. Certificate of employment ("kyuyohosho") wherein the school states your salary and work schedule.

      7. Letter of invitation or contract from the school to you ("shohei ryusho").

      8. List of instructors currently with the school ("koshimeibo").

      9. Company brochure ("annaisho").

      Incredible though it may seem, a lot of school administrators are unaware of the fact that practically *any* reputable school--especially if it's been in business quite awhile--can sponsor a foreign instructor. You may have to educate them on how to put together the papers they'll need to send you (or give you to take to Korea or Hong Kong).

      The fact that the school is somewhat naive about sponsoring procedures doesn't necessarily mean they're small-time. They may just be complacent. Many schools have been getting along quite nicely using teachers already holding visas, hiring just about anyone who walks through the door. And many of these "local-hire only" schools are somewhat surprised when told just how easy it is to sponsor a teacher.

      Once you've gotten the papers from the school in Japan, you'll need to make sure you have at least two copies of each (make extra copies if necessary). Then, to all this, you must add two copies of: application for work visa (which you got from the consulate), resume, latest grade transcript, a head-and-shoulder black and white photo taken within the last six months (not machine-made), a one-page letter of intent addressed to the Ministry of Justice (in which you should mention how teaching in Japan would fulfill a lifelong dream, etc., etc.), a brief personal history, a copy of your college diploma and two or three letters of recommendation.

      Depending on whether you're applying from home or Japan, you then either mail your papers to the nearest Japanese consulate (if you're applying for a work visa before you go over) or take them all to a Japanese consulate outside the country, plunk them on the counter and wait for the bureaucrats to work their magic--about two or three months' worth.

If you're one of that scurrilous breed who's willing to teach on a tourist visa (you'll have plenty of English-speaking company), you probably won't have much luck working for the major schools; they have too much to lose if they're caught hiring you. Most of the little schools, however, are almost always looking for somebody and, although their facilities usually consist of one room behind Uncle Hiroshi's noodle shop, the pay will be comparable and sometimes even better than what the biggies offer. Either way, the students are for the most part bright, eager and attentive. Just keep a close eye on your paychecks at the smaller places; inattentiveness tends to make them shrink.

Some brave souls, in fact, simply come to Japan for three months on a tourist visa (six months with renewal), work illegally for the hole-in-the-wall schools (there are literally hundreds in Tokyo alone) and go home several thousand experiences (and dollars) richer. Some money maniacs who really try to sock it away are able to do so at quite a good clip when they may be averaging upwards of $20 an hour, working 40 hours a week (often more), and paring living expenses down to about $500 a month. Memories of the country, however, are usually limited to train schedules, MacDonalds and nervous glances behind the back, scanning for the Immigration man.

At the other end of the spectrum are the people who want mainly to learn about the culture and so teach the bare minimum needed for survival (about 10 hours per week) and use the rest of the time to study some intruiging little nuance of Japan which has long fascinated them. Foreigners can be found intensely studying almost every facet of the culture, usually supporting themselves with a few well-paying hours of English teaching, either on work or cultural visas.

Most sensei's choose a happy medium: reasonable schedule (20-25 teaching hours a week) and a work or student visa to avoid possible legal unpleasantries. With an arrangement like this, you'd have plenty of time to see the country, meet the people, and still have saved up enough to take your folks out to dinner at the ritziest joint in

town when you get back home and not even notice the
dent the bill makes in your wad of Japanese dollars.

Lessons To Be Learned

Unfortunately, far too many people seem to go to Japan primarily for the money, often not caring about the culture and sometimes actively disliking it. It's their loss, of course, that they never come to appreciate such a refined, aesthetically stimulating land as Japan--and the Japanese are certainly none too keen on having such mercenary visitors in their country. On the other hand, the sensei, who *does* have an interest in things Japanese will truly be welcomed by a people eager to share their rich heritage.

Many foreigners go to Japan to study some pet interest of theirs, and the government is delighted to help them by granting a cultural (student) visa quite freely to just about anyone who regularly attends an accredited institution. Visas have been granted for the study of martial arts, theater, flower arranging, massage, music, almost any bit of "Japanalia" you could imagine. But, of course, the most common area of study is the Japanese language as taught at one of the many schools for gaijin.

Should you want to investigate the possibility of studying in Japan, either through a university exchange program or at a private school, a good first step would be to write to the Association of International Education, at 4-5-29 Komaba, Meguro-ku, Tokyo 153 (tel. 467-3521) and request a copy of their "Student Guide to Japan" and "ABC's of Study in Japan" (also available from Universal Business Corporation, 17907 Cicelia Place, Cerritos, CA 90701). These will explain in some detail how to go about getting into almost any kind of school. Be sure to ask about scholarship and fellowship opportunities.

The only catch with this way of getting to Japan, however, is that the government will ask for a letter of guarantee from a resident--but not necessarily a citizen--of Japan. Many times, if you are applying for admission to a lengthy program, the school itself will be willing to act as guarantor, assuring the Japanese government that, not only will you not mount any kamikaze raids on the Imperial Palace but, should it be necessary, your sponsor will pay your living expenses and pay for your transportation home. Ask the school about this letter of guarantee at the time you request other information.

To be issued a visa to attend a private non-university school, you'll also need to provide your nearest consulate with a letter detailing why you'd like to study in Japan, certificate of admission to the school, a brief personal history, graduation certificate or latest grade transcript and the school's tax certificate. The consulate will want all these, the visa application form, passport-size photos and the letter of guarantee in duplicate.

It's also possible to attend English-language classes in Japan and earn college credits transferable to institutions at home. Many foreigners earn four-year degrees which are fully recognized by most English-speaking universities without ever speaking Japanese in the classroom.

Sophia University, Ichigaya Campus, 4 Yonban-cho, Chiyoda-ku, Tokyo 102, is probably the best known of these schools because all classes at the Ichigaya Campus are in English and many people, gaijin and Nihonjin alike, earn US degrees without ever stepping foot on American soil.

Also offering US accredited courses are the International Christian University, College of Liberal Arts, 3-10-2 Osawa, Mitaka-shi, Tokyo 181 or Toyohashi University of Technology Graduate School, Tenpaku-sho, Hibarigaoka, Toyohashi, Nagoya 440, both of which offer some (but not all) classes in English.

College sophomores might want to consider doing their junior year in Japan. In Tokyo, International Christian University, Sophia University and Waseda University all have full-year programs for those interested in studying the language and the culture. Also, Nanzan University in Nagoya and Kansai University in Osaka have similar programs. Information should be available at your school's Guidance Office or from the Association of International Education in Tokyo.

As a full-time college or university student in Japan, you can obtain a visa quite easily by submitting to your consulate two copies of the visa application form, passport photos and your Student Residence Certificate ("zairyu shikaku nintei shomeisho"), issued by the Ministry of Justice after you've been accepted to the institution.

In the Appendix, you'll find just a few of the dozens of Japanese-language schools available throughout the country. Should you be interested in obtaining a student (actually a "cultural") visa to study Japanese, all the ones listed can give you full information on requirements and several will act as guarantor so you can get your visa. Be advised, however, that some will *not* sponsor you to study due to unfamiliarity with the sponsoring process or an unwillingness to assume the responsibility for your behavior while in the country. You'll need to find your own sponsor if you wish to attend those schools. Obviously, schools that will sponsor *and* teach are going to be more attractive to overseas applicants.

Unfortunately for those students more interested in doing teaching themselves, the cultural visa usually requires at least 15 hours of classroom instruction per week. On the plus side, however, those Japanese class hours are probably during the day when your teaching talents are less in demand. Just be sure that wherever you go, they emphasize spoken Japanese and don't waste your precious time and teaching earnings making you learn more kanji characters than you could ever use.

As for tuition, expect to pay more in the larger cities. The Aoyama Language Academy (Landic Hirakawa-cho Bldg. 2F, 2-6-2 Hirakawa-cho, Chiyoda-ku, Tokyo 102) for example, charges students approximately $630 per three-month semester (and a $45 registration fee) for its daily 3-hour intensive class (with one-hour daily lab) while the Kyoto Japanese Language School (Ichijo-dori, Muromachi Nishi, Kamigyo-ku, Kyoto 602) charges a little

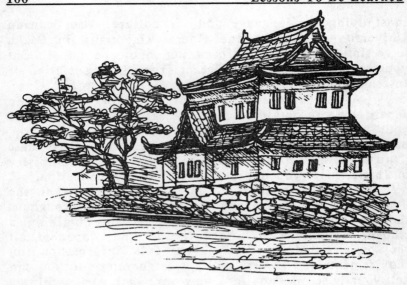

more than half for the same instruction. Of course, less intensive classes are also available at proportionately less cost but don't count on getting any school to sponsor you for anything less than a full-time intensive language program.

As you'd imagine, some foreigners get cultural visas just so they can work legally. A somewhat less than scrupulous school will tell the government that the student is in class the minimum number of hours when in fact, he or she might check in with the sensei once a week. Needless to say, the school certainly doesn't mind the arrangement; tuition is paid as if the student is full-time. Immigration, however, would take a very dim view of the situation if it ever got wind of the ruse. Deportation wouldn't be out of the question.

It's perfectly legal, though, to work while a legitimate student. Many people teaching English in Japan are, in fact, doing so on "cultural" visas, usually obtained from such language schools. *Any* sort of student, however, is entitled to teach part-time, as long as the number of hours does not exceed the maximum as established by immigration.

But, like so much involving the Japanese government, the rules are muddy. Things are usually decided on the infamous "case-by-case" basis, meaning that,

if you decide to go over on a student visa or apply for one
once you're in Japan, the person you talk to at
immigration can pretty well decide on the spot how many
hours he'll let you work on a student visa.

The usual number of work hours you're allowed is
between 10 and 15 per week--but it's almost impossible for
the government to determine just exactly how many hours
a student really is working, and they rarely try. The real
limiting factor for students trying to teach English is the
work load of the language school. Some Japanese classes
move so quickly that hours of study are necessary each
day just to keep up with the course. Beware of overload!

Japan For Kids

There are few intangibles that a parent can share with his or her offspring that are as valuable as an awareness of other cultures, other values and different ways of solving life's problems. Kids, in fact, may benefit more from living abroad than adults--they seem more accepting, more resilient, more willing to become a natural part of their environment. (Don't let your ego be too crushed when your seven-year-old starts giving *you* Japanese lessons.) Certainly there's no better way for a child to develop empathy for the feelings and beliefs of those not of his culture than to interact with the natives in sincere peer relationships.

There's very little red tape involved with bringing a child or any other dependent (i.e., non-working) family member with you to Japan. Dependent visas are relatively easy to obtain from the Japanese government so long as the working member can assure Tokyo that income and/or savings will be sufficient to support the whole family.

One usually unexpected problem that most foreign parents don't consider before they bring their children with them, however, is the scarcity of baby sitters or day-care centers in Japan. The role of women is slowly changing in Japan but it's still the norm for mothers to stay home and mind the kids while Papa goes out and earns their daily rice. Thus, the gaijin parent may have some trouble initially locating child care, unless she can find a willing neighbor. Baby sitting, when done by students, runs about $3 an hour in Tokyo but this can often be taken care of by offering English lessons (the coin of the gaijin realm) in trade.

There's certainly no need to worry about such matters as children's clothes, baby food or health care for kids--the Japanese dote on children and the well-being of tykes is of very great concern to the entire society. By far the biggest difficulty in bringing children to Japan is maintaining their schooling so they can rejoin their schoolmates back home in whatever class they would have entered had they not gone overseas.

But even that's no real problem for the reasonably well-heeled parent who wants to keep a child in the American education system. Almost all private schools in Japan which conduct classes in English model themselves on the American system. For the most part, they are fully accredited by the Western Association of Schools and Colleges, meaning that all credits earned are transferable to American institutions.

The biggest problem is expense. Free public education for 1st through 12th grades *is* available in Japan, of course, but all classes are taught in Japanese. Only private schools--of which there are many--offer complete curricula in English--and they are expensive.

As you might expect, the most expensive schools are in Tokyo, with top honors going to the largest such school in the country: the American School in Japan. ASIJ charges in the neighborhood of 1,200,000 yen (over $5,400) for one year's registration and tuition for a student attending grades 7 through 12 (secondary). Elementary school tuition and registration (grades 1-6) are about 70,000 yen ($320) less than this per year but even kindergarten at ASIJ costs 825,000 yen ($3,750), an amount that will still buy a decent college education in the US! The other schools in the Tokyo area are comparable in terms of both quality (high) and cost (steep).

Outside of the Tokyo metro area, costs drop by about one-half and quality is severely dependent on the skill of the individual teachers comprising the usually tiny faculty. For example, the Hokkaido International School-- also accredited in the US--consists of just two licensed American teachers, aided by their American principal (compared to ASIJ's more than 80 teachers). But tuition at HIS (probably the lowest of any international school in the country) is only about 600,000 yen ($2,700) for grades 1 through 9.

If you've had or have any affiliation with the US government, it might be worthwhile trying to get your little bundle of bills enrolled in one of the Department of Defense elementary and secondary schools sprinkled throughout the country. Such schools usually accept only children of active duty military personnel, civil service employees and retired versions of these (on a space-available basis), but if they have a few classroom chairs vacant, they might just be talked into letting your little Billy or Suzy fill one. The tuition would be far less than the private schools' (possibly free) but you'd probably need some substantial strings to pull to get your child in. Have any relatives in Congress?

The school year at the private and DoD schools is essentially the same as an American school's: classes begin either the last week in August or the first week in September and end usually the first week in June. Most American holidays are observed as well as some Japanese. Classes generally begin at 8:30 and end at 3, Monday through Friday. Some schools hold classes on Saturday as well, in keeping with the Japanese public school system's five and one-half day school week.

It's not actually impossible to enroll a foreign child in a Japanese public school (tuition-free) but school officials are understandably reluctant to allow such kids to attend classes held in a language with which they are totally unfamiliar. If your child knows some Japanese or is so young that the officials can be convinced that he or she will pick up the language quickly, you may have a chance of getting the child enrolled.

But there are no bilingual education laws in Japan; the classes will be in Japanese and your little "kodomo" will be expected to sink or swim along with the Japanese students in what's probably the most rigorous educational system in the world. Decisions on admissions are made by local school administrators on that infamous "case-by-case" basis so, if that's what you want for your child, make sure your "case" is a sound one before proposing it to them in Japan.

A complete list of private "international" schools for children where the language of instruction is English and credits are generally transferable to foreign (especially American) institutions appears in the Appendix. Most schools offer instruction in grades Kindergarten through 12, many offer pre-school instruction as well. Some smaller schools, however, teach grades K through 9 only. For complete information, write to the school directly.

Welcome To Wonderland

So, the die is almost cast. Maybe you're getting very close to actually giving it a try. Still, nobody likes too many surprises--especially when they're all taking place on the other side of the world. Just to get you fully psyched for the experience, let's take a look at what exactly will greet you once your overseas odyssey is under way.

The non-stop flight over (depending on route), should take about 11 hours from the US West Coast, 13 from New York, 10 from Australia and a whopping 18 hours from London (with one stop in Anchorage, Alaska).

All carriers will ply you liberally with food and drink, trying to keep you in your seat and sedated so as not to pester the stewardesses unduly. After feeding time, the lights will dim and you'll probably be offered a film which will likely be in the native language of your airline with English subtitles. Most of these are bizarrely interesting for a few minutes but "lights out" is when a lot of trans-Pacific pros make a dive for the center seats. The idea is to stake out a block of three seats, enough to put up the arm rests and catch the Z's needed to cope with post-landing.

At the end of your flight, you stumble bleary-eyed from the craft, your fuzzy bedroom slippers taking that first triumphant step onto Japanese soil, your grade-school teddy bear silently cheering your courage from inside your Camp Runamucka overnight bag. The air is cool and moist, the sky and most buildings you see, grey. You gaze about in awe at the airport personnel scurrying around you faster than you've ever seen anyone move before. The scene at the airport seems as well choreographed as a Las Vegas dance number--everyone knowing just where to go and what to do. So *this* is Japan!

Many people at the airport will speak English, more at Narita than Haneda. At Narita, it will take you a few minutes to wend your way to the baggage pickup area; at Haneda, it's just a few very obvious steps to the one and only luggage carousel.

Go through customs (please don't be so foolish as to bring in any no-no's--even Paul McCartney was thrown in the slammer for *his* little indiscretion a few years back) and declare whatever you think is really worth mentioning.

Technically, you might have to mention that $8 Timex your Aunt Louise gave you for junior high school graduation, but the customs guys are really only looking for the big stuff like jewelry (highly taxed) and firearms (highly illegal--"Saturday Night Specials" reputedly sell for close to $5,000 on the black market). You can lump most of your appliances and what-not's under "miscellaneous personal effects" and odds are, they'll just wave you through without even opening all your bags.

Be a little careful with immigration if you're going on a tourist visa. Be sure you tell the suspicious character at the booth that you really are in Japan just to see the sights and hope to travel all over the country and spend *fantastic* sums of tourist-type money everywhere you go. Although there's nothing illegal about a tourist *looking* for work and then leaving the country again to get the proper visa, it's easier just to say you're there to see the many magnificent sights of the country. He may very well suspect your true purpose but probably won't say anything since it's unlikely you'd be taking work from a native Japanese anyway.

Tourists and work-visa types alike: take careful note of the date stamped into your passport and etch it indelibly into your grey matter. That date will determine by what date in the future you must register with your local city hall (non-tourists only) and renew or change your visa. Miss that deadline by even one day and you will have some extensive apologizing to do, possibly from outside the country.

If your destination is not Tokyo, you will be even happier you landed at Haneda, from which all domestic flights depart. To make connections, you simply walk from the tiny international terminal to the much larger domestic, check your bags in and wait for your flight. If you land at Narita, of course, you're going to have to take one of the express busses that connect the airports.

Airport formalities completed, you boldly stride forth into your brand-new brand of reality: the home of Sony, sushi and samurai. And, what do you know, you really *can't* read any of the signs! Fortunately, telephones have the same general body parts in Japan as elsewhere and it is to one of these beasts that you should head immediately, before you start playing brave scout.

If you already have a sponsor or have the name and number of a school that definitely wanted to see you if and when you made it over, call immediately to let them know you made it (most offices in Japan are open from about 9:30 a.m. to about 7 p.m.). If you arrive after hours or you haven't made prior arrangements with them or anyone else, don't let the strangeness of the place upset you. Make your number one priority finding shelter--start calling hotels. (Plenty of cheap, clean and centrally located ones are listed for you in the Appendix.)

But how to use the rainbow of phones which greets you there in the airport lounge? Well, if you can find one, go for a yellow phone, the Cadillac of communication devices. A yellow phone will let you deposit the standard 10 yen piece (which will give you three minutes worth of local calling) or 100 yen which, logically enough, is the equivalent of 10 10-yenners (couldn't we just call them "dimes?")

The only drawback to using a 100 yen coin in the yellow phone is that you won't get any change back for your unused time. Why would anyone ever use a 100 yen coin? The Japanese phone system is set up strictly according to time and distance. Thus, you can call anywhere in the country for 10 yen but the time you're allowed depends on how far you're calling; e.g., in your own dialing area, you get 3 minutes but if you're calling Kyoto from Tokyo, you might get about 10 seconds. You can put up to eight "dimes" into any phone but even so, it's a pain to have to work with that many coins when one 100 yen will do the same job.

The "dimes" you insert will drop steadily into the belly of the box as you continue to speak. Finally, when you have only one remaining, you'll get a "five second warning": a raucus buzz that lets you know your last coin has just been devoured and you'd better insert more or tell the other party you'll call him back as soon as you can remember how to ask for more change (hint: "komakai arimasuka?")

Next down on the list of phones is the red devil, which, contrary to what its appearance might suggest, is not second cousin to the "hot line" but can be used just like a yellow phone; it just won't take 100 yen coins. This is by far the most common type of phone and you're bound to become fast friends as it makes you a part of the great network of garrulous gaijin.

Finally, we come to the lowly blue phone, a tranquil appliance, but if you're trying to call anywhere outside of, say, the building you're standing in, forget it. You'll just get the dulcet voice of a robot operator chiding you for being foolish enough to expect to call across the street from a phone intended for decoration only. All seriousness aside, stick to yellow or red. They're colors you can rely on.

It's unlikely that your first call in Japan wouldn't be local, but in case you're calling someplace you know is not in your calling area, be sure to dial the prefix "area code." For example, if you're in Tokyo and you want to call 777-8899, fine, that's all you dial. But if the number's in Osaka, you'll need to dial 06-777-8899 ("06" being Osaka's area code) or in Yokohama 045-777-8899 (Yokohama also has other area codes).

Note that not all area codes have the same number of digits (they range from two to four), but they do all begin with "0" ("operator" in Japan is "106"). Just be sure you omit the area code if you're already in the area to which you're calling; e.g., if the number you want in Tokyo is 03-222-5588 but you're calling *from* Tokyo, just dial 222-5588. ("03" is Tokyo's area code.)

Now back to you, trembling in the airport.

If you are able to catch someone at your place of future employment, ask to speak to an English-speaking person and, with a note of helplessness in your voice, ask what you should do now. Most businesses and some of the classier schools actually arrange to pick up their new personnel and escort them to their sumptuous quarters, but the usual response to most teachers' notification of arrival is a sincere "welcome", followed by a somewhat desperate "you can start tonight maybe?" Don't count on the red carpet.

But just maybe, as one of the more popular fairy tales goes, the teacher winds up talking to the president of the company himself who magnanimously offers his own palatial digs until the gaijin's able to get his or her own place. Yes, it *has* been known to happen. Should you be so fortunate as to have this offer made to you, feel honored and go for it. You'll have a far easier time adjusting to the culture if you're staying in a home environment.

Another suggestion the company may make for parking your Samsonite is that you stay with the secretary's older brother's girlfriend, boyfriend or some such convoluted relationship. It may just happen that he, she or it is studying English and has a spare room, just waiting for the likes of you to take up residency temporarily--or permanently. While it may not be for everyone, there *are* quite a few "rent in exchange for tutoring" situations to be had and, if you're looking for ways to cut expenses to the bone, you should definitely check this out. Some schools actually specialize in such "total immersion" instruction with students and teachers living together. Frankly, though it may be a great way for the student to learn English quickly, the teacher usually contracts a bad case of "Japanglish" overexposure rather soon after moving in.

If you really would like to live with a Japanese individual or family, you might be able to do so. Hopefully, you will have tried to make some Japanese connections in your home town (either with students, housewives or people working there), and so should have the names and addresses of some of their friends and relations with whom you could stay for a few days upon arriving.

Establishing such a pleasant base of operations in a sometimes-confusing land is probably the single most important thing you can do to get the confidence necessary to sally forth and do some serious job hunting. The hotels we've listed are pleasant enough, but, of course, nothing beats being taken in by a caring family, especially when you're fresh off the boat. But don't plan on staying with someone just because they're in Japan--find their home on the map and carefully consider travel time to downtown, where most of your interviews will be. If the addresses you were given are not in the metropolitan area where you are (or hope to be) working, save visiting those people till vacation time.

But if you do stay with friends of friends, be very polite, of course, but don't worry if they are what you consider overly kind to you. The houseguest in Japan is very honored indeed, and the Japanese will want to take care of you totally while you're staying in their home. Whatever you do, don't fight it; just enjoy. On the other hand, if you sense that an offer of help around the house would be appreciated (as it may be, especially with younger families), don't hesitate to suggest it. A safe rule of thumb is always offer to help several times, but never insist.

If you stay in a home, be sure to bring a gift for the family, preferably something imported and not easily obtained in Japan. A good bottle of scotch purchased at the duty-free store at the airport makes an ideal "puresento" (you can bring up to three liters into the country) as do T-shirts (especially popular with kids), good Indian jewelry, picture books, leather handicrafts, and, the hands-down favorite of international luggage-luggers, commemorative stamps.

Take full advantage of the perfume allowance, too, by buying as many individual bottles as your allowance will allow and, even if you don't smoke, you'll meet a lot of (primarily male) people who will appreciate your American brands, also purchased tax-free. Any tasteful, unusual and readily-identifiable example of your country's art or culture is almost always a hit. You'll find yourself *constantly* exchanging gifts with the Japanese and among the most appreciated are those you can bring from home.

As for your behaviour in their home, don't worry about offending your guests by saying or doing the wrong things--just use your own common sense and behave as Mom would want you to. The Japanese certainly don't expect you to know all the minutiae of their etiquette. As long as you respect them and their home, you shouldn't feel at all nervous about stepping on their figurative toes. Your hosts will be delighted to educate you into the ways of Nippon, if they see that you're honestly interested.

But don't despair if you didn't fill up your address book before you left home or the president's out of town or the secretary's brother just broke up with his girlfriend; you can always head for one of the places we've recommended in the Appendix and find shelter for under $20 a night (sometimes *way* under) which will be clean and safe (even for single women) and keep you in the heart of the city, well-situated for the next few phases of your adventure.

Even if you do have to stay in one of the places we've suggested, you'll still get a wonderful introduction to the culture, especially if you stay in a "minshuku" or "ryokan" or even temple rather than one of the somewhat spartan "business hotels" or hostels.

Minshuku are traditional Japanese-style hotels, usually family-owned and operated, which offer very reasonable rates, especially considering the price includes one and sometimes two meals. In summer and other peak tourist periods, you may be asked to share a room with a few other guests of the same sex, but this usually happens only at popular resorts on weekends.

In a minshuku, you're expected to sleep on soft, smooth tatami mats, with bedding laid out by the maid, who also puts it back in the closet each morning. Bathing is Japanese-style, probably communal (sorry, never co-ed), with the hot water pool or tub used for soaking only, *not* washing. Always soap up and rinse outside the bath unless you seek your fellow bathers' ire.

The only real problem with minshuku's is that the owners and guests might not speak much English, but they will most certainly welcome you and be eager to learn all about you and your reactions to their country. For complete information on minshuku's and listings outside major cities, write to the Japan Minshiku Center, Kotsu Kaikan Bldg., 2-10-1, Yurakucho, Chiyoda-ku, Tokyo.

Business hotels are what most Westerners are accustomed to as they seek only to provide the weary traveler with lodging: no meals, no maid service and probably a more anonymous atmosphere than you'd find in the minshuku's. I would certainly recommend the minshuku's (which are not much more expensive than hotels) unless you think the culture change would be too much, too fast for you.

Ryokans are also Japanese-style lodgings, a kind of minshuku-hotel hybrid. The prices will be more than at a minshuku but the accommodations will be a bit nicer and the service more formal--but not necessarily any better than at a minshuku. Still, if you want an immediate taste of the culture and there's no room at the minshuku, the ryokan with its bath, Japanese breakfast and tatami floors will certainly be more appealing to you than the Far Eastern version of the Holiday Inn which most business hotels tend to resemble.

Temples are just that. "Shuku-bo" are places of monastic contemplation and introspection and, as such, are not exactly hotspots. Prices, meals and service are comparable to a minshuku's but temples may require you to help with some light housekeeping or attend the early morning service (that's early as in about 5 or 6 a.m.). Needless to say, you can't get much more authentically Japanese than one of these places but it might be a bit intense for you to handle fresh off the plane. I suggest you try one later.

Hostels are the cheapest places to crash you'll find, thanks to their policy of putting many members of the same sex in the same room. In Japan, there are about 75 public hostels operated by national or regional governments and around 450 hostels affiliated with Japan Youth Hostels Inc. JYH hostels are a little cheaper (about 1,500 yen a night) due to their membership with International Youth Hostels (IYH) but public hostels are still bargain-basement at around 2,000 yen a night. Both types usually have meals available (about 700 yen) and neither have any age limits. You'll need to be an IYH member to stay at a JYH hostel but you can join in Japan for about $10. Write Japan Youth Hostels, Hoken Kaikan Bldg. 3F, 1-2 Ichigaya-Sadoharacho, Shinjuku-ku, Tokyo 162 for a complete list and information.

All lodgings listed in the Appendix are accustomed to foreign guests and are easily accessible by public transportation, either train or subway. As is the case everywhere in Japan, tipping is neither expected nor appreciated--service is provided because it's part of the job. You wouldn't expect to tip a bank teller back home, why would you tip a bellboy, waitress or cab driver in Japan? (Does make sense when you think about it, doesn't it?)

You could make reservations at least four weeks in advance at any of the hotels and minshuku's mentioned, but unless you expect to arrive during Golden Week (a string of national holidays around the beginning of May when everyone and his 2.1 children leave home to recreate), it's probably not necessary. You shouldn't have any trouble finding a place somewhere in the city if you just call a few places when you land.

Information on additional lodging in major cities is available from any tourist information center in the area, which you should certainly visit as soon as possible after arriving. Get directions to their office from one of the English-speaking staff and stock up on their many helpful brochures as well.

In Sapporo, call the Sapporo Tourist Association (tel. 011-211-3341); in Tokyo, it's the Tourist Information Center (502-1461); in Yokohama, call the International Welcome Association (045-641-5824) or the Kanagawa Prefectural Tourist Association (045-681-0007); Nagoya: Tourist and Foreign Trade Section (052-961-1111); Kyoto: Tourist Section (075-752-0215) or their TIC (075-371-5649); Osaka: Tourist Association (06-261-3948) or the TIC (06-345-2189); Kobe: International Tourist Association (078-232-1010); and in Kagoshima (at the southern tip of Kyushu), call the City Tourist Section (0992-24-1111). Remember not to dial the two, three or four digit area prefix beginning with "0" if you're already in the city.

All of these offices are open from 9 to 5 and 'til noon on Saturdays and will have someone in the office who can help you in English. Some of the larger offices, such as Tokyo, Kyoto and Osaka also can help in other major languages as well. These places provide a wealth of information on just about everything from accommodations to tours of the town but remember that they're set up to serve tourists and your needs as a resident will be quite different. They aren't, for example, going to help you out much with your apartment hunting.

One wonderful service offered by the Tourist Information Center is a toll-free "panic number" which will put you in touch with an English-speaking person who should be able to get you out of your pickle, no matter where you may encounter it; just be sure said pickle occurs during normal office hours.

Here's how it works: in Tokyo or Kyoto, you can call the Tourist Information Center locally (see listings above). Anywhere else, just dial 106 (operator) from any phone and say "Collect call, TIC." Don't jazz it up; say exactly that and don't deviate one iota from it. (Any more elaborate English and you might blow one of the operator's logic circuits.)

Masterful Transit

Now that you've figured out where you'll be spending the first night, let's look at the next dragon to be be tamed: the maddening and magnificent mass transit system.

There's a very good chance that the trains and subways of Japan will spoil you forever and, if you're American, they'll probably make you wonder why we can't do better than the rickety eyesores that pass for subways and commuter trains in *our* country. Tokyo residents have by far the most extensive and efficient mass transit system in the world and you are going to revel in it and wrestle with it from the moment you step foot outside the airport.

First the fundamentals. There are two kinds of subways and trains: private (proprietary) and public (run by the Japanese government as part of the Japan National Railroad or "JNR"). Both types of lines require you to buy a ticket from a vending machine before you can enter the station proper.

Once you get to know the system, you'll be able to determine the price of the ticket by locating your destination on a large map above the machines. On this map, you'll find the names of the stations (illegible to those unfamiliar with the Japanese alphabet) with numbers by the names. These numbers represent fares from your station to those stations. If each destination has two fares, the lower of the two is for children.

Knowing the fare to your destination (it'll be at least 120 yen), you then insert enough coins into the machine to make the appropriate fare button light up. Most machines accept and give change in coins (although some JNR machines also accept 1,000 yen notes.) To get change for large bills, simply use one of the change machines (the ones without the fare buttons) or hand your 500, 1,000, 5,000 or 10,000 yen note to one of the station men and he'll give you change which you then use in the machine. Station personnel are allowed to sell only long-distance tickets and special passes, never local tickets.

Of course, if you don't know the Japanese spelling of your destination, you won't be able to find it on the fare map above the machines or determine your fare. One perfectly acceptable way of finding out how much you should pay is to ask anyone, in English, what the fare will be. Don't be bashful about it, this is Japan; courtesy comes with the territory.

Anytime you need help from a stranger, first try to approach young adults--they are the most likely either to be studying English or to have it still fresh in their minds from their high school or college days. Next best are the three-piece bedecked businessmen, many of whom are likely to use English in their jobs.

Unless you know the person you're speaking to is proficient with English, keep it simple. This means avoiding contractions ("you are" instead of "you're"), colloquialisms ("do you understand?" instead of "get it?") and, of course, complex constructions ("What station is two stops before Shinagawa?" and "What is the fare to that station?" instead of "What's the fare to the station two stops before Shinagawa?"). Keep it rudimentary until you've gauged the other person's English ability and be prepared for your helper to be flustered at having to use English. Give them time; it'll come.

Another way of avoiding the confusion of figuring your fare is just to buy the cheapest ticket you can (the lowest denomination fare button) which will be just enough to get you to the next stop down the line. Your purpose, of course, is merely to get into the station. Then, after you've reached your destination, you simply hand your ticket to the wicket man at the exit and he'll tell you how much extra you owe.

Since most train lines interconnect, you can usually go from one to another without exiting the system. This means you can ride on several different lines without having to buy a new ticket for each leg of your trip. (But you do usually have to exit and buy a new ticket between JNR and private trains or subways.)

There's absolutely no penalty for paying the fare at the end of your trip and it's very common for gaijin to do so when they can't make out the fares. Occasionally, a conductor on your train or subway will ask to see your ticket but even if you have an insufficient one, he'll just ask you to pay the fare to whatever your destination is. No embarrassment, no accusations.

Your first challenge, however, will be to get from the airport to your hotel intact.

From the New Tokyo International Airport at Narita, it's fairly simple. First you take a bus to the Narita train station, then transfer to an express train that will take you into Tokyo's Ueno Station. There are several other ways to get to town from Narita, but with the exception of the express bus that takes you direct from the airport to Tokyo City Air Terminal (TCAT), the bus/train route is probably the most hassle-free and fun.

From Haneda Airport, getting to town is even easier. Many years ago, just after Disneyland installed theirs, the good citizens of Tokyo decided their fair city just had to have its own monorail. (There are a few other interesting parallels that can be drawn between Japan and the Magic Kingdom as well, but you can discover those for yourself.) And what better use for one-track transport than to ferry VIPs from downtown to the then-international airport at Haneda?

The airport's past glory may have faded a bit, but the monorail's still fun. You could take a $20 taxi ride into the city but for less than a buck, you can have a quite spectacular introductory view of Tokyo served up to you 50 feet above the teeming metropolis. To find the monorail terminal at Haneda, just follow the crowd (it's only about a five-minute walk) and when in doubt about anything, ask! *In English!*

In all honesty, there will be times when your North American or British English won't be comprehensible, but usually only because of your pronunciation. Such a tremendous number of English words (like "monorail") have become integral parts of the Japanese language that,

believe it or not, some Japanese don't realize that certain foreign words aren't Japanese.

For example, there is no Japanese equivalent for "monorail" so the people have absorbed the English word totally into their vocabulary, in this case retaining its original meaning, but giving it a Japanese pronunciation. Thus, if you're American and ask the whereabouts of the "ma-nuh-ray-uhl," you may be greeted with blank stares of non-comprehension. Ask for the "mo-no-ray-roo" however, and all roads lead to rest for the weary traveller.

Take the "monorayroo" to the end of the line and you'll get off at Hamamatsucho Station, which, like Ueno Station (where those coming from Narita will wind up), is also on the Yamanote Line which circles around the Imperial Palace. (Interestingly, the Japanese use the same word to describe the Yamanote's circular movement as they use to describe the movement of the blood through the body. And like our own blood system, it circulates life throughout the central body, never ending.)

Because the Yamanote is roughly circular, many people describe the locations of stations on it as being on the face of a clock. The monorail brings you from Haneda into Hamamatsucho at about 5 o'clock. Coming from Narita, you'd come in to Ueno at about 2 o'clock. Shinjuku is at 10 and Tokyo Station itself is at 4.

Almost all other lines, private and public, subway and train, anywhere in the city, connect with the Yamanote. Locate these transfer points on your map first;

they'll be of greatest use to you: Shibuya, Tokyo Station, Shinbashi, Kanda, Ueno and Shinagawa (where the Tokyo Immigration Office is headquartered) and, of course, Shinjuku, through whose portals pour an average of two million commuters each and every day.

The major lines you really should know about right off the bat are: the Yamanote from which most other lines radiate out to the suburbs, much like spokes from the hub of a wheel; the Chuo or "Main" line which bisects the Yamanote and continues west from Shinjuku past Tachikawa and Hachioji (still technically Tokyo but definitely the boondocks) and beyond to the hinterlands.

A private line which offers considerable competition to the Chuo is the Keio which also runs between Shinjuku and Hachioji. Why would two train lines serve the same route? Because the Keio is owned by the Keio Corporation while the Chuo is part of the Japan National Railway, run (some say mismanaged) by the government. Wherever in Japan you wind up, it's fairly important you understand the difference between public and private lines for those times when you have a choice of which to take, especially on a regular basis.

The majority of subway and train lines are part of the huge JNR network, a gigantic conglomeration of everything from the ultra-modern "bullet train" express to the coal-fired rattletraps that serve Hokkaido's rural lines. Like all national railways throughout the world, it is a financial black hole. In 1981, the system lost over one *trillion* yen.

The private lines, on the other hand, are owned and operated by huge, multi-interest corporations, most of which have gigantic department stores in metropolitan areas. For example, the Odakyu "depaato"--as the Japanese call it--occupies about three city blocks in Tokyo's Shinjuku district. The Odakyu train line serving southwest Tokyo, naturally enough, deposits passengers in Shinjuku practically on top of the store's cash registers.

These private lines are not burdened with the same social responsibility as JNR; if a line's not profitable, they shut it down. JNR, on the other hand, is expected to provide full rail service throughout the country, even in unprofitable low-density rural areas. In Tokyo, though, almost all lines, private and JNR show a healthy profit because of heavy ridership.

But the different *overall* profit pictures between the two kinds of lines is the reason why there are such striking differences between the two lines linking Shinjuku and Hachioji.

The Keio is fast, clean, plush and cheap; a model of free enterprise serving the consumer. The Chuo, run by the financially strapped and heavily-politicized JNR, is much slower, somewhat grimy and sometimes more than twice as expensive as the private line. Why? To help compensate for all the money JNR loses on its other (principally rural) lines. Not too surprisingly, it's a sore point with Tokyo-ites but it'll make a great conversation topic in your class!

If you're using a large station with more than one platform and you haven't yet learned to read the destination signs, you'll have to ask the man at the ticket wicket--in English--for the track number. (In case of confusion, just emphasize the name of your destination.) Learn your Japanese numbers before you go!

All subways stop at every station along the way, but there are several different kinds of trains which you should know about. The slowest is the "kakueki densha" or "every station train." (Who said this was a difficult language to learn?)

You'll probably become quite familiar with this quaint but arthritic milktrain if you're the partying kind who likes to stay downtown till it's time to do the hundred yard dash for the last train of the night. Miss that last, crammed local and it will probably mean a $20 cab ride or hotel room. Then again, the all-night fun spots downtown *do* know how to help make the best of a potentially problematic predicament. After the trains stop running, Tokyo turns into a whole 'nother breed of cat, one you should savor at least once.

After about 11 p.m., the local "kakueki" is the only kind of train you'll find and it makes your homeward journey a long one, especially if you wind up next to a well-pickled businessman who not only looks the color of week-old tofu but seems about to toss some of it in your general direction. (It should be mentioned that the Japanese men love to get looped, but never on company time. The ladies usually demur.)

You may also have to take the local to and from your home station if you want to transfer to one of the express trains which only stop at major stations. You'll probably want to travel by express train as much as possible--they're faster and more comfortable than any local. In fact, by using a "kaisoku" (regular express) or it's even faster cousin, the "tokkyu" (limited express), you should be able to cut your travel time between major stations by as much as one-half. Between cities, of course, the super expresses make only three or four stops every hundred miles and the world-renowned JNR "bullet train" makes only one stop per major city, waiting a scant thirty seconds before pulling out again.

(Incidentally, studies have proven that it's actually faster to travel between some major cities by the "bullet" than by plane, once check-in time and travel to the airport are figured in. But, thanks to the efforts of JNR to reduce their ocean of red ink, it's not always cheaper. If you're thinking of travelling more than 200 miles or so, ask a travel agent how the fares compare between JNR, All Nippon Airways and Japan Air Lines.)

Next in the transport panoply, we come to the travel means of true adventurers and tourists, respectively: the humble bus and the ubiquitous cab.

There may be no better test of a gaijin's mettle (and sanity) than to attempt the traversing of Point A to Point B by "wan-man (one man) basu." Think of the challenge! For 160 yen, you'll get at least five times as many stops on the average bus line as on a train or subway line, with none of the signs written in English and the driver rarely seeming to understand *Japanese* let alone the frantic yammering of a terrified gai-person.

Yes, perhaps after you've read Lady Murasaki's Tale of Genji in the original and once you find yourself consistently mistaken for a native Japanese over the phone, you really should attempt, say, a one-mile ride on the bus. But, please, don't tell anyone you'll be home in time for dinner.

At the other extreme, we have the easiest and most expensive mode of transit in cities, the taxi. The Nipponese "takushi" (that's really what they call 'em) is the epitome of spit-and-polish and the driver will usually comport himself like the captain of the QE 2.

He may not actually run out and open the door for you but the general idea is there with the automatic door which swings wide for the entering passenger, much like the creaky front door in a B-rated fright-fest. Somewhat eerie, but a nice touch.

You pay for such courtesies, however. Fares start at 470 yen (about $2.15) and increase by 80 yen every two kilometers or 2.5 minutes. Another incentive for you not to miss that last train home: after 11 p.m., all taxi fares go up by 20%. Still, they are convenient. You can find them just about anywhere, especially in front of the train stations.

Once you've nabbed one, just pass the driver a slip of paper with your destination written in Japanese (matchbooks are quite handy for this) or tell him to head for the station nearest your end point. If you're trying to get to some out-of-the-way place (like your well-concealed abode), you'll probably have to personally direct him to it from the nearest well-known landmark, be it train station, major intersection or park. (The idea of naming their streets apparently has not yet occurred to the Japanese so forget about just telling your cab jocky "2503 Tsunami Way" and catching a snooze in the back seat. You *will* have to verbally guide him in once you're nearing the mark.)

One very nice way to beat the ever-deepening bite of train and subway (and even bus) fares is to take advantage of one, three or six month passes called "teki," offered by almost all carriers. With one of these, you can save up to 50% of regular fare if you regularly travel between two points. They're also a real time-saver if you find yourself stuck in line behind 25 school kid clones out on a field trip, waiting to buy a ticket. Instead, you just flash the ever-clicking ticket puncher your teki and in you go. Highly recommended.

One other form of transportation which probably is very much a part of your preconceived vision of the country is the bicycle. You may have expected to find droves of pin-stripe suited cyclists filling the streets of Tokyo every day on their way to their corporate strongholds, but, sorry, only the neighborhood delivery boys and suicidal gaijin are fool enough to do such battle with Tokyo traffic. It really is a dangerous way to get from here to there and we wholeheartedly discourage you from duking it out with one of the city's mighty mite dump trucks which careen regularly through the thoroughfares.

About the only time the average Japanese uses a bicycle these days is to get to the nearest train station or neighborhood shop. *Local* usage of bicycles is very common, so much so that bike pollution is becoming a real problem. It seems that so many people are riding their bicycles to the station and downtown area that the parking lots for them are becoming incredibly congested with not only commuters' bikes but abandoned heaps as well.

When the parking situation gets bad enough, the city piles up all the bicycles that appear to have been abandoned and, if they're not claimed, hauls them off to be turned into anything from a trunk lid for a Toyota to a chassis panel for a Sony. (The resource-scarce Nipponese are very much into recycling.)

Some cost-conscious foreigners have discovered that, if you ask politely, you can often have one of the abandoned bikes free. A little steel wool to remove the rust (everything rusts and mildews in the Land of the Rising Humidity), some paint and air in the tires and voila! Many a heap has been remade into a conveyance just perfect for some very nice weekend rides on one of the several excellent bike paths outside the city.

Those raised on the potent juice of the American V-8 may find it exceedingly difficult, if not impossible to use a car as some automaniacs are used to. With streets almost as narrow as bike paths (with utility poles planted in the street, prompting many a lively game of "chicken"), gasoline going for about three dollars a gallon and an almost complete lack of on-street parking, it's difficult to understand why about 20% of the Japanese bother owning a car, especially with such excellent mass transit available.

It's usually a poor idea for short-timers to own a car but, in case you ever want to rent a car or borrow one of your friends', you probably should pick up an international driver's license at your local Automobile Club or Licensing Bureau before leaving home. (It will also let you drive small motorscooters in Japan.)

The cost is minimal and you don't have to take any sort of test. Just bring a picture and a valid local license and you'll be issued a license on the spot.

The Nipponese Nest

So let's assume you're gradually getting the hang of getting around, your sponsor has taken you to the bosom of his company and you're ready to think about where in the great megalopolis you should reside. Think long and hard--mistakes in this area are expensive.

Whatever part of the Island Kingdom you go for, you'll probably wind up in an "apaato" (the Japanized abbreviation of "apartment"). Land prices in Japan have gone up even faster than in other countries so demand is keen for apartments; they're all most people can afford. But, because the units are smaller than what we Westerners are used to, the rents are really quite reasonable. It's the *size* of your place that will require some getting used to.

The factors you consider in choosing a place are pretty much the same you'd use anywhere: rent, distance from work, neighborhood, availability of shops and (possibly a new consideration) distance from public transportation.

For many, the ambience of the area is critical. Newcomers especially often need relief from the pressures of Tokyo and so choose a locale with as much of a "country feeling" as possible. Such areas are not difficult to find, but you will have to decide early on how much daily train commuting is acceptable for you. Many very pleasant semi-rural areas are located a mere 30 minutes from the city's center.

Fortunately for you, most Japanese don't care to live in the more spacious areas many Westerners prefer.

The Japanese, as a rule, like to "cluster," that is, live as near to each other as price and circumstance allow. Compared to most nations, Japan is actually a relatively large country with many lightly populated regions. The high population density of the cities is largely due to the Japanese predilection for being close to "the action."

What this all means, as you've probably surmised, is that very nice apartments can be had quite reasonably away from town or city centers. Given the fact that you'll probably be surrounded by the din of the city every working day downtown, you might give some thought to living someplace where you can enjoy some greenery and tranquility.

On the other hand, if you're the kind who has to live among the bright lights, you'll wind up paying astronomical rent for meager accomodations. And while the convenience of living ten minutes from work and play is great, monthly rents of $500 are by no means uncommon for tiny apartments inside Tokyo's Yamanote line.

Factors determining apartment rents (in descending order of importance) are: distance from city center, size, features (bath, Western toilet, etc.), number of easily accessible train or subway lines, distance from nearest train or subway station and distance from shops and other amenities. Strangely enough, the *type* of neighborhood doesn't seem to play a large part in pricing probably because most Japanese (90% in a recent poll) consider themselves "middle class" and thus, 90% of their neighborhoods are also "middle class."

So, if you're willing to walk or ride a bicycle a bit to the station and grocery store and ride the train more than 30 minutes in to work, you can find a very comfortable apartment in a delightfully relaxing neighborhood for less than $200 per month. And this is the world's most expensive city?

Your first step in finding your little hideaway must be to decide *exactly* what kind of place you're looking for. Must it be close to town? Large? In an area with other gaijin? Have Western features like carpeting and a Western seat-type toilet? (All these are going to make your place very expensive.) Should it be in a small town? Japanese style, with woven rice straw mats ("tatami") on the floor and Japanese "squat" toilet? What do you want to see when you look out the windows? How long are you willing to spend riding the trains each day? (Don't worry about the expense; the employer(s) will pay your transportation costs.)

Only after you've formed a mental picture of the apartment of your dreams can you go looking for it with any hope of actually finding it. Because most people are somewhat disoriented while searching for a place, they often take the advice of well-meaning friends or get desperate and wind up taking an apartment that doesn't suit them--a very large mistake. Your living environment probably will be even more important to you in Japan than it was at home; you'll have a greater need for privacy in your own personal world and it should serve as a haven from the pressures of the city. Make sure it's exactly what you want!

With your map of the city (every time you find yourself near the Tourist Information Center you should pick up another one; you'll wear them out in no time), figure out how far from your main teaching job you can live and still not spend more time on the train than you want to. If you think you can accept 45 minutes on the train each way, plot a circle 45 minutes in all directions from your school or office.

Now that you've established your parameters, try to decide what the most convenient train or subway would be for your primary destination (probably your sponsor's office or school). Now the second most convenient. And the third. (It would be ideal if you could live at the junction of two train lines you used regularly.) Locate the major express stops on the line, then look at the stations one or two stops beyond those. (You might also consider stations before the express stops but then you'd have to backtrack if you transferred from an express to a local train, which, of course, is a bit more time-consuming.)

You now probably have a list of three or four stations on each of the two or three lines you could use to get to your job(s). Next, find out what cities ("shi") those stations are in and have a Japanese friend call the city hall ("shiyakusho") to inquire about national health insurance ("hoken") for gaijin. Some cities extend the

insurance to foreigners; some don't. If your employer isn't
providing you with any, make sure that at least your city
will.

Once you're satisfied with the insurance part, take
one full Sunday (the one day when all the townsfolk will
be out and about) and visit each place. Soak in the
ambience. Is it relaxed? Clean? Check the quality and
prices of the shops. Are you being stared at? (Might
suggest they're too unused to having gaijin around.) How
much greenery is in evidence? Don't expect entertainment
facilities. Almost all theaters, clubs and the like are
concentrated in entertainment districts, where you might
not want to live even if you could afford to.

Decide which little burg you like best, then pick a
second choice, and a third. Now you're ready for the
tricky part: negotiating with the realtors.

For this bit of business, you should ask a Japanese
friend or one of the school secretaries to assist you. (Most
schools consider helping sponsored teachers find
accommodations to be one of their responsibilities.) The
two of you should go to the nearest station that serves
your primary choice living location and find the area's
two or three "fudosan-ya" (real estate offices).

In Japan, the realtors are about the only people who
have places for rent. Don't make the mistake of looking
for a place in the daily newspaper want ads. Advertising
space is *very* expensive in Japan and the only places you'll
find that way are those for foreign executives whose
companies are footing 90% of the rent. However, if you'd
like a nice 3 bedroom American-style apartment in the
heart of downtown, this is about the only place you'll find
one. Just don't let the $2,000 a month rent scare you off.

If that kind of highway robbery doesn't appeal to
you, stick to the fudosan-ya's. Rents for their places
usually range from $100 to $350 with the latter being large
(probably 3 rooms and a kitchen), located just 3 or 4
minutes from the station, clean, and well-lighted. The
former would probably be one room, which you would be
expected to share with a large tribe of resident cucarachas.
Scientists say cockroaches will be the only survivors of
World War III; evidence suggests they've already started

taking over in Japan. Nevertheless, their lovable antics make for great war stories.

The real estate offices, like just about every other enterprise in town, will be located quite near the station. You'll recognize them by the large windows, plastered with ads for available dwellings. Although they also rent and sell houses and condominiums (which they call "mansions," inscrutably enough), you'll only be interested in those ads on the window with the word "apaato," spelled out in katakana.

Before we get into how you can read the information on the window ad, we'll have to give you a little inside poop on the way the Japanese describe land and housing in general.

The Japanese are officially on the metric system, but old habits die hard. They have never given up the old measurements for living space so you will probably find everything in the ads expressed in "jo" and possibly "tsubo." A "jo" is an area about 3 feet by 6 feet, while a "tsubo" is merely two "jo" or a 6 by 6 square. One "tatami" mat is exactly one "jo" in size and you'll often hear a 6 jo room called a 6 "mat" room. Rooms come in all sizes, but you're unlikely to encounter any larger than 6 jo (mats). Six is the standard sized room, with 4 1/2 (yo-jo han) and 3 (san-jo) also fairly common.

Rooms in Japanese homes are multi-purpose. You eat, sleep, watch TV, everything, all in the same room, stowing the bedding during the daytime in the spacious closets all apartments have. Thus it would be meaningless to talk in terms of a one or two "bedroom" apartment. Instead, you'll see apartments listed as 1,2 or 3 "DK," meaning the place has 1,2 or 3 rooms *and* a "dining/kitchen" room, which could be any size.

On the ads, you'll see large numbers written vertically. These refer to the size of the rooms. The slightly smaller number below them is the size of the "DK," usually about 3/4 the size of the smallest other room. (A kitchen it may be but don't expect to be stuffing any dining room tables into it.)

In the upper left hand corner of the ad, you'll find the rent (the number with lots of zeros at the end) and, below it, a modest little monthly maintenance fee which

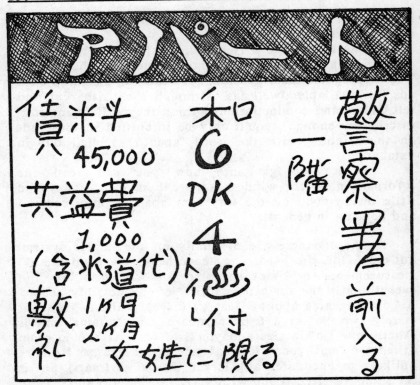

you may or may not be asked to pay (rarely more than a few dollars).

Below this on the ad comes the part that makes most gaijin wish they'd stayed in Sacramento. It's the notice of what it will cost you to move in, expressed in months of rent. It's always a bundle, but don't despair, many schools at least will loan their sponsored teachers this "key money."

"Key money" has developed in Japan simply because housing is a seller's market (the landlords can get away with it) and the Japanese value stability over simple profit. The system is used for Japanese and gaijin alike (don't feel exploited) and it's *extremely* effective in getting people to stay put once they've taken an apartment. And once you've put down 4 or 5 month's key money, you too will feel rather unwilling to leave, knowing that you're liable to get back only *one* of those month's rent and that the next place you live will expect the same amount of key money. When you take an apartment, be absolutely certain you'll be staying a good long while. Then *stay put!*

Don't be like one teacher who paid her four month's rent and stayed one. Her $200 a month rent very quickly became a $600 a month rent when she found that only the one month she'd paid as a damage deposit could be returned. The other month's went to first month's rent, real estate agent's fee, and landlord's fee. (Like we said, they *can* and *do* get away with it.)

Sure it's an outrageous practice and it's especially unfair to gaijin who are planning to stay only a short while, but don't argue with the fudosan. Remember, he won't have the slightest difficulty renting that place to a Japanese and, considering the reputation most gaijin have for noise and general obnoxiousness, he's probably doing you a favor by even showing you the apartment. *Everyone* not getting some sort of special private deal pays "key money;" don't gripe to him about it or he might just refuse to rent it to you. Which he is perfectly entitled to do.

The anti-discrimination laws in Japan are fuzzy at best and they are intended to protect Japanese. You, as a visiting "outside person" have questionable rights if any at all. But, if you are polite, friendly and wear your "young professional" costume (i.e., nice clothes), you shouldn't have any trouble getting the place you want.

Many, possibly most, apartments these days have baths. This was quite a rarity just a few years ago when almost everyone tromped down to the "sento" (public bath) for a segregated soaking. (Yes, you can find a very few co-ed tubs in the hinterlands, but the only members of the opposite sex you're liable to spot will be Farmer Matsumoto and his 80 year-old wife. But they'll think *your* anatomy is *very* interesting.)

Sento's are expensive these days--about a buck a bath. For an extra $20 a month or so, you can have one in the apartment, and while the communal experience is lacking, it's nice not to have to make that long walk back home through a monsoon.

Apartment "ofuro's" (baths) are the model of simplicity. Just fill up the squarish tub with cold water, light the gas heater below, wait about half an hour and hop in. Heavenly. Just remember if you're only one of several who'll be using the same water to do all your washing *before* you climb into the bath. The water in the tub should stay clean through at least three washings if everyone rinses off carefully before hopping in.

And once you see what you're paying for the natural gas to heat the ofuro, you won't think sharing the water sounds nearly as unsavory as you might now. You can spot apartments on the realtor's window that have ofuro's by looking for a symbol that looks like steam rising from a pool, usually printed near the size of the "DK."

Western or "seat" toilets are becoming more common in Japan--with many Japanese preferring them. It's a shame in a way because doctors have shown that it's far more natural for us to squat than sit whilst answering nature's call. ('Course, it *is* rather difficult to read your "Jokes for the John" in the knees-up position. It's a sad fact that Japanese toilets are simply not designed for philosophical ruminations.)

Your knees really might ache a little at first at the strain that's being put on them, but, after a week, you should be quite used to it. Just remember to face the hump and don't be embarrassed to have to hang on to the water pipe in front of you (we hear the Japanese use it for balance too). Some apartments do have Western toilets but you'll probably have to pay a premium for that exotic pot. In any case, steer clear of non-flush (septic) toilets, which although mercifully disappearing from the scene, still will assail your nostrils occasionally, especially in rural areas.

You're on your own for home decorating, but don't despair, nice furnishings are readily available, usually cheap, sometimes free. Just start letting everyone (as in everyone) know you're in the market for necessities. You'll be surprised how much can be found just by talking to your neighbors and asking about what you think might be unneeded items when you see them, especially behind shops. And you certainly should watch for the gems which frequently will adorn your neighborhood trash pickup area.

Now, we're not recommending you become a bag-gaijin and start dumpster diving daily, but you should know that the Japanese throw out many things that would certainly be sold through want ads in the US and Europe. The reason they aren't in Japan is because of the Japanese prejudice against anything used and the lack of classifieds in their papers.

The Japanese aren't wasteful by nature, but with very limited storage space, they must clear out household excess immediately. Consequently, they have no choice but to give or throw away perfectly good appliances, often wrapping them in plastic bags and leaving them near but not *in* the neighborhood garbage area, hoping that someone will be able to make use of them.

Garbagemen are very particular about what they pick up and when. You'll probably be expected to segregate your trash into burnables ("moeru gomi") and non-burnables ("moenai gomi"), putting bags in the garbage collection area only when it's the day for that kind of garbage to be picked up (moeru thrice weekly, moenai once). Similarly, the garbagemen will pick up large or bulky items ("sodai gomi" like appliances and such) only on, as the natives call it, "Big Garbage Day."

Needless to say, it would behoove you to find out what day this is in *your* neighborhood and scour the streets the night before the trashmen cometh. (The pickings are so good in some of the ritzier neighborhoods that one enterprising young gaijin used to cruise with his pick-up truck, snatching all sorts of goodies, then selling them "as is" to recently-arrived fellow foreigners).

Don't be ashamed to check out those two-burner stoves, heaters, TV's, even refrigerators that sometimes adorn the rubbish. It's a very accepted practice to take what you can use. Occasionally, you'll see respectable Japanese doing it too, although not many of them could boast having furnished an entire home with the stuff, as can many a gaijin. Still, if this method of interior decoration doesn't suit your fancy, however, or if you suffer slim pickings, you will have to turn to other sources of good, cheap household paraphernalia.

Most Tokyo-based gaijin find out fairly quickly about the Salvation Army's warehouse full of used stuff in

Nakano, west of downtown Tokyo. It's a bit far from the nearest station, but if you can talk one of your Japanese friends into driving you, you'll find bargains aplenty. Even if you're unused to shopping at thrift stores, you should check out this one because it's probably the biggest in town, with better-than-average quality merchandise. Call them at 531-3516 before you try to find the place, though. Nakano is a student area so there is also an abundance of good, cheap second-hand shops ("chuko-ya") thereabouts, many of which are listed in the excellent "Tokyo Journal" weekly. Those going to Osaka and elsewhere will just have to ask around.

Go to some of the larger EFL schools in town and post a notice in the teacher's lounge asking any home-bound sensei's to call you if they have anything for sale. Such "sayonara sales" are especially common, as you'd imagine, just after the end of the teaching semester or in June, when company personnel are rotated home. Don't forget to ask about such sales at the embassy, churches, English language elementary and secondary schools and any other likely organizations which might be in touch with large numbers of foreigners.

At your neighborhood police box ("koban"), you can find out where the nearest "chuko-ya" (second-hand) stores are located. Your little town probably has a couple which, while they might not be as well-stocked as those in the student district, could have something you were looking for.

But, if you've been to the Salvation Army and the "chuko-ya's," kept eyes peeled for the bonanzas of Big Garbage Day *and* made it known to everyone in the greater metropolitan area that you're desperate for domestic doo-dads, and you *still* haven't found what you need, you're just going to have to shell out for new.

As basic furnishings for your apartment, you'll probably need several dishes and silverware but not many pots or pans (it's possible you won't be doing much cooking at home). You'll probably want some kind of cabinet to put these in, something small and cheap. You'll need a low table, one that stands about a foot above the tatami mats where you'll eat and write while sitting on the floor. You won't need chairs; you'll get used to sitting on tatami very quickly (it's surprisingly comfortable) although if you do much sitting at home, you may eventually want a "tatami-chair" with a back rest but no legs.

Bedding may be a bit expensive but we certainly don't recommend you get that used. The best place to get your "futon" (a large, warm quilt), mattress (usually cotton-filled and intended to be used in conjunction with the already-soft tatami), pillow and top and bottom sheets is a big department store which can offer far better prices on just about everything than your tiny neighborhood stores can. Another reason to go to a larger store is so you'll find the kind of pillow you're used to. The Japanese sleep on very hard pillows stuffed with rice husks which are guaranteed to kink even the sturdiest gaijin neck.

An alternative to sleeping on the floor is to find a Western- type bed, although almost everyone agrees that using a futon on tatami gives a better night's rest than any Posturepedic ever could. Anyway, if you really want that feeling of a four-poster, you'll find a few large furniture stores selling beds. They're very expensive with a decent queen size mattress and box spring running about $500. If you talk a good rap, however, you might be able to take home one of the trade-ins most stores have in the back, waiting to be recycled anyway. A few brash individuals have been able to get nearly-new, complete sets free, just by asking.

By way of appliances, you may want a refrigerator if you intend to use your apartment as anything more than a place to collapse after making your daily tofu. The Japanese versions are, not surprisingly, much smaller than their American counterparts but their prices don't reflect their size. Again, expensive new but may be quite cheap used.

You could get a TV, but as we warned before, if you do, be sure it can be used back home. Most are useless outside of Japan. Even if you don't buy your dream stereo right away, be sure you pick up at least a cheap little AM radio *immediately* so you can enjoy FEN, the US military station which does wonders to alleviate the inevitable homesickness.

You may have to buy a few light fixtures for the ceiling which will pop right into the sockets left when the former tenants took *their* lights with them. And you will definitely appreciate having a small instantaneous hot water heater for your kitchen sink when you yearn to wash your face some chilly winter's morn.

All of these appliances (and some furniture as well) can be bought new at near-wholesale prices at Tokyo's electronic wonderland, Akihabara. This area (at about 3 o'clock on the Yamanote) is crammed with shops, almost all selling electronics and appliances. The competition for your shopping yen is fierce and those boys are always in a dealing mood. You'll almost always find the best prices in the city on anything electric in Akihabara. And best of all, they usually deliver straight to your door for no extra charge.

Although they're quite expensive, you may need to get a telephone, especially if you work for several different companies who need to contact you for work scheduling. Like paying "key money" to rent an apartment, getting a phone requires the outlay of hundreds of dollars in the form of a government bond, which does earn modest interest for as long as you keep the phone.

Many times, one of your employers will buy your phone for you (the bond is a fairly decent investment for a company) in the hopes of enticing you to stay with them instead of leaving for a better offer. But if such generosity is beyond them, you can occasionally find departing gaijin who will sell their phone and bond at a discount.

Calling charges are the same for home phones as public, a nickel for three minutes to a local number (within your prefix area). Try to make sure that your home is within the *major* dialing area (in Tokyo, for example, "03"). Just take a look at any phone in your neighborhood and if it has a different telephone prefix, it will mean that every time you call downtown, you'll be making a long distance call. That gets expensive fast.

Your alternative to having your own phone is to work out some kind of arrangement with one of your neighbors (one hour of English conversation weekly with number one son in exchange for telephone privileges?) or just use the local "koshu denwa" (public phone). But, as the long-time veterans will tell you, you'll probably miss out on some very appealing employment opportunities if you don't give people a way to get in touch with you. Let thy wallet be thy guide!

You may have a hard time both figuring out the address of your new home and finding schools when you're job hunting, all because of the agonizingly imprecise Japanese address system. Frankly, I wonder why the Japanese even bother using addresses at all for all the good it does someone trying to find a place. Hard as it may be to believe about the modern mecca of precision and efficiency, even natives can't find a place with just an address. At best, addresses are useful only for telling what *block* a house or office is in. The precise location can only be ascertained by a local resident who knows the neighborhood like the back of his chopsticks.

In the West (and in a few Japanese cities built post-war), the system is simple: we have named streets with structures on those streets numbered according to their distance from some common starting point. Thus, 3650 Market St. is probably 36 1/2 blocks from Main St.

In Japan, they locate buildings by narrowing down districts, in ever-smaller areas, much like a bull's-eye. The trouble is, there aren't enough rings in the bull's eye; you just can't get precise enough to accurately locate a single building.

As an example, let's look at a typical Tokyo-ite's residential address (although there are others even more confusing, less logical than this): Yamato-so #205, 14-7-2 Minato-ku, Tokyo-to, Japan 162.

As you might guess, the suffix "-so" means "apartment house." "Yamato" is the name of the building and "#205" is the number of a second floor apartment. So far, so good, right?

Next come the two numbers indicating the "chome" ("choh-may") and the "banchi" with the banchi being a smaller area inside the chome. So, in our case, we're describing a place in the seventh banchi of the fourteenth chome of Minato-ku ("ku" means ward or district, of which Tokyo has 23).

The third number of the "address" (in this case the "2" in "14-7-2") is a fairly recent addition to the numbering system.

Some neighborhoods have grown too large for just one "banchi" number, so they're further delineated into "sub-banchi" (my term) to give more precision. It's helped a little, so that now the first-time visitor to a home or business wanders around a one-half square mile instead of a one-square mile area, looking for his destination. And by far the most logical element of the address is the other three-digit number ("162") which is a postal or "zip" code, very similar to the American variety.

The "-to" in "Tokyo-to" refers to the fact that Tokyo is not really a city but a kind of state or, as the Japanese translate it, "prefecture." Forty-eight of Japan's prefectures have the "-ken" suffix, but Tokyo-*to*, Osaka-*fu*, Kyoto-*fu*, and Hokkai*do* are the exceptions. Why call some prefectures "ken," others "fu," "to" or "do?" Well, they do have a reputation for incomprehensibility to protect, right?

The logical questions that arises from all this is, of course, how does anybody find anyplace new and how does the mail get delivered? The answers? They don't and it doesn't, at least not without lots of help from knowledgeable neighbors.

When you're trying to line up interviews, don't even bother asking for an address beyond the nearest train or subway stop. Just ask for and expect an escort from the school or company who will meet you at the station or some easily-found landmark (like a bank) and guide you back to the office. Whatever you do, don't let them try to convince you that even a greenhorn like you will be able to find their miniscule digs.

Don't be afraid of imposing this way; it's the accepted way of helping newcomers find the school. Unfortunately, some of the smaller schools are occasionally reluctant to send a staff member out to meet a stranger, especially if the weather is nasty. But unless you'd like to explore the neighborhood and ask at least three or four people for the whereabouts of the place (OK in the spring, not OK during a typhoon), insist on an escort. Just be sure to remember how you came so the secretary doesn't have to lead you in again.

It may take a few days for the mailman and newpaperboy to figure out where in the "banchi" you're living, especially if you somehow wind up *not* living in a well-known apartment building. Your address may very well be *exactly* like everyone else's in your area--only your name would tell the deliverer to whom the letter or newspaper should be brought.

We once tried to start home delivery of one of Tokyo's five excellent English-language newspapers, gave the subscription department at the main office our precise home address, including apartment name and number. When, having waited several days without the paper, we called to inquire, we were told that the newspaperboy had tried to find our house twice and had finally given up.

How he could fail to find the only gaijin couple in an all-Japanese neighborhood remains a mystery but we finally had to arrange to meet him early one morning at the train station and (you guessed it), personally escort him to the house. The address we'd given him was complete; the Japanese address *system* is far from it.

If you absolutely *have* to find someplace by address alone, be sure you make use of the excellent and ubiquitous police boxes ("koban"). These tiny offices with red lights out front are usually located near train stations. There, you'll find one or two of Japan's finest, whose primary duty in that nearly crime-free country is to help confused citizens try to make sense of unfamiliar addresses.

One word of caution, however: if you do stop a cop and ask direction, be sure you're carrying proper identification; you may be asked to show either your passport (if you're on a tourist visa) or alien registration card (if you're on a resident or work visa). And if you don't have it with you, you may just as well cancel the rest of your plans for the day.

First stop after you're nabbed: police headquarters for a two-hour question and answer session, then an escorted trip back to your home to retrieve your papers, then back to the station where you are expected to compose and submit what's been dubbed by the gaijin community a "gomen nasai" ("I'm sorry") letter to the authorities. The process seems to be extremely effective in encouraging foreigners to carry ID. One such massive inconvenience and you too are likely to make a habit of always packing your papers.

Anyone staying in Japan for an extended period of time must obtain an "alien registration card" (which is actually a small book). It's the individual's responsibility to get one of these items at the person's city hall ("shiyakusho") within 90 days of arrival in Japan on a "resident" (i.e., non-tourist) visa. Tourists needn't worry about it until they get sponsored and come back into Japan on a work visa.

Failure to report to the "shiakusho" within 90 days of arrival in the country, or 10 days of arrival from another municipality, is, of course, a "gomen nasai" letter offense at the very least. And, if you get too many of those letters in your file at the Ministry of Justice, the government just might decide you're not the kind of gaijin they want in their country. Then it's sayonara, sensei.

You won't have any trouble finding the "shiyakusho" in your town; just ask at the police box. Take your passport and 4 photo machine pictures to the place and ask one of the lovely ladies at the information desk where you might find the "gaijin torokusho" (alien registration) desk. Whether or not you dress in true "alien" attire (antennae and purple fur) at the time of registration is, of course, optional.

Chances are the person at the "torokusho" desk will speak excellent English (after all, he works with gaijin every day) and, after answering a few simple questions about your employer and home address, you'll be given the "card." You'll be told that you must always carry it with you and, gomen nasai, but they're not kidding.

After you're finished registering, ask the person at the desk where the "kokumin kenko hoken" (national health insurance) desk is. It's almost sure to be in the same building and, in a matter of ten minutes, you can be covered by Japan's excellent and extensive national health plan.

Most cities now offer the insurance to non-residents as well as Japanese and it's quite comprehensive, paying 75% of all medical expenses. The premium you're asked to pay is based on your last year's income which, in the case of a newcomer is zero, making you elegible for the lowest premium, about $5 a month. Of course, if you stay more than one year and you make as much as any ambitious gaijin *should* make in Japan, you could well find your premiums tripling or quadrupling. Still, it's probably the best medical insurance to be had and, unless your employer has a better plan, we suggest you go for it.

Where you go after you've gone for it is quite another matter. Most hospitals are not equipped to listen to a patient's symptoms in English so you'd do best to stick to those hospitals featuring an English-speaking staff. Luckily there are quite a few; the better known ones (in Tokyo at least) we share with you in the Appendix. All those listed accept national insurance and all have English-speaking staff, as do all pharmacies listed.

A Stroll Through Anytown

Well, it all may sound tolerable (if not downright fun), but reading about living conditions, of course, is nothing like being there and experiencing them first hand. Unfortunately, we can't take you to Japan for a reconnaissance mission, but we can try to paint for you as accurate a picture as possible of what your life there probably will be like. Forward: through the looking glass and into your new Nipponese neighborhood.

Our scene opens with you preparing to leave your apartment one weekend morning. The apartment is probably one of about eight in a building built maybe twenty years ago. With its thin walls and lack of insulation, it's not nearly as substantial as what you're used to seeing back home, but your very quiet neighbors and the kerosene heater you bought in the fall make things pleasant. (Central heating is almost nonexistent.)

The building and the neighborhood are immaculate, thanks to everyone's taking turns sweeping the walks and keeping the rubbish area tidy. Your turn was last week and you just this morning passed on the communal broom and dust pan to Mrs. Noguchi next door.

The realtor was right, the apartment does get a lot of sun and the sweet-smelling tatami mats covering the floor of two of your three rooms are always toasty warm during the day, even in winter. You had the wisdom to get a second-story apartment so you should get a good breeze in the humid summer just by opening some of the many windows, several of which are opaque to compensate for the absence of curtains.

The rooms of your apartment are arranged in a line, with the six-mat back room used for sleeping and working. The small balcony beyond it has been the sight of some very nice sunset-viewings.

The middle room is smaller than the other with only 4 1/2 tatami mats, but it's still large enough to entertain the neighbors when they come by to visit. One of the housewives has suggested that the room be used for a neighborhood English class which she has volunteered to organize for you. You, however, are not sure you want to take on any more teaching responsibilities at this point, even for friends.

The kitchen is small but you managed to find, borrow or buy just about everything you need. You saw a two-burner stove sitting behind a shop one day and asked the owner if you could buy it. Instead, he gave it to you and you fixed it up with a little steel wool. The refrigerator was bought from a secretary in your office who was getting married and needed a larger one and the china cabinet came from a neighbor who is loaning it to you while its owner is on assignment for his company in Australia.

Off the kitchen is your toilet (which you're still not quite comfortable with) and bath ("ofuro") which you use every morning, much to the puzzlement of your neighbors who *all* take their baths at night.

You very quickly got into the habit of leaving your shoes at the front door and slip into them now as you leave. Outside, one of your neighbors, a young mother of about 25, is doing the laundry with her 6-month old baby in a carrier on her back. You exchange "ohayo gozaimasu" ("good morning") greetings and you silently vow to yourself to get down to Akihabara this weekend and see how much a little washing machine would be. This hauling your laundry five blocks to the nearest laundromat ("coin laundry") is getting mighty wearisome.

After a few more greetings and some small talk with other neighbors (almost all young mothers going about their household chores), you enter the heart of your little town. You pass the dry cleaners, the "chuka" (a cheap

Chinese restaurant where you regularly stop after class to fill up on great food for 3 or 4 dollars), and the elementary school with its hundreds of happy little tykes running around in the yard, squealing with glee as they wave at you and let loose with their usual chorus of "hellos." One of these days, you think, I'll have to teach them something new, like "Greetings, alien."

Finally you arrive at the bank, your destination. The lobby is crowded with people waiting for their numbers to be called so they can go the tellers' windows for service. Since you just need to make a withdrawal, you head for the "cash card" machine. You need cash for the entire week, so you decide to withdraw 30,000 yen, about $140. Back home, of course, you almost never had that much on you, so, at first, you were a little concerned carrying all that "okane." But after seeing the gigantic wads of 10,000 yen notes some of the little old Japanese ladies regularly take out of the machines, you've decided there's no cause for worry.

You've chosen a small town to live in because of its tranquility but you've had to put up with some inconveniences. The express train doesn't stop here, so you have to get off the "tokkyu" two stops before and transfer to a local. You also have to pay slightly higher prices for your shopping items (and go to more stores) than you would in a large town where you could do all your shopping, even for groceries, at a department store.

But you've decided you like the personal touch of getting your things at different shops anyway--lets you get to know each and every merchant. It reminds you of your home town as it must have been 50 years ago, and here it is only 40 minutes from downtown Tokyo.

After picking up some things at the hardware store, you stop by the butcher to see if he might be featuring any affordable meat (affordable by Japanese standards, at least). No such luck. Well, chicken isn't *too* bad at about $2 a pound and you've decided to heed the advice of the secretary at the office to use meat sparingly, primarily to flavor the other things. Healthier for you that way anyway, you reason, while trying hard not to drool noticeably over the $15 a pound sirloin.

You get a few chicken wings, cleverly sliced to look like miniature legs, and a bit of sukiyaki meat in preparation for the dinner one of your students has volunteered to cook for you.

At the greengrocer's, you select a few tomatoes and a "daikon," a kind of giant mild radish which, when minced (you've been told) makes the perfect compliment to sukiyaki. You're delighted at the freshness and flavor of almost all the vegetables you've had in Japan, thanks to the country's decentralized agriculture. Farmers grow their crops in tiny fields even in Tokyo's crowded suburbs, getting their produce to your market within hours of its harvest.

The fruit lady seems glad to see you again at her tiny store front. Somehow, she manages to explain to you that tangerines are coming in season in a couple of weeks and she'd be glad to set a basketful of the best aside for you, if you'd like. You've heard stories about the exquisite flavor of "mikan" and readily agree. Meanwhile, you content yourself with a pineapple and bananas, both less expensive than back home, due to Japan's proximity to Taiwan, where most are grown. You decide to leave the $20 honeydew melon where it sits like the Hope Diamond, regally wrapped in lace on the fruit store's "delicacy" shelf.

Arms laden, you head for home again, passing the unisex beauty parlor where the stylists were all astounded at the softness and light color of your Western hair. They all had asked to touch it and their sounds of amazement seemed to suggest that they were envious. You, of course, assured them that many Westerners think the Japanese have the most beautiful hair in the world. This compliment and your general friendly manner won you a complimentary bottle of expensive shampoo from the manager and an invitation to drop by anytime to say hello. The Japanese, you thought at the time, certainly seem to know how to develop good customer relations; you'll be back.

The last shop you see on your way back home is your neighborhood bakery. Although the morning's baking was finished hours ago, the air in the shop is still rich with the enticing fragrances of bread and pastry. You imagine for a moment that this could be a "patisserie" in France; the items look just as appealing as you remember their Parisian cousins did when you saw them years ago.

The baker gets quite a kick out of your finally being able to ask for two small loaves of bread without using your hands. You only get a little of the Japanese he speaks to you but you think he's saying something about how you must be a very good teacher to have learned so much Japanese in such a short time. He seems genuinely impressed, while you think your progress with the language has been abysmal. In parting, he asks if you've considered holding classes for the neighborhood youngsters. He's got a 6 year old daughter who can hardly speak *Japanese* yet but you know he's eager to give her a head-start with her English by having her learn just a little from a native speaker. Could he already have picked out a university for her as well?

You tell him you'll think about the class but dismiss the idea to yourself; any more teaching and you won't have time to see anything of the country. He tells you to come again soon and you start home, past the orchards and rice fields that, in addition to your neighbors, have made you very glad you chose this as your home in Nihon.

This is not an unrealistically romantic view of what your adopted town will be like, if you are a bit selective. Too many gaijin take the first 2DK that comes along even if it's nose-to-nose with a foundry, then spend the rest of their time in the country complaining to anyone in earshot how they can't get a decent night's sleep and can't afford to move because they'd lose their key money.

There's no reason whatsoever that you can't find a gentle, unhurried little community 30 to 40 minutes from downtown with plenty of greenery and neighbors who will welcome you and do everything they can to help you feel at home. The people have a great sense of pride in themselves and in their community; most of your neighbors have been there all their lives. They want you to like their hometown as much as they do.

The Class Act

By now, I hope we're all agreed that Japan is a gorgeous country, the people are generally friendly and helpful and they have a great deal of cultural wisdom to share with us. But, if all *that* isn't enough to interest you, consider what also makes Nippon a great place for the ambitious: the jobs. There are many, almost everywhere, for almost everyone. And they're probably almost all more interesting than what's available back home. Opportunities truly abound for English-speakers, especially in the area of teaching conversational English.

No one knows exactly what teaching a "conversation class" entails, least of all the Japanese school administrators. The general feeling is that its purpose is to make the students comfortable with using English for *communication*, not, as has been their purpose up till then, for scholastic achievement. The students usually already know most English grammar; their vocabulary is sometimes better than the instructor's. What they seem to need is practice with someone who will help them get beyond their inarticulate literacy and allow the English that's in them to flow more smoothly and naturally.

Professional English teachers are sometimes annoyed that schools are frequently quite willing to hire inexperienced novices, even when pro's are available. As a teaching professional myself, I commiserate with my colleagues but only to a point. I must agree with other administrators that all the teaching experience and credentials in the world aren't going to do much good if the teacher can't or won't try to understand the psycho-emotional problems the Japanese student of English is trying to overcome in the class. What most students need is compassion and encouragement, qualities shared by professionals and amateurs alike.

By nature, individual Japanese are quite shy and unassertive. They are also perfectionists and extremely reluctant to display any skill without having nearly mastered it through self-study. Language acquisition, of course, won't allow this method of learning; the student *must* try to use the language and make many, sometimes foolish errors which are corrected repeatedly--ideally in a kindly fashion.

Because this obvious lack of mastery is extremely embarrassing to Japanese students, a teacher must be very supportive with them if he or she hopes to be a success at the job. Disciplinarians and drill sergeants don't fare well as sensei's unless the teaching supervisor tells them specifically to crack the whip on students, possibly in preparation for college-entrance "exam hell" or overseas assignment. As little as "real" teachers may want to hear it, usually all anyone wants out of an English class (especially an "in-company" class) in Japan is conversation, occasional pronunciation practice and a regular good time.

Most classes are supposed to be "low stress" and relatively informal. Consequently, there are some school administrators who actually *prefer* conversation teachers with little previous experience, believing that such teachers will be, in the words of one, "fresh" in the classroom and more likely to treat students as peers rather than as warm bodies to be lectured to and drilled.

The Japan-US Educational Commission, in fact, believes that "the attitude still prevails that any native speaker can teach his own language, and what matters is that the foreign teacher be reliable and sincere, qualities that can best be ascertained in a face-to-face situation." (Which, of course, reinforces the idea that overseas hiring of you sight-unseen is going to be tough.)

There may be some validity to the idea that you don't need credentials or experience to teach conversational English, but it fails to take into account the fact that the vast majority of professional ESL teachers are also sympathetic to the needs of the students and may be more adept at recognizing those needs. Still, there is probably no other place in the world where the untrained novice can meet with as much success as he or she will find in the English teaching profession in Japan. Conversely, the seasoned sensei may find her experience not as fully appreciated as it might be elsewhere.

Although the majority of people studying English today are kids in public school, it's rather unlikely that you'll be teaching many of them. One reason: the system currently almost always has a Japanese teach the rudiments of English (including grammar) and then, and only then, does the native-speaker come into the learning picture--either in a private school or university--to breathe life into their studies. A bigger reason for the lack of jobs in public schools, however, is that a Japanese teaching certificate is required and powerful unions make them extremely difficult for foreigners to obtain.

Recent programs conducted by the Ministry of Education ("Monbusho") have brought some foreign teachers to Japan to serve as teacher's assistants in public schools but their number has not been significant: about 100 per year. These "Monbusho Fellows" are assigned for a year to certain prefectural boards of education to work as assistants to junior and senior high school English teaching consultants.

"Fellows" are not teachers as such but do help Japanese teachers by talking with students, judging speech contests, making pronunciation tapes and basically anything else the classroom teachers can think of. May sound like glorified "go-fer" work, perhaps, but the pay isn't bad (about $14,000 per year) and you'd probably see parts of Japan most gaijin miss. Teaching experience isn't required but a college degree is and familiarity with Japan helps. Apply to the Japan English Fellows Program, Asian and Professional Programs, Council on International Educational Exchange, 205 E. 42nd St., New York City, NY 10017 (tel. (212) 661-1414).

Japan's 989 junior colleges and universities (1983 count) offer positions ranging in pay from about three to six million yen for an average of a mere 90 teaching days a year. Generally, the more prestigious the school, the better the pay and working conditions but, often, the worse the students. This is largely due to the Japanese university system itself which allows a student, once he has passed a monstrous entrance exam to get into the school, to forget his studies for at least the first two years. Students are almost never expelled for any reason and they are virtually assured excellent jobs upon graduation if the school has a "name." Students at lesser schools, however, usually have to do a lot more serious studying if they're to get that primo position with Panasonic.

Luckily for those hoping for that top teaching spot at Tokyo U, the parliament passed legislation in August of 1982 allowing non-Japanese to be appointed faculty members at national and public universities. Still, it's almost essential that you have a personal introduction from another faculty member. Very few teachers are hired from abroad but rather, (says the embassy's Japan Information Service) through a foreign teacher already working there. In other words, start making friends as soon as you can if you're in the market for a sinecure.

On the other hand, private language schools offer tremendous job opportunities, day and night. The vast majority of classes are held at night, but there's no shortage of daytime work for those willing to call around. In most day classes, you're liable to get almost anyone for a student: prim (but bored) housewife, hot-shot student cramming for his college entrance exam, or eager businessman, desperately absorbing as much as he can before his company sends him off to the fabled land of the gaijin.

At night, dark blue polyester dominates the classroom fashion scene. You are almost guaranteed to be doing most of your evening teaching to businessmen, usually at their work location in a meeting room supplied by the company for your "in-company" class. No one is exactly sure why so many huge companies urge all middle and upper management employees to study English (probably less than one-tenth of one percent will ever actually use it) but who's complaining? It all adds up to lots of work on weeknights, always at top dollar.

Remember that you are always most valuable between the hours of 5 and 9 p.m. Monday through Friday and on weekends. Probably half the English classes in Japan are held weeknights and you should certainly hold off committing yourself to working those hours until you're sure the pay and conditions you're offered are top-notch. On the other hand, there are fewer day classes than night and so, complying with the law of supply and demand, they usually pay somewhat less.

Fairly early on (either while job hunting in Japan or considering job offers before you go), you'll have to decide how much you want to teach. Decide, then stick to it; it's all too easy to get over-extended and then be unable to back out of commitments already made. Many teachers, starved for decent work in their own country, turn into unabashed workaholics when given the opportunity to work literally whenever they choose for excellent pay. Sensei's sometimes forget that they went to Japan for things other than work also.

Most schools will not sponsor you unless you agree to work for them full-time (generally about 20 teaching hours per week), but you can, on occasion, find a school that likes you so well (or is so desperate for teachers) that it will sponsor you and ask that you teach as few as 10 hours per week (in which case it merely tells the government that you will be working more than you actually will to satisfy sponsorship requirements). This situation could be very advantageous for you, as it will get you your precious visa, yet give you plenty of freedom-- freedom to pursue a special interest, see the country or find even better jobs with schools that don't want to sponsor but pay well.

Full-time hours taught at the school that sponsors you frequently pay less than part-time hours taught elsewhere. The sponsoring school has you over a barrel and knows it: no visa, no legal teaching (except for students on a cultural visa, of course). Many schools figure the fact that they're sponsoring you gives them license to pay as little as half what the going rate is for teachers of your caliber. It really doesn't and rest assured that there are plenty of schools out there that will be happy to pay you what you're worth (at least 3,000 yen for weeknight classes) *and* sponsor you *and* treat you well. Too many teachers, not knowing what the standard rate is for such work, commit themselves to working 20 or 30 hours a week for less than what they could earn at home. "Sensei emptor!"--"Let the teacher beware!"

One case of a sensei who wasn't (beware, that is) is an Iowa woman who wrote in August of 1985. With her tale of woe, she makes a strong case for going over to Japan to check-out the school first even if they *do* offer you a job while you're still at home.

She was still working for a school in Shizuoka when she wrote to tell me how the president of her school was "quite unscrupulous." She continued, "I wish now I'd been more cautious in getting involved in an 18-month contract, but at the time, I lacked sufficient perspective to make a well-reasoned decision. Oh well..." But then, in the optimistic tones of a born survivor, she added, "Until my contract is up in June next year, I intend to make the best of the situation. The saving grace of it all are my students."

The lesson here: know your sponsor. Talk to other teachers and find out *exactly* what will be expected of you as a full-time teacher. Be especially careful about agreeing to do more than was specifically listed in your contract as regular responsibilities. And be sure your sponsor agrees that you may quit his employ with a month's notice (a fairly common stipulation). You, as a

highly valuable foreign instructor, should not have to put with any sort of nonsense, especially if it's apparent that the school is just trying to get some free gaijin labor.

A good sponsor will respect your position and won't give you busy work. A good sponsor will also be glad to let you speak to other instructors about the school and their treatment. But if you do somehow find yourself stuck with a rotten one, don't despair. Despite what your pseudo-samurai warlord boss may say to discourage you, it's not too terribly difficult to find a new sponsor. However unpleasant he may be, however, try to remain on good terms since he will have to "release" you for you to transfer sponsorship to another, hopefully better, school.

As an example, let's look at a good typical school: the Tokyo Foreign Language College (a two-year vocational college with about 1,500 students and 70 teachers), which, says Director Charles Binder, "enjoys a very low turnover of teachers, in part because of relatively good conditions in our school, and in part because of less-than-desireable conditions at other schools." Blunt, but probably accurate.

At TFLC, teachers must have a BA or MA in English, Education, TESL/TEFL or some such and should have teaching experience. This is a fairly common "wish list" of instructor qualifications for a school (and TFLC may be able to get it) but most schools will settle for any BA in a storm.

TFLC teachers work 9 to 4 Monday through Friday, teaching 20 hours a week. The school year begins in April. The first semester ends in July. August is summer vacation and the second semester extends from September until March with three weeks off for Christmas and New Year's. Contracts are signed for March to March but applications need to be in by early January.

In 1985, teachers started at about $1100 a month (248,000 yen) and got a one-month bonus if they fulfilled their year's contract. (The bonus and airfare home are the two most common carrots to induce teachers to stick out their essentially unenforceable contracts.) Like almost every school, TFLC also picks up the tab for transportation costs between the teacher's home and school.

Although I'm not personally familiar with TFLC, it seems on the up-and-up. That's not really an endorsement and I'd be reluctant to make any considering how quickly schools (and their administrators) come and go. But when judging a school's quality, always bear in mind that teaching English is primarily a business in Japan--a huge one. And, in case you hadn't noticed, the Japanese are exceptionally good businessmen. The people have been eking out an existence on those barren rocks for centuries and they understand extremely well how important it is to get the most for their money. And that most certainly includes getting the most out of gaijin staff.

Pay is usually quite negotiable at private language schools, much as the employers would like you to think otherwise. Big, established schools (like TFLC) probably don't have much salary leeway but be prepared to dicker with the smaller fry. The manager who interviews you (probably the number two or three person in the school) will likely start his salary offer very low, just on the off chance you won't know any better and bite. Like fares on the same airplane, salaries in the same school sometimes vary widely.

If you would like to be sure you get top yen, just demure politely each time he ups the ante. Finally, he'll reach his limit of what he can pay you and still make a gigantic profit on what he charges the students for your services. (It's a *very* profitable business in Nihon.) This top offer will depend on how much he's charging the students, how well he likes you and how desperate he is to find a teacher immediately. In some interviews, you'll be asked if you can start that night.

Always "soft-pedal" your request for a better salary. The last thing you want to say to a possible employer is something like, "Sorry, I know I'm worth twice that." You may, in fact, be but never be so blunt as to say it. The *second* to the last thing you want to tell him, though, is a lie about your "countless years of experience." The Japanese are uncanny BS detectors and remember, you'll probably be judged and hired based on your character, not your qualifications.

Of course, pay is not the only consideration in accepting a position. Obviously, an offer of sponsorship, pleasant working conditions and fringe benefits such as an apartment, phone, furniture, paid home leave and others should also be weighed. But all those "perks" do cost you; you'll rarely find a school offering top money *and* benefits. It's usually one or the other.

Don't be mercenary, but at the same time, don't play into the hands of a sharpy businessman, which many private English school presidents are. Sure, sharing your knowledge with other people is a wonderful, spiritually rewarding activity, but make sure that it's the students who are the beneficiaries of your kindness. If you work cheap, the only one who's benefitting is the fat-cat owner. Why not save your philanthropy for that class with the kids in your neighborhood?

Know thyself. It's important that you know what you're looking for by going to Japan. Everyone has different needs that must be met in making one of the biggest moves of his or her life. What are yours? Security? Financial gain? The people you work with? The workplace? It's up to you to decide and you'll save yourself a lot of wasted energy and time if you figure this out before you accept any commitments. As you've seen in the case of key money and sponsorship, it's a little more difficult to undo mistakes in Japan than it is back home.

If you apply to some of the schools mentioned in the Appendix (especially in person), you will probably get a few offers of full-time salaried positions. The salaries will probably range from $1,000 to $1,500 per month, depending on your qualifications and the size of the school. Considering the large number of hours you may be asked to teach, this probably represents considerably less per hour than what you might be paid at schools that pay on an hourly basis. But other considerations may make the arrangement desirable for you.

Schools paying monthly salaries, for one thing, are usually more helpful to their foreign staff members. The school may be willing to provide things like paid air transportation (either for home leave or visa trips), furnished accommodations, free Japanese language classes and a telephone.

The life of a salaried teacher is also somewhat less hectic than that of a free-lancer working for several schools. In addition to not having to race all over town to teach, the "in-house" person gets to know students very well and usually develops close relationships with them. Fellow instructors at such schools also seem to exhibit more camaraderie because of their commitment to a single institution. (By comparison, free-lancers sometimes run a bit low on conversation after the initial standard greeting of "Hey, guess how much I'm making over at _____ now.") While the salaried teacher might not take home a huge nest egg, she likely would have had plenty of time and money to see a great deal of the country, learn about the culture and the people and develop many lasting friendships.

But if you are out to maximize your income then, having found the sponsor of your dreams and gotten the work visa, you'll next want to start filling the "holes" in the schedule your sponsor has given you. Be *very* particular about what kind of work you accept during "prime time" (weeknights) in the unlikely event your sponsor hasn't occupied those hours with his own classes.

Another good time to teach is early weekday mornings (8 to 10 a.m.) when you'll get businessmen (often trainees) before they settle down for the day's grind. Also weekends, especially Saturday mornings, are considered choice times for which you should get at least your "prime time" rate.

Daytime hours (i.e., 10 a.m. to 5 p.m.) are somewhat more difficult to fill as the people who can attend regularly are often housewives having to use their pin money to pay tuition. During these hours, the large, private schools with "in-house" classes at a central location are probably best. Pay for part-time (in this case, unsponsored) teachers is frequently much higher than pay for regular teachers for whom sponsorship is considered part of their compensation. As a part-timer, you may be making 15-20% more than your co-teachers and for this reason, it's wise not to discuss pay with other staff members--they might become justifiably annoyed with the administration.

Your best general source of jobs will be the English newspapers, especially the Japan Times, especially Monday mornings, *especially* Monday mornings right before the new semesters begin in September and March. It's a fairly safe bet, though, that most of the schools listed in the Appendix will be hiring, if not year-round, than at least just prior to the beginning of the semesters.

You might want to make a habit of taking a few hours each week to just call around to see what's available--you'll have much greater success if *you* take the initiative and go directly to the school instead of waiting for them to advertise a position. Most of the schools will tell you they are hiring but won't give you any specifics about number of hours or pay over the phone; they want you to come to their office to size you up before they make an offer. But try not to waste your time going to those schools you don't think will pay your minimum hourly pay (as determined by you).

If they won't tell you over the phone what they're paying, tell them what you're accepting; then ask if they can match it. If they say "yes," fine, even though they might have offered more if you hadn't shown your hand. But if they say "no," then you've saved yourself a pointless trip to their office, only to find that you were worlds apart on pay. Remember: you can telephone a dozen schools in the time it would take you to visit one. Be very selective, but be reasonable.

Those who are *really* serious about stuffing their futon's with yen, however, should seriously consider starting their own mini-school, thereby by-passing the middleman between students and sensei. Just start telling your neighbors that you're willing to teach a class in the area and charge them less than what they'd have to pay to go to a real school. You can hold the class in your apartment or someone's house and, because you have no overhead to pay, your rates can be very competitive indeed. In all fairness, though, you should slide the "per student" hourly charge down as the number of students increases.

The students, of course, will be delighted to be learning from a real native speaker--who is also a neighbor--and to be paying so much less than what they'd have to pay a school. If your fees are substantially less than a school's, you'll soon have more students in both classes and tutoring sessions than you'll be able to handle.

To get into the teaching megabucks (10,000 yen per hour and more), however, you're going to have to gain access to the monied class. In Japan, this is primarily the dentists, doctors, airline pilots and entertainers, in that order. Aside from making personal calls to select individuals, probably the most efficient method would be to advertise your services in a professional journal, emphasizing your familiarity with the English their particular profession requires.

Another means of reaching them is to identify where such likely "targets" might frequent and make sure your business card and/or flyer reaches them. One daring young fellow tutored several very wealthy housewives several times a week and was very handsomely remunerated. He contacted the ladies by going to their exclusive "mansion" (i.e., condominium) and stuffing their mailboxes with his flyer. He then followed up with a personal visit several days later and, within the week, he was averaging 8,000 yen ($36) for each of the ten hours a week he had chatted with them.

More than likely, however, you will find most of your best-paying jobs through friends and friends of friends. Japan is the land of connections and you, as a very special, somewhat mysterious and certainly interesting foreign person should have no trouble finding your way into the upper echelons of ESL opportunity--if that is where you wish to be. Most people do quite well teaching for a single school which takes care of them generally and allows them time to see the sights. You must decide for yourself which is more important: the income of the free-lancer or the security of the salaried teacher.

Arbeit Delight

So far, we've been concentrating on teaching as the primary source of employment and, more importantly, sponsorship for foreigners. There's no doubt that teaching conversational English at a private school is by far the easiest way to live and work in Japan unless you have a very specialized skill the Japanese desperately need and for which the sponsor can find no qualified native.

But there are several other interesting and potentially lucrative areas which you may want to explore. These part-time pastimes are known in Japan as "arbeit" which, as German-speaking polyglots already know, simply means "work." In Japan, of course, where foreign words mean anything the Japanese want them to mean, the word means *only* part-time work.

The demand for a variety of gaijin skills has become great enough that employment agencies are starting to spring up. Your personal "grapevine" will probably be a richer source of arbeit but if you'd like to be a little more organized about filling up your work schedule, contact Oak Associates in Tokyo at 354-9502. They're liable to have more part-time than full-time (i.e., sponsorable) jobs but if you'd like to write them about sponsorship possibilities, their address is 5-21-5 Sendagaya, Shibuya-ku, Tokyo 151. (Mind telling them where you heard about their service?)

If you have enough competency with English to teach it, you probably could get a piece of growing editing business, especially if, in addition to English, you have proficiency in another language. Even if you don't regard yourself as fluent, you might be able to get some good work doing translations or copy edits.

Not many gaijin do translations involving Japanese (there are too many capable natives) but translating or editing in other languages is very possible. Western European--especially Spanish, German and French--and the Middle Eastern varieties are the current lingos where you'd probably have a pretty good chance of finding what is sometimes very well-paying arbeit--depending, of course, on your level of language and technical proficiency.

In English, there's a growing need for people even remotely familiar with technical matters to edit manuals, correspondence and legal paperwork as more and more exporting companies realize with what gales of laughter their earlier attempts at communication have been received by English-speaking customers. It's humor's loss, of course, but your gain as editing jobs abound, especially with the mammoth "sogo shosha" (trading companies) like Mitsubishi, Mitsui, C. Itoh and Marubeni.

Be warned however: you may think "editing" means polishing up the original a bit, but in Japan, it almost always means condemning an unsuspecting native-speaker to hours of wading through great globs of unrefined gobbledygook that the client (usually some large exporter) will tell you in all seriousness has "already been translated into English."

Most of the time, what you are given is totally incomprehensible and probably would be even to a Ph.D. in whatever subject is being mangled therein. It's usually hideous stuff that will pain your eyes and warp your mind but, if you're into cryptography, technical editing may be for you. At least the pay's not bad and the more arcane the subject, the better the money. Bring aspirin.

Journalistic endeavors with Japan's many English-language newspapers, magazines and book publishers are generally far more rewarding, at least in terms of preserving one's sanity. Although most of the staff of English publications are natives (remember their prowess with written English), they are generally in need of a few people to make sure that what gets printed not only is grammatically and syntactically correct but doesn't sound like it was spat out by a computer. The pay, however, is rarely what one would term "front page news."

Also enjoyable but regretably hard to come by are jobs writing ad copy. English-language ads fill all sorts of publications and good copywriters who can create under sometimes severe time constraints are well-rewarded. Almost all the major American ad agencies are represented in Japan now and they are always interested in meeting with anyone who thinks they have something to contribute to their operation. That contribution might not be in the form of copywriting, however, as the agencies also need people to edit translations of ads for American companies that have appeared in the Japanese media. Either job might be a good way to get some exposure to an interesting line of work.

The other traditionally lucrative pursuits (or so some avow) are modelling and acting. As you may know already, the Japanese are positively ga-ga over gaijin in their advertising. You'll see a veritable galaxy of American and European stars such as Paul Newman, Alain Delon, even Woody Allen doing ads regularly--selling everything from coffee to radial tires.

The reason for this fascination with faces foreign is, according to *The Wall Street Journal*, that advertisers want to "link a product with images of prestige, style and quality" by showing (what are to the Japanese) exotic-looking foreign models, both male and female, as they demonstrate Watanabe's industrial-strength widget or whatever's being peddled.

Many believe the modelling balloon has burst in Japan, at least for your basic beautiful foreigner and foreignette. The reason, some say, is that the Japanese are finally starting to consider themselves equals of Western folk, finally overcoming the inferiority complex, in large part (armchair-psychologically speaking here) due to their defeat in World War II.

Possibly because of Japan's stature in the world today, it no longer seems necessary--or even desirable--for an advertiser to suggest that his product is so good that even gaijin like it. The attitude more and more seems to be "We Japanese have tastes at least as discriminating as those big-nosed foreigners; what do our *own* beautiful people think about it?"

More and more, you'll see Japanese models (albeit still rather Western-looking ones) advertising such things as booze, cars and high-fashion that were once the sole domain of the foreign beauty. As the *Journal* adds, "The Japanese are coming to believe what the rest of the world is telling them, that they've more than caught up with most industrial nations...As time goes along, foreign influence decreases."

Aside from the waning demand in modelling, there is now a positive glut of pretty people clamoring for what work is available. Some weekend p.m., you'll probably wind up in the legendary land of gorgeous gaijin: Tokyo's Roppongi district. There you'll see the place absolutely packed with perambulating mannequins, strutting their stuff, straight out of *Vogue* and *Gentlemen's Quarterly*.

What brings all these nice foreign kids so far from family, friends and Fifth Avenue fashion? Mostly the promises of Japanese agents all over the world who ply the pretty folk with tall tales of boundless wealth for just a few month's duty in Nippon. And when the naifs arrive, well, they're usually treated all right--but El Dorado of the Far East it most assuredly ain't.

And if *they're* having a hard time of it, there probably isn't much chance for you, even though all your friends did say your graduation picture made you look just like Christy Brinkley and not a bit like E.T.'s maternal pod. Gaijin modelling in Japan is highly professional now; without experience and training, you probably wouldn't do much more than model polyester double-knits for some store's Big Cherry Blossom Viewing Day Bargain Blowout.

Where you might have a better chance (especially if you've had some high school or community theater experience) is with acting. Japanese cinema is only now starting to treat Westerners as anything other than the cardboard stereotypes of yore (e.g., foreign scientist-type to frightened eight-year-old hero, "Don't worry, Hideo, the CIA is Godzilla's friend. We won't hurt him.") Some of the parts they're giving gaijin today, even in TV, are quite respectable.

Even though it *is* a lot of fun and you're guaranteed at least a walk-on if you're blessed with even mediocre talent and looks, I don't recommend this either as a serious way to make money. Still, there's probably no better way to impress the gang back home than to send or bring them a poster or video tape of you trying to look like Sophia Loren or Clint Eastwood.

If you *are* interested in exploring the possibilities, drop off your 8 by 10 head-and-shoulder photos and resume with a few agencies like Ad Plan (tel. 585-9241), Trac One (496-3827), or K&M (404-9429) in Tokyo. Then get back to your teaching and editing where you'll actually have some reliable work.

When seeking work in Japan, the question to keep foremost in your mind is, "Could a Japanese do it?" If the answer is yes, you probably won't have much luck competing. As the well-respected magazine, *Keizai Orai*, pointed out in an article on foreign workers which appeared in the summer of 1985, "For workers possessing skills widely held in Japan, cracking the labor market is virtually impossible." Not only will the Japanese be willing to work for less but it's incumbent upon any society to hire first those citizens who meet the requirements. It's really not unreasonable; your country would certainly do the same to protect your job at home.

Your most valuable attributes to the Japanese are your knowledge of English, familiarity with Western social and business practices, and your looks. Almost all your work will revolve around one of these in some way. Don't become annoyed that your extensive knowledge of, for example, computer programming isn't landing you a job as a programmer--there are too many Japanese who can program and are likely to have a career with the company.

But the reasons for Japan's lack of foreign workers goes beyond mere self-reliance. Consider that right now, according to the *Keizai Orai* article, only 1.7 percent of Japan's labor force is foreign (i.e., non-Japanese). This compares with between 6 and 7 percent of the work force in Europe being from other countries.

The article's author, Professor Shoji Suzuki, attributes this "closed door policy" (with, of course, the English-speaking exceptions noted here) to the Japanese society itself. "The closed circle of insiders," he says, "begins with the family and extends gradually outward to one's friends, company, and ultimately, to the nation. Those outside each group of reference are kept at arm's length."

With surprising honesty, Professor Suzuki goes on to suggest that Japan's efforts to internationalize may even be somewhat superficial. "Japanese often comment," he writes, "on how international their country has become. But ordinary people seldom have meaningful contacts with non-Japanese. The absence of person-to-person interaction with cultural outsiders explains the inadequacy many Japanese experience in the presence of Westerners, and the smug superiority they feel toward Asians and Africans."

What all this means in terms of arbeit is that whatever you do, you'll probably be considered a "transient" employee and "kept at arm's length" from the core of the company. Foreigners, the Japanese know very well, rarely stay more than a couple of years and so are usually treated as intermediate-term employees there to satisfy a very specific need of the company.

There have been some developments in accepting gaijin as regular employees but such progress is slow in coming. Certain foreign instructors at universities have been granted tenure after many years of service (and griping about their second-class status on the faculty) and a few companies will reward loyal long-time foreign employees with regular status. By and large, though, the gaijin is thought to be "just passing through." This, of course, makes the company reluctant to offer benefits that might make it more likely that the employee *would* want to stay.

It's a typically Japanese "Catch-22" but not really important for the true short-timer (as I'm encouraging you to be). Just remember, the company may not need a gaijin programmer but it almost certainly could use a teacher of English computer terms and foreign programming methods. Find the need and fill it but don't plan on a career with the company.

But don't always wait for companies to recognize that arbeit need and publicize it with a want ad. Take the initiative and go directly to those places you'd like to work for. Many times large companies don't even know they need someone until that someone steps on the scene and gets the management to thinking of ways in which

having such a person on board could benefit the company.
There usually are many.

Interested in business? Visit a few big trading
companies and ask them if they've ever considered having
a foreigner work in their office, even if only to answer
their international calls for a few hours a week. Banking?
As you'd imagine, every major bank in the world is
represented in Tokyo. If you've got any sort of education
or experience that might be of help to them (maybe just
your way with the language is help enough), there's a good
chance they'll take you on and *that* may prove to be your
first step on the very rewarding career path of world
trade. At the very least, it would certainly look impressive
on your future resumes.

One friend went to Japan with nothing more than a
four-year degree in Economics. Recognizing the "business-
major glut" then developing in his native USA, he decided
to investigate opportunities in Nippon. He was intelligent
and first made a solid work foundation by getting himself
sponsored by a small school which needed him for only a
few hours each week even though he didn't consider
himself a "real" teacher and did it strictly for visa and
spending-money purposes. Then he began his search for
connections.

By going to as many business-related seminars and
meetings as he could find (many are listed in the Japan
Times), and tutoring the right kind of business people in
English, he was finally able to get that all-important
introduction to the president of a precious metals trading
firm in Tokyo. A week later, he found himself helping to
close multi-million dollar deals with Paris, London and
New York, with whom he was in telephone contact every
day.

How was he able to land the job? Well, he did have
some knowledge of business in general but certainly no
idea how things were done in Japan. The primary reason
was his manner (trustworthy and friendly) and his ability
to speak our World Language. As with teaching, the
Japanese are not so impressed by credentials as by a
person's manner.

Minding Your Millions

Yes, income can be excellent for the English-speaker but another substantial financial advantage to working in Japan is the tax situation. Gaijin of all lands universally praise the rock-bottom taxation of those fortunate enough to make their daily bread in Nippon. With no defense burden to speak of, the government has been able to keep taxes among the lowest in the world, while still providing national health insurance and many other social services unknown in some Western countries.

The basic rate of income taxation for individuals is between 10 and 70 percent but the *actual* rate is usually far less because the government allows a hefty tax deduction for which almost everyone qualifies. Thus, if you were to make, for example, the entirely possible annual teaching salary of 5,000,000 yen (about $23,000), you'd pay just 8.7 percent in national tax. The rate at 3,000,000 yen (about $13,650) is 5.9 percent.

What about local (state and municipal) taxes? In America, for example, these average from about 10 to 17 percent, depending on the appetite of the state or town where you live. In Japan, you are exempt from *all* local taxes for the first year you work. Should you decide to stay another year and were making 5,000,000 yen, you'd pay about 5.7 percent in addition to your national tax. A person earning 3,000,000 would pay about 3.6 percent additional.

To get a reasonably accurate idea of just how favorable a situation this is, you must think in terms of *after-tax* income, that is, what you actually get to save and/or spend after you pay all taxes. To demonstrate this, let's consider just how much a person would have to earn in America to equal his/her first year's income in Japan.

To take home that after-tax $20,740 that she would get on an income of $23,000 in Japan, a person living in Chicago, paying federal, state and local income taxes and sales tax, would have to make a salary of over $28,000 per year. If he or she were living in Los Angeles, a pre-tax salary of about $29,000 a year would be necessary. And if a person in New York were trying to take home as much as he'd get after paying first year Japanese taxes on that $23,000, he'd actually have to make well over $30,000 a year. And *that's* why Nipponese nest eggs are so delightfully easy to produce.

But that's not the only "tax" or hidden cost advantage to working in Japan. How much do you imagine you spend on tips every year for waitresses, taxi drivers, hotel clerks and the like? In Japan, service people are never tipped and a sales tax is rarely charged and then only for true luxury items.

But the real icing on the cake for Americans is the change in US tax law. Prior to 1981, America was one of the very few countries in the world that actually expected its citizens to pay US tax on the income they had earned abroad--despite the fact that they weren't even in the US to enjoy the benefits for which the tax was paid!

Finally, Washington realized this policy was a severe disincentive to getting people and companies to go overseas and possibly help improve our lopsided balance of payments. It seemed that those executives unlucky enough to get an overseas assignment were being hit with the double whammy of high relocation and living costs *and* high US taxes. Consequently, the law was changed and today all overseas incomes up to $75,000 are totally free from American taxes.

And one good way to make sure you don't pay more than your fair share of Japanese tax is to go by your local tax office ("zeimusho") a few weeks before you head for home. There you may request a refund of the taxes that were withheld (national and local, if you stayed more than one year) *if* you leave the country prior to the end of their fiscal year.

Depending on your income, the refund can be substantial since it is based on the amount the government withheld from your salary assuming that you were going to stay for a full year and earn 12 times your highest monthly salary during that time. But if you stayed only 8 months of that year, for example, your rate of taxation would have to be refigured (in Japan, like most countries, it's progressive) since your total annual income would be much less than anticipated. They would probably owe you a refund for having withheld too much--often several hundred dollars. But don't expect the "zeimusho" to let you know about it until you ask.

But no matter how much the goverments of Japan and your home let you keep, it's not at all difficult to spend everything you make in Japan. Japanese merchants have myriad ways of relieving you of your yen--all tantalizing. The designer clothes in the well-stocked department stores will beckon; the exquisitely arranged and incomparably delicious delicacies in the downtown restaurant will entice; the glittery toys of the consumer's paradise will try to ensnare you with promises of flawless stereo sound or magazine-quality photographs. *Resist!* It's all too easy for a hard-working foreigner's nest egg to wind up as part of some Japanese merchant's Western omelette.

Especially if you are already in the education field or are a recent college graduate, you no doubt are quite used to getting by on quite little--through no choice of your own. Well, in Japan, you *will* have a choice to spend or to save. Personally, I'd strongly suggest you take the opportunity to make a financial cushion for yourself while you have the opportunity, unless you're absolutely certain that you won't need it when you go home.

Remember, too, that at home things are likely to cost considerably less than in Japan. Even Japanese goods may cost less in North America or Europe than in their homeland because of the taxes the Japanese apply to luxury goods and Japanese merchants' high overhead. If

you're going over with the idea of buying your dream
stereo, for example, bring some discount prices from home.
You may be surprised to find the same equipment selling
for more in Japan.

If you do retain your frugal ways, you'll eventually
find yourself developing a hefty cash surplus in Japan. We
all may have some pretty good ideas about how to manage
our money back home, but what do you do with yen?
Failing to make intelligent decisions about your earnings
could wind up costing you hundreds if not thousands of
dollars which could otherwise accompany you home. It's
important to know the options.

First and foremost, everyone should have an
ordinary savings account. If you open yours at a local
bank, make sure it's a big one, like Japan's largest, Daiichi Kangyo, or another mega-buck depository like Mitsui,
Fuji, Sanwa, or Mitsubishi, all of which have plenty of
branches nationwide to allow you to make withdrawals
wherever you may be and can do your foreign currency
transactions.

An even more convenient place to park your yen is
the post office. This may strike Americans as odd, but
actually, postal savings operations are fairly common
outside the US. They work much like banks in that
basically the same sort of information is required to open
the account and deposits and withdrawals are handled as
any bank would. Advantages to the "yubin chokin" include
knowing that you can get to your money at any post office
anywhere, lines are sometimes shorter at the post office
than at the bank, and, pleasantly enough, the PO pays
slightly higher interest than the "ginko."

You may want to ask someone from your school or
a friend to go with you to open your account, but it's not
at all difficult to do it solo. Most larger branches of banks
have English-speaking tellers who will want to know your
address, alien registration (or passport) number, and
possibly your employer's name, address and tax ID number,
especially if the office will be depositing your paycheck
into the account automatically.

The bank will also want a specimen of your
signature to refer to when you--or someone claiming to be
you--wants to pull out some of your money. But simply

signing the card is not always the best--or easiest--
specimen you can give them. The reason for this relates to
a most charming anachronism, the "hanko."

For centuries now, the Japanese have been using the
"hanko" (or "chop" as it's known in China) instead of
signing important documents. This small stamp, made of
anything from ivory to plastic, has the owner's name hand-
carved on its face. Thus, when he wants to indicate his
agreement or authorization for something, he simply
stamps the paper. The "han" stamp is as binding on that
person as our signature would be on us; it's legally
enforcible.

The Japanese think this is a marvelously convenient
way to do things because it allows others to act as their
agent, without having to prepare a power-of-attorney or
proxy agreement. Many Westerners with their rampant
paranoia, of course think it's an open invitation to have
someone rip off your hanko and drain your bank account,
if they can get down to the bank before you report the
theft. In fact, this is exactly what's happened more times
than the Japanese would like to admit--especially to a
gaijin--but still the system remains.

Anyway, as a gaijin, you're certainly not expected
to have a hanko, even though there's no reason why you
couldn't have one made if the stamp carver could think up
some kanji characters to go with the syllables of your
name. Some people have done just that but the Japanese
regard the gaijin hanko as such a novelty item, that its
only real use is usually that of conversation piece for the
folks back home. Foreigners almost always sign documents
instead.

But you, signing sensei, are going to have to cope
with a legal system designed for a hanko. Practically
speaking, this means that when asked to sign your name,
you will usually find provided for you an area the size of
a dime in which to write your entire "Jun" Hancock. Now,
if micro-penmanship was not your forte in elementary
school, you may choose as your "Japan signature" not your
full name but merely your initials--which are far more
likely to fit comfortably in the hanko space.

The bank and other official-type institutions won't
care what you scribble in the circle, just as long as you're
consistent and don't start signing your name one day, and

printing your initials the next. That sort of thing will
cause a lot of confusion because the tellers, for instance,
are very picky about exactly matching what they see on
the specimen card on file with what you've "signed" on
your withdrawal slip. No match, no yen. And they might
not even tell you why.

Even if you're intimidated by computers and the
like, be sure to get a "cash card" as well when you open
your account. Japan is an almost completely cash-oriented
society with very few checking accounts or credit cards
but, with an almost nonexistent crime rate, they really
aren't needed. Consequently, you too probably will find
yourself carrying several hundred dollars worth on your
person and, eventually--about the same time you stop
looking over your shoulder every five minutes on your
evening walk home from the station--it won't bother you a
bit.

(As you've probably heard, there is almost no theft
in Japan--certainly not personal--and the stories that you
hear around bonus time (when employees are given up to 3
month's salary in cash) will amaze you. One of your
students probably will accidentally leave his cash bonus--
sometimes several thousand dollars--in some taxi or train
or in some greasy chopstick cafe, and it will invariably be
turned in to the nearest police box. Now *that's* "Civilized"
with a capital "C"!)

The "cash card" is a real time-saver when you find
two dozen housewives ahead of you waiting to deposit
hubby's paycheck or withdraw grocery money. (The
Japanese business structure assumes that there is always
someone in every household who wouldn't mind spending a
couple of hours to do something in person that could be
done by mail or machine.) But since you'll probably be too
busy to wait and chat about the price of horse mackerel
with the girls, out comes your credit-card-sized piece of
plastic which you simply slip into one of the machines in
the bank lobby.

You punch in your secret code (four easily
remembered digits--like your birth month and day), the
amount you wish to withdraw (you'll need to be familiar
with the counting system as explained earlier) and you've
got the loot. Convenient? Sure, but wouldn't it make more

sense if you could use the machines after banking hours? Well, we don't want to make things *too* easy for you.

One note of cash-card caution: be sure not to foul up the sequence more than twice; three strikes and the machine assumes you're not the rightful owner, keeps the card, changes the code and freezes your account--a hassle and a half to straighten out. If you blow it twice, call over one of the ever-grinning guards (it's so nice not to see people with guns in Japan) who, although he probably won't speak English, will surely get your drift when he spots your lean and hungry look. He'll get you your lucre in short order.

Another nice thing about ordinary banks is that they offer a complimentary service whereby they will automatically pay all your utility bills. It's a real convenience and, considering the general accuracy of all things Japanese, you're probably safe authorizing them to withdraw whatever's necessary to keep the lights working. Paying bills yourself requires you to go to any bank or post office and wait along with the housewives. No fun.

You may as well let the bank do as much as it's willing to do for you. After all, they should do *something* to make up for the positively paltry interest rate they'll be paying you. While Americans have been griping about banks offering a measly 5 percent on ordinary passbook savings accounts, the vast majority of Japanese have been contentedly salting away their life savings where they get 1.75 percent! Truly inscrutable.

Unfortunately, most gaijin just leave their money in their ordinary bank account simply because they don't know what else to do with it. That may be not be too terribly tragic since Japan's interest rates have always been far lower than just about any Western country's (due in large part to their usually low rate of inflation) but what *is* sad is to see naive non-natives trot into the bank the day before they're ready to go home, ask that their yen be converted into their home currency and made into a bank draft and then walk out the door with several hundred--sometimes thousand--dollars less than they could have had.

Currencies today are very flexible things; they're worth only what popular opinion *thinks* they should be worth. And that opinion of what they're worth changes daily as forces such as inflation, unemployment, interest rates, balance of payments, even the weather (if it affects crops) have turned the world's currencies into very bouncy variables. Although recent actions by the national banks of the major countries should tend to stabilize currencies, it's still the personal responsibility of every individual earning one currency but hoping to spend it as another to watch very closely just exactly where their two currencies are in relation to each other. And everything, but *everything*, is relative.

To explain this relativity, let's use one of yours (relatives, that is), Uncle Sidney, the Liverpudlian ball bearing importer and you, his hard-working, yen-earning nephew. Sidney, of course, wants the British pound to be just as strong as possible so he won't have to convert a quid more than he must to get his bearings and head for home. You, on the other hand, want a *weak* pound (i.e., a strong yen) so that it won't take quite as many of your yen to buy the sterling you so long to spend back home.

You and Sidney are at cross-purposes. He, and all people wanting to buy foreign goods, hope their currency will remain strong. You, and all exporters who don't want to price their goods out of the world market, hope the currency will weaken. When you're converting pounds--such as when you first arrive in Japan--you want a weak yen. When you're converting yen at the end of your working stint, you'll want a weak pound, or dollar, or wampum or whatever.

This conversion rate business can make a very big difference in your total earnings. By way of example, let's look at how much the yen has varied, vis-a-vis the US dollar in recent history. Say a typical English teacher (you) works in Japan for a year and is able to accumulate 1,000,000 yen in savings--a fairly modest figure. In this little exercise, you decide when would be the best time to convert that yen into dollars and how much you'd save by doing so at optimum times.

From 1949 to 1971, the yen's value was "fixed" by the Japanese government at 360 yen = US$1. Then, in 1971, most of the world's currencies were "floated"--including the yen--so that their value would be determined by what everyone else thought they were worth. The yen strengthened first to 350 in 1971 (it took 10 less yen to buy one dollar than before), then moved to 300 in 1972, 270 in '73, back down in value to 290 in '74 and stayed there 'til '77 while the Japanese economy was being ravaged by the first OPEC-induced oil "shock."

When it became apparent that Japan was much tougher than the rest of the world had thought prior to the oil crisis, the word got around that Japan might be the most solid economy on earth. Suddenly, everyone, from sultans to stockbrokers, developed an appetite for yen. Its value moved up to 270 then continued into the stratosphere until, on October 31, 1978, it reached its historic high of 175 yen to the dollar, worth more than twice what it had been just seven years earlier.

Then American interest rates started heating up as a result of stampeding inflation. At a time when Japanese banks were paying 2 percent on yen accounts, American money market funds were offering 18 percent for dollar accounts. Which interest would you have preferred? So the yen, along with just about every other currency in the world, started slipping as more and more non-Americans traded their native currencies for those high-interest greenbacks. The yen "dropped" to 220 in 1979, 227 in '80, and to about 260 in February of 1985. Then suddenly, with American interest rates declining and national banks acting in unison to depress the value of the dollar, the yen rocketed in November to about 200, where the Japanese government supposedly wants it to stay, more or less.

What it all means in dollars and yens figures is that if you had converted that 1,000,000 yen in February, 1985, you would have gotten $3,846. But if you had waited just nine months, you would have received $5,000 *plus* the interest you would have earned while keeping it in the bank. For you number buffs, that translates into 30% "interest" just for keeping it as yen! Do yourself a financial favor: think twice before you blithely take whatever exchange rate the bank is willing to give you on the day before you leave for home. It's really not that hard to convert before or after you go.

OK, so you decide to watch the exchange rates and make periodic conversions into your "target" currency when the time is right. (Don't forget to figure in the commission the bank charges to make those conversions.) What to do with your "real" money after you have it?

Well, in most countries today, there are investments available for the "little guy" (namely the person with less than $100,000 to play around with) that pay nearly as much as the moneybags can earn--safely. Certificates of Deposit, Money Market Funds, and Money Market Accounts are just a few of the perfectly safe places to park your money at home or abroad. And, although it's certainly not for everyone, if you're the daring sort, you could even dabble in the Japanese or overseas stock markets.

Although there are many banks and what-not at home who'd be delighted to help you invest virtually any amount, about the only place in Japan that is currently willing to offer a full range of services to the "low income" gaijin (you should realize that most foreign executives and such pull down $50,000 and up in Japan) is Merrill Lynch, America's largest brokerage house which also happens to have a very large Tokyo operation. What's nice about working with them for Americans is that it's an American company and transferring money between the US and Japan is quite easy.

Places like Merrill Lynch have investments for everyone from tigers to scaredy-cats, ranging from speculative stocks to US government-backed bonds--as safe as any bank account while paying better interest. This is no plug for them, but M-L does seem to take an interest in the little guy and if you call them in Tokyo at 581-7331, they'll certainly take the time to explain what's available to you.

But what if it's time to head for home and you never got around to changing any money earlier? And now, sure enough, the exchange rate stinks. Where can you park your money until a better rate comes along? One obvious place is right where you've had it all along: in your ordinary bank or postal savings account, earning tofu for interest.

The smart alternative might be the "wariko" or "warichin" account at banks. These are time deposits which you can't touch for at least a full year but they do pay far more interest (about 6%) than any other investment instrument a gaijin might be able to buy. Especially when playing the international money game, planning ahead pays plenty.

After Hours Antics

As I said earlier, I'm not even going to attempt to duplicate what the dozens of tourist books on the market today have discovered for the gadabout gaijin to do in sakuraland. In any of the larger city book stores in Japan you'll find some truly excellent guides written by long-time residents who will quickly enlighten you about interesting, out-of-the-way places that you could never hope to find on your own.

One of your very first stops once you've settled in at your hotel should be to a major book store. In Tokyo, the biggies are Kinokuniya in Shinjuku (with American branches in New York, LA and San Francisco), Maruzen and Sanseido in Kanda, Yosho Biblos in Takadanobaba, and Jena in Ginza. In Osaka, head for Asahiya Shoten in Umeda, Kinokuniya in Shibata and Maruzen in Bakurocho. Kyoto's Maruzen Bookstore is located in the Takoyakushi district of Nakagyo-ku while Kobe's Bunyodo is near Sannomiya station, hard by the International House.

Once inside, ask any clerk for the foreign book section. Most will have an entire floor devoted to books from abroad, with about 90% being in English. There, you'll find an amazing assortment of TESL textbooks and books on teaching theory, the latest magazines from all over the world (and all the major newspapers), maps by the dozens, guidebooks for every budget about every spot, and, of course, enough paperback books to keep you entertained for years of commuting on the "densha."

Japan is the land of lovers of literature. With the highest literacy rate in the world (99 point some-odd percent), the Japanese absolutely devour the printed word in all its manifestations. Fortunately for visiting foreigners, they're almost as interested in reading *our* literature as their own. The selection of English reading matter is terrific; you'll probably find almost as much in the Japanese stores and major hotels as you had in some book stores back home. Unfortunately, libraries don't appear to have as great a love for the printed English words as do the merchants.

Kanda and its neighbor, Jimbocho--at about 3 o'clock on Tokyo's Yamanote Line--have more book stores than any other area in the country. You can make a fascinating low-cost afternoon for yourself just by poking through the dusty shops there, looking for long-buried literary treasures. It's an area few gaijin and fewer international book dealers get to, so the persevering bibliophile can sometimes find some rare gems indeed: books long out of print, brought over 200 years ago by a seafaring missionary, now worth a small fortune in the West and the Japanese store owner can't even read the title. It's happened!

But, of course, we humanoids don't live by printer's ink alone; there's an outstanding assortment of entertaining activities in Nippon. Anything from the high brow culture of kabuki to a disco roller rink. *Whatever* you're looking for, you'll find it--for a price--in Japan.

Those stricken with Saturday Night Fever will find speedy relief at any of the many well-attended discos of Roppongi, Shibuya, Shinjuku, Ginza and Akasaka. For between $10 and $15 the clubs will turn customers loose on all the booze and edibles they care to over-indulge in. And don't worry about finding the clubs; just wander around the station and the doormen/hucksters will surely find *you*!

Most recreational activities these days--regardless of residence--seem to revolve around eating out and films. Tokyo, of course, offers plenty in both realms. There are dozens of beaneries in every block of the city, ranging from the elegant to the ptomaine domain. (Don't fret; even the grimiest dives are survivable.) There are so many of the teeny type of eatery, in fact, that you sometimes wonder how they all can do enough business to endure. But that they do, principally on the patronage of starving students and harried businessmen, wolfing down a bowl of noodles after work, just in time to make their evening English class.

Most penny-wise sensei's become quite partial to the "chuka" restaurant--a sort of low-rent Chinese joint. The food is almost without exception quite tasty and one can always stuff one's face quite adequately for less than $5, usually while quaffing a Kirin and enjoying the grunts and thumps of a late-night "sumo" bout on TV. And when "atmosphere" is required, there's always the "robatayaki," cozy little quasi-restaurants where drinking is the name of the game but delicious ala carte goodies are served as well, to keep you from getting too potted too quickly. It's a favorite haunt of carousing college kids.

The "robatayaki" is probably your best bet for fun, good, affordable food *and* a healthy dose of the culture. It's a great place to go with your students (be prepared to be cajoled into going out with them after almost every class) and, after the second or third scotch and water (only gaijin and geezers still drink sake, you know), you'll be amazed at how your Japanese improves--right along with their English. The Japanese, contrary to the rather stuffy image we have of them, are a *very* partying people!

If you're out on your own in the city, however, be very careful about what sort of place you wander into. No, you don't need to worry about the dives, it's the *nice* places that'll make off with the contents of your wallet. As *Sunset Magazine* pointed out, "Expense has much to do with where, not what, you eat. Real estate prices are higher in Japan than anywhere in the world. A meal in a small restaurant on a major thoroughfare will generally cost more than food at a second-floor restaurant on a side-street. And there's little to fear from trying a cheaper, side-street restaurant, for the Japanese maintain a high standard of food preparation and cleanliness."

What you *do* have to fear is "quaint"-avoid it like the plague. Oh, you'll recognize it no problem. You'll be looking for a little place to get a bite to eat and there before you will rise as if from a dream a vision of all that is refined, serene, and aesthetically pleasing about Japan. Before you will stretch a lovely pebbled path leading past ancient stone lanterns, up to a delicately etched sliding glass door through which shines the soft mellow glow of a paper lantern. Your Far East fantasies fulfilled!

Well, you've been warned. Any place that looks that Japanese-y will probably set you back a good $50 just to walk in the door. And everyone will be sooooo very nice to you inside that you'll feel like you couldn't possibly just walk out. You can and you should if you hope to hang on to your earnings.

Places like that are the almost exclusive turf of the businessman on an open-ended expense account (one of the many "perks" by which the Japanese are compensated for their rather low salaries). And it is assumed that he or she who enters won't faint dead away when, at the end of the evening, the hostess--never so crass as to itemize the bill--simply hands the customer a slip of absolutely gorgeous rice paper, upon which is written in exquisite handwriting a single five, sometimes six digit figure. Which she expects to be paid. In cash. On the spot.

The more reputable places like that take pity on the unsuspecting foreigner and sometimes will actually try to dissuade him or her from entering. Others, of course, will take any creature that falls into their web, so it's up to you to develop a "feel" for the type of beanery that'll try to make off with your month's paycheck. When in doubt, ask to see a menu. If they don't have one, you *know* it's not your kind of place!

Anyway, there are dozens of other kinds of eateries, most of which specialize in a certain kind of cuisine: Korean barbecue, "shabu-shabu" (a kind of boiled sukiyaki), "nabe" (stews made with anything and everything), sushi (wait for your students to introduce you to an affordable place), "okonomiya" (dare one call it an omelette?) and, of course, for the uninspired, lots of Western grub, which, unfortunately, seems to be becoming more popular by the hour.

Regardless of the type of place you wind up dining in, you'll really be a hit if you can read the selections either on the menu or on wall plaques (usually written in katakana but sometimes hiragana too). There are few things as ridiculous as the many gaijin who've lived in Japan for years who never got around to learning the less than 100 kana (despite speaking the language reasonably well) and so still must have even the simplest signs read for them. It's bad enough when newcomers have to point and pantomime for their comestibles but when an old-timer has to drag some unwilling restaurant minion outside to indicate the plastic model of the desired delicacy, you know somebody's not trying too hard.

We all get a hankering for home-style cooking and many will be the time when your heart will soar at the sight of a MacDonald's, waiting to assuage those waves of homesickness which will periodically sweep over you. Happiness, at such moments, is nothing more than a local American greaseburger joint, of which there are hundreds, sprinkled along the highways and byways of Nippon, rather like cholesterol deposits in one's arteries.

Japan has been thoroughly invaded by all manner of places you might have hoped to leave behind. Denny's, Dairy Queen, Dunkin Donuts, Kentucky Fried Chicken, Wimpy's (a British chain), even Pizza Hut (don't miss their corn and squid number) are all thriving in the major cities. And, as expected, those magnificent and ubiquitous golden arches thrusting proudly into the skyline at hundreds of locations each offer the nation's youth "bee-goo-ma-koo" and "cho-ko-ray-to shay-kee" in abundance. ("Tay-koo ow-toh" available, of course.)

Quick to recognize a good thing, the Japanese have recently introduced their fast-food home-grown clones, with only slightly Japanized fare (could that be the taste of whale in my "furenchi furai?"). Lotteria, Dom Dom, and, everyone's favorite in the "read it and weep (with laughter)" department, Mossburger, all offer you all-American grub just like Mom never made (we hope).

Coffee's generally expensive in Japan, costing between $1.20 and $2 a cup. Now, while that may seem awfully steep by American standards, when you realize that some coffee shops in Shinjuku are sitting on land worth $20,000 a square yard and must pay rent accordingly, it begins to seem downright reasonable, especially since you're never pressured to get anything more than a single cup.

If you're an independent teacher with a few "holes" in your schedule, you may very well wind up nursing a cup of coffee for hours until your next class begins. Such "kissaten's" (coffee shops) are a real institution in Japan, with hundreds of different motifs offered, ranging from fine music (jazz and classical are very popular) to one which surrounds the customer with mirrors. A narcissist's delight, but rather a tough place to concentrate on one's lesson plans.

If you're a real coffee hound, however, and just have to have your five cups of java to get the day underway, try to work into your schedule a stop at one of the *American* coffee shops which are far nicer in Japan than the home-grown versions in the States. Denny's, IHOP, Royal Host and the like are all over town and they are about the only places in Japan where you can get free refills on your bean juice, a luxury we in gaijinland usually take for granted. (By the way, it's pronounced "koh-hee"--ask for "coffee" and the waitress will probably think you sneezed.)

But if you really want to have your coffee and drink it too, drop in to one of the many "conversation lounges" which offer fresh-perked drinkables (and sometimes snacks) free to any native English speaker who comes by. It's hoped that you'll also chat a bit with the paying Japanese customers in English but it's never mandatory. These places really are just for English conversation and are an excellent way for a newcomer to Tokyo to make contact with people whose English is really quite good and probably want to be friends.

For "kohi" and conversation, check listings in the Tokyo Journal or the Kansai Time Out (at bookstores). In Kobe, you might want to try the Sun Mihall at Sannomiya (tel. 078-221-5408) and in Osaka, the Cafe Continental (945-9833). In Tokyo, try the Com' Inn at Ebisu (793-3371), ESS in Shibuya (498-2056), English Inn at Meiji Jingumae (470-0213), California at Takadanobaba (209-9692), International Pacific Club in Yotsuya (358-1681) and Pentagon in Shibuya (409-7200), which urges visitors to "Do mistake, learn better." Sure, it's a bit strange to be paid in coffee for your knowledge of your own mother tongue, but, well, it's Japan. Things are *supposed* to be a little different, right?

Reading, television, and tiddly-winks are probably the ideal entertainments in a city where a square foot of downtown land sells for well over $2,000. Bear in mind that anything that takes space to engage in will more than likely cost you more than you might care to spend. Concert goers, tennis and golf players (as well as model-rocket hobbyists) take note.

Theaters are usually a good bet for excellent, affordable fun but it's strange that, although the Japanese are avid film-goers, the selection of films even in Tokyo is not tremendous. You'll probably find the same big-budget releases (most from Hollywood) playing everywhere you look. As in so many other areas of the culture, quality is high but selection is somewhat limited. The Japanese are not renowned for their willingness to take chances and theater owners are no exception. When it comes to booking films, blockbusters only need apply.

You'll almost always be able to see these first-run super-spectaculars at the deluxe theaters downtown. Most of the major American films make it over and are never dubbed except when they're shown on TV (which almost always dubs and for which you may need a special receiver to get the original soundtrack). Tickets at the door for first-run shows are about $7 for general seating, more for reserved. Those in the know, however, buy tickets before the show from certain bookstores near the theater which discount them substantially.

The best films, however, are to be found in the second-run dives where for two or three bucks you can see both "Godfather" films *and* put your feet up on the chairs. (Is there any other way to enjoy Brando?) As with the restaurants, the dives are clean but very short on amenities. They also have an annoying habit of overselling seats. If you get to a popular show less than 15 minutes before curtain, be prepared to sit in the aisle or stand. The places have a somewhat informal atmosphere, as you may have gathered.

  The Japanese know what they like and they stick
with it. Innovation and experimentation *are* starting to
develop but, by and large, you're liable to find offered
only those things which have proven to be hits in the past.
In second-run films, this means that you'll almost always
be able to find "Cabaret," "Sound of Music" and the
"Godfather" series playing somewhere in the city. "Sleepers"
(the good but not terribly successful films) are a little
hard to find although "art cine" houses showing the
classics are starting to appear.
  Also hard to find are good foreign films dealing
with anything other than the country of origin's

stereotype. Thus, there's never a shortage of ultra-violent American pulp, super-sexy French moan-fests and Italian pasta parades (at least Fellini is fairly popular there). Also, of course, almost all films are shown in the original language--wonderful if you're an 007 freak but disappointing for those hoping to grasp Truffaut's latest.

The best way to find out what's showing at both the first and second-run theaters is to check the English papers. Major English dailies like *The Japan Times* come out with pretty good listings of weekly events, but they're usually geared to free-spending businessmen spending OPE (other people's money). Since the dozens of little theaters don't have the resources to publicize their shows and they *are* a bit tough to find in the big-city maze, I encourage you to subscribe to one of two excellent weeklies (depending in which plain--Kanto or Kansai--you settle) that cover the entertainment scene extensively.

I especially appreciated a great paper called *Tokyo Journal* which, after years of struggle, has graduated to the big time and is now very slick indeed. In addition to its theater and club listings, it's also crammed with other yen-saving entertainment ideas, very well-written (and refreshingly frank) articles on the culture, and even good classifieds (something Tokyo is sadly lacking). It can be bought at most major bookstores or by subscription by calling their office at 667-7397. In the Osaka, Kobe and Kyoto, *Kansai Time Out* (tel. (078) 332-4533) is not quite as glitzy but still holds a treasure trove of survival tips and hot happenings in the area. Very commendably trying to meet the needs of resident gaijin *not* aboard the corporate gravy train, these kinds of papers really need to be supported.

If you think your katakana is up to it, you might also try to wade through a copy of *Pia*, an excellent guide to absolutely everything that's happening in Tokyo. Naturally, several imitations have appeared since *Pia's* success but all seem to do a pretty good job. The magazines, unfortunately are in Japanese, for Japanese (unlike *Tokyo Journal* which is primarily for the foreign community). But if you have a friend who can explain to you how to use the guides (especially for films), you should be able to use them by yourself in no time. The wealth of entertainment information therein will amaze you.

Foreign films almost always retain their original titles and are listed as such (in katakana usually) in the entertainment guides. Sometimes, though, the titles are changed or actually translated into Japanese (i.e., given a totally new name). You probably won't be able to decipher those written in kanji but film names that have been renamed using katakana might be intelligible, if you use a little imagination.

For example, several years ago, major theaters in Japan had a film playing whose title was listed as "Chansu" (in katakana). No major film of that title has ever been released, but Peter Sellers aficionados may have their bells rung by it. It seems the Japanese distributor of the film took the liberty of retitling the film, naming it after the main character.

The film was "Being There" (which wouldn't have made much sense to the Japanese even in their own language) and the main character as played by Sellers was indeed named "Chance." The English word "chance" is very common in Japanese--used more to mean "opportunity" than anything else--and so the local distributor cleverly added another level of interpretation by changing the title. It pays to have well-developed deductive skills to get around in Nippon.

Other entertainment related publications cater mostly to the typical turista from Buffalo and do have some interesting things to say to those who've been in the country less than about 3 minutes. Tips on counting your change and using the toilet get a little old if they take up half of every issue. Both the *Tokyo Weekender* and *The Tour Companion* are available free of charge in the lobbies of hotels catering to gaijin and sporadically at the Tourist Information Center. In all fairness, they do have good information on upcoming festivals and other such tourist fare.

Live theater (of which there isn't much in English) and live music are plentiful but expensive. The music's technically excellent, as you'd expect, and highly listenable, especially the classical, which demands the kind of precision the Japanese so love to exercise. As for concerts, you'll feel right at home. Bruce Springsteen, the London Philharmonic, Huey Lewis and the News, Count Basie Orchestra--all the major international stars of pop, jazz, rock and classical make regular treks to Japan.

One note of caution about going to rock or jazz clubs: go early, and we do mean early. Music clubs really start jumping on weekends at about 5 or 6 and by 9 p.m., they're mopping down the floors. In a land where almost all transportation stops running at midnight, most frolicsome activity starts winding down by 11 at the latest. About the only exceptions are the all-night joints which we'll let you find out about (should you be so daring) on your own. Again, check *Tokyo Journal* and *Kansai Time Out* for the latest listings.

Often, one of the biggest disappointments when getting settled is the sudden realization that there are few public libraries with much in their English collection. Very fortunately for the Tokyo breed of species "bookwormus Americanus," literary salvation is near at hand: The American Center Library at Shiba Koen, tel. 436-0901.

The library is part of the American Center (there is a smaller version in Osaka), operated by the US Information Agency and intended for the use of Japanese interested in learning about America. But the kindly staff also usually give gaijin access to the many American literary, historical and technical works along with the very complete collection of periodicals--but only on a space available basis. All the librarians speak impeccable English (the American brand) and seem genuinely glad to have you there.

For those in Tokyo with a penchant for things Anglo-Saxon, don't miss the British Council in Jimbocho (tel. 269-3721) with its well-stocked library and information center. For Francophiles, there's the Maison Franco-Japonaise (tel. 291-1141). Although it is a private (and pricey) club, if you can find your way into the American Club in Azabudai (tel. 583-8381), you'll find a very nice library there as well.

Japanese FM radio is quite good with a heavy emphasis on classical and jazz, some classical Japanese as well. But don't expect to be able to pick stations up on your American FM radio; Japanese FM is just below US FM on the tuning dial. The only radios that can pick up both FM bands are the models which extend all the way from 78 mHz to 108 mHz. The usual American types start at 88 mHz.

If you intend to buy, use and ship home a quality tuner, be sure it has both US and Japanese bands. Although converters to allow you to receive Japanese FM on US radios are available, they're expensive. You should probably just leave your FM radio home.

The AM dial, however, is the same the world over. Any radio from anywhere will pick up the dozens of stations crowding the AM airwaves of Tokyo and other big cities. Most of the the stations are solid talk (average rate of speech: 200 words per millisecond) and very short on music--with one outstanding exception.

Since after the war, US occupation troops--now considered Japan-US alliance forces--have had their own broadcasting network throughout the country. In the hinterlands, this "Far East Network" has TV stations as well, but in the congested airwaves of Tokyo, the GIs are allowed to broadcast over one AM frequency only. This one English oasis in a sea of Japanese gibberish is to be found at 810 on the dial and is a true godsend to the homesick gai-person yearning for a few voices from home, no matter how banal their patter.

Most of their programs are pre-recorded in Hollywood and their hourly news is notoriously lacking in anything local, but the folksy music-oriented format is welcomed by all. The younger Japanese are especially appreciative as they think it's all very "hip" and a good chance for them to pick up some of the latest stateside slang.

In terms of mass-media news, not only are any of the English papers very authoritative, but FEN features live satellite broadcasts from America of significant events (such as presidential noise conferences) and an excellent compilation of news and commentary every weeknight. If you care to invest in a good shortwave receiver, you can also pick up the Voice of America, the BBC and Radio Australia quite easily from just about anywhere in Japan. They generally feature news and general interest stories, usually in English. Without an expensive tuner, though, shortwave static and drift eventually get to be very hard on the ears.

Japanese television used to be an even greater wasteland than the US variety for the visiting sensei, but with the advent of bilingual broadcasts several years ago, suddenly it's worthwhile owning a TV again. Again, however, US and Japanese stations don't mix so Americans shouldn't bother bringing theirs from home or taking one back unless they're positive it *will* work there.

Bilingual and stereo television is an innovation that the West has been talking about offering for years but it's a very popular reality in Japan. Of the nine Tokyo stations, three stations broadcast on the average of one film in two languages (the original and Japanese) and one stereo concert per week. The Kansai area also offers regular bilingual TV shows.

The catch here is that the bilingual or stereo signal is distinct from the TV signal; you need a special receiver. Most new TVs in Japan have the receiver built into the TV itself. But if your TV is an older one, all you'll get is the Japanese dubbed soundtrack coming out of your speaker. There are a few separate receivers on the market which will let you turn down the sound on the TV and just use the stereo receiver as you would a radio. These separates are becoming increasingly difficult to find outside of the big electronics areas such as Tokyo's Akihabara.

Sports-wise, big cities are, as you'd imagine, a little hard up for recreation room. Golf and tennis are the two most popular sports in the country, which makes absolutely no sense (considering the amount of land they require) until you realize that the Japanese think of them as prestige sports. Anyone who can claim to be a regular golfer, for example, has got to be rolling in yen simply because the average green fee in the city for 18 holes is about $100. With very few municipal courts, tennis is also outrageously expensive. Now do you see why table tennis has always been so popular in the populous East?

But unless you're hooked on these high-priced pastimes, you can stay in shape and have fun for next to nothing. The secret is discovering your town or "ku's" municipal recreation center or "ku-ei rekurieshon senta." (Say it fast and you'll see what we mean about having to mangle your own language.) Some of them are gigantic, with basketball courts, swimming pools, running tracks and martial arts practice rooms, all accessible for a very modest fee, usually 50 cents for residents of the area, $1 for non-residents. Your "shiakusho" (city hall) can give you full details when you get your alien registration card and national health insurance.

With 75% of Japan mountainous, there's little wonder most people escape the hub-bub of the city by hiking in the summer and skiing in the winter. Costs for these aren't too bad if you take advantage of the many travel packages available. Do try to make it to Mt. Zao in Yamagata-ken to see the surrealistic "ice trees"--great skiing too! Check with the Travel Information Center for details. A train ride to Mt. Takao, just one hour from downtown Tokyo, makes for a wonderful afternoon in the mountains.

The beaches of Japan have gotten infinitely more appealing in the last few years as the government has enacted some of the toughest anti-pollution controls in the world. As with all such activities, however, try to avoid going on a Sunday unless you love wall-to-wall humanity. And whilst gamboling about in the sand, don't step on the remains of the unfortunate clubbed watermelons (carnage from a kid's game). Does Greenpeace know about this cruel summer pastime?

Edo Alternatives

While it's true that the overwhelming majority of foreigners living in Japan have planted themselves in Tokyo, there *is* life for the gaijin outside Tokyo city limits. In fact, if you're one of the growing number of people yearning to leave the hustle-bustle of big city life behind (and there are few cities in the world as hustly or bustly as Tokyo), you might be far better suited to working in a city somewhat less daunting than the big "T". Let's look at all the practical alternatives for the first-timer.

According to the 1980 census, the ten largest cities in Japan were: Tokyo with 8,179,000 inhabitants; Yokohama, 2,755,000; Osaka, 2,578,000; Nagoya, 2,084,000; Kyoto, 1,450,000; Sapporo, 1,354,000; Kobe, 1,346,000; Kitakyushu, 1,057,000; Fukuoka, 1,032,000; and Kawasaki, 1,016,000. You can get an idea of where these are by referring to the map of Japan in the back of the book.

Tokyo, Yokohama and Kawasaki are contiguous and have grown together much like Dallas/Ft. Worth or Minneapolis/St. Paul in the US. Most people today just lump them all together and describe the Tokyo metro area as having 12 million people, or roughly five times as many as the next largest, Osaka.

Tokyo's big. And fast. And, especially at first, confusing. But, five times the population means five times the jobs, maybe more for the foreigner if you consider that Tokyo is the unrivaled center of Japan's international trade efforts.

Non-teaching work is scarce outside the big international ports of Tokyo, Osaka and possibly Nagoya but, if you're a college graduate and especially if you've had any teacher training or experience in the classroom, it's safe to say you wouldn't have a bit of trouble getting a good teaching job in *any* major city or probably anywhere in the country.

Some fellow teachers whose opinions I trust assure me that the pay for teaching outside the capital is almost as good as what you could make in Tokyo and the cost of living is lots less. (Compared to Tokyo, the U.N. claims you'd save about 20% by living in Osaka and about 40% living anywhere else.) Detractors of Tokyo point out that competition for jobs in smaller cities would be less and that you'd get a lot more personal attention from the townsfolk. But it's that "attention" that would make me a bit leery of settling in Hicksville. Even Japanese in Tokyo will occasionally stare at a gaijin; in a small town, the looks and whispering of your neighbors as you pass might make you eventually feel like kin of the "elephant man."

It's just far easier to blend in with people in Tokyo since the Japanese there are used to seeing and dealing with foreigners on a regular basis. This certainly makes life considerably easier and more comfortable for the newly-arrived gaijin who doesn't want to serve as some small town's surrogate celebrity but would rather just fit in.

Contrary to the boondocks boosters, I think you'd probably do best at least to *start* with Tokyo until you figure out what Japan is about. Then, after six months (when you have to reapply for your work visa and your Japanese is functional), if the crowds and the concrete *still* bother you, take a trip to a more tranquil environment and, if you find one that suits you, apply for a position. You really should be able to find teaching work all over the country.

If and when the time comes for you to consider living in the provinces, you'll need to know something about the land beyond Edo, that one-time fishing village, and for the last three-and-a-half centuries the "East Capital"--Tokyo.

The Japanese islands (like the Hawaiian chain) are essentially the tops of undersea mountains which have pushed their way up through the Pacific Ocean. And, disturbingly enough, they're really not yet done pushing. The mountainous, heavily-wooded country has 40 active volcanoes (and about 110 quiescent ones--for now) and is regularly wracked by earthquakes--1,500 of them annually.

Admittedly most of these quakes--especially Tokyo's 150 yearly--are imperceptible tremors, but wherever you decide to settle, you can expect to see your furniture rockin' and a'rollin' at least a few times a year. The Japanese, of course, have been living with "jisshin" for thousands of years and don't give them a second thought (they often don't even notice).

I suggest that instead of flipping out during your first one, you instead flip on the tape recorder and give the folks back home a vicarious thrill. You should also be able to base a lively class discussion on how regular earthquakes may have affected the Japanese attitude toward life, making the people more flexible, realizing that nothing, not even the earth, is unchanging. And here you thought this book was going to be light-weight reading!

Three-fourths of the country is covered by hills and mountains with slopes greater than 15 degrees (the steepest highways anywhere in the world, by comparison, almost never exceed 5 degrees). This makes livable and arable land a precious commodity indeed.

Naturally enough, Japanese civilization developed on the plains formed by the deposits of the largest rivers. Kanto, Japan's largest plain, has been almost completely filled with Tokyo sprawl. Osaka and Kyoto are on the Kinki Plain and Nagoya sits on the Nobi. Other plains in northern Honshu and Hokkaido have been slow to develop, largely due to their harsh winters.

The country is usually divided into eight geographical regions. From north to south, they are: Hokkaido (an island), Tohoku, Kanto, Chubu, Kinki, Chugoku (these last five comprise the island of Honshu or "main island"), Shikoku (a beautiful island in the Inland Sea) and finally Kyushu, the southernmost major island.

Let's look at each region; you decide which strikes your fancy.

Hokkaido, with over one-fifth of Japan's land area has only about one-twentieth of its population. It's still thought of by the Japanese as "the frontier" and it's definitely as close to the kind of space you may be used to in America as you'll find in Nihon. Dairies and farms are in abundance there as well as hordes of Tokyo tourists who escape the summer's humidity down south for their once-in-a-lifetime glimpse of a heifer.

Because it was settled only about 100 years ago, it doesn't really look all that Japanese. In fact, if you could tune out the signs and the people, you might imagine yourself not in Sapporo, but Butte, Montana. (OK, maybe Butte doesn't have *quite* as many shops selling octopus knuckles.)

The Tohoku region comprises the "prefectures"-- similar to American states--of Aomori (whose capital is the town of Aomori); Akita (capital: Akita); Iwate (Morioka); Yamagata (Yamagata); Miyagi (Sendai) and Fukushima (Fukushima).

Sendai is the largest city in this very hilly and mostly rural area. It's still pretty much of a backwater (or perhaps "back ice water" would be more accurate) but it is an interesting place for the typical gaijin to visit because of the people's fierce adherence to centuries-old custom and tradition.

The Kanto region has seven prefectures: Tochigi (whose capital is Utsunomiya); Gumma (Maebashi); Ibaraki (Mito); Saitama (Uruwa); Chiba (Chiba); Kanagawa (Yokohama) and Tokyo (which is a kind of city-state).

With the exception of Tokyo and its suburb, Kanagawa, the other prefectures are surprisingly rural to this day, considering their proximity to the megalopolis. If you don't mind a somewhat lengthy commute into town, you might consider checking into Chiba and Saitama for their home-grown country charm.

Yokohama, Kanagawa's capital, is an exceptionally clean and progressive city and very international due to its huge port where dozens of ships arrive daily from all points on the globe, eagerly filling their maws with everything from tractors to tennis shoes.

Kawasaki--Kanagawa's other major city--is probably best avoided unless you're a great fan of smokestacks and generally gray-on-black-on-brown color schemes. Heavy industry and seedy neighborhoods in abundance.

Further south is Chubu, which is sometimes further subclassified as the Hokuriku, Tosan and Tokai regions. This is a very rugged part of the country with soaring peaks and icy blasts whipping in from mainland China. On the opposite, Pacific Ocean side, however, lies Nagoya, home of many of Japan's monster corporations, including Toyota.

Prefectures in the Chubu region include: Niigata (capital: Niigata); Nagano (Nagano); Yamanashi (Kofu); Shizuoka (Shizuoka); Toyama (Toyama); Gifu (Gifu); Aichi

(Nagoya); Ishikawa (Kanazawa); Fukui (Fukui); and Mie (Tsu).

Kanazawa, the capital of Ishikawa prefecture on the Sea of Japan side of Honshu, has one of the most pleasant atmospheres of any town its size in the country. An education/resort town, its population fluctuates seasonally but is definitely worth a look-see, despite its somewhat nasty winters.

The Kinki Plain (often called the Kansai region) boasts Osaka and Kobe on the economic side of the scale and Kyoto and Nara on the cultural. A very nice balance, actually.

Its prefectures are: Shiga (capital: Otsu); Nara (Nara); Kyoto and Osaka (both city-states); Wakayama (Wakayama); and Hyogo (Kobe).

The Nara and Kyoto basins are the real heart and soul of Japan--while Tokyo and Osaka might be termed its attache case. Even if you wind up living at the other end of the country in Hokkaido, don't dare leave Japan without spending at least a few days reveling in the sights of Kyoto. If you don't see them, you certainly don't see Japan and if you really are in love with the culture (or would like to be), this area might very well be for you. It can only be compared to Paris in terms of representing the spirit of a people.

You might want to find work in Osaka and live in Kyoto (about 30 miles away) or somewhere between the two. This would definitely offer you the best of both worlds and many of your fellow foreigners have chosen this area between the south's center of commerce and Japan's cultural mecca for their home.

The Chugoku region--Tottori (Tottori); Okayama (Okayama); Shimane (Matsue); Hiroshima (Hiroshima) and Yamaguchi (Yamaguchi)--could be considered semi-tropical and should suit you sun buffs to a "t." Like most scenic places, however, it makes a nice place to visit if time allows, but doesn't have much in the way of work and entertainment activities, other than ogling the gorgeous Inland Sea between Honshu and Shikoku Islands.

Shikoku Island, comprising Kagawa (Takamatsu); Tokushima (Tokushima); Kochi (Kochi); and Ehime (Matsuyama) prefectures is, many believe, the jewel of Japan, nestled in the Inland Sea, the Mediterranean of the Orient. Although a gigantic bridge is on the drawing board, the current lack of any but ferry and air connections between the island and the mainland has left the region isolated and poor but spectacular in its rustic poverty. You probably could find teaching work here, but expect to be paid in pomegranates for your efforts.

Kyushu Island has the prefectures Fukuoka, Oita, Saga, Kumamoto, Nagasaki, Miyazaki and Kagoshima, all with capitals of the same name. One of the first parts of Japan to be settled, it served as a stepping stone for immigrants from Korea centuries ago--a theory purist Japanese historians fervently deny. (There is widespread but thankfully dwindling prejudice against the Koreans.)
Kitakyushu (literally "north Kyushu") is both an area and a city. It is by far the most heavily populated area (Fukuoka is near it) and, partially due to large coal deposits in the region, also heavily industrialized with all the worst kinds of industry (from the mammalian point of view): tires, steel and ship-building. Like to see the air you breathe? This is the place for you!

Assistance for non-Japanese-speaking foreigners, is, as you might imagine, a little hard to come by outside of Tokyo and Osaka. Japan is a very homogeneous culture and, unless there's a real need for people to deal with foreigners on a regular basis, they generally are not too well-versed in the care and feeding thereof. You really *will* find life in the smaller cities and towns rather confusing and possibly frustrating if your Japanese is not up to at least the basic survival level.

Gambate! (Go For It!)

I sincerely hope you've found at least some of the information shared with you thus far to be of help in your pursuit of fun and profit in Nippon. All jests aside, there *are* plenty of both awaiting you. I hope that this book, in addition to helping you live in Japan, also encourages other authors to delve more deeply into other kinds of opportunities there and address their efforts not so much to the tourists but to those of us who believe it's necessary to be in a culture at least several months to even begin to grasp it.

I apologize in advance for any erroneous information I have included here. Although I've tried to be as accurate and current as my sources allowed, government regulations, addresses and statistics do change over time and I know that a few things will "slip through the cracks." I'm quite confident, though, that any errors will be minor ones and not adversely affect you in your adventure.

If you find a mistake in anything I've put in print, please let me know immediately so we can help out those who follow in your brave footsteps. Just a postcard to me care of the publisher would do, but I'd love to hear in detail how you're making out over there. You see, Japan "vets" form a very select group of individuals and there's nothing more fun than swapping war stories about how we deal with the frustrations and enlightenments, each in our own unique way.

If you'd like to help other overseas adventurers when you return, you might also want to send me your home address so I can refer them to you for advice. I'd like to be able to create a pool of vets in various parts of the world who can help first-timers make the transition from West to East. Understandably, most people just want a little real-live reassurance from someone who's actually been there before making such a major commitment. Every once in a while, you can even make a friend of such a person. After all, if they're crazy enough want to do this too, you must have something in common, right?

Sorry, I couldn't give you more information on non-teaching jobs in Japan, but I hope you understand that, unless you've got 20 years in with IBM, ones that will get you a visa are hard to come by. Your greatest strength will almost always be your special knowledge of the English language but once you're over there, you can and will find many non-teaching (and non-language) part-time jobs to complement your classroom schedule.

Those interested in obtaining such work should concentrate on gaining access to "networks." This means getting to know as many Japanese in your area of interest as possible. One of the best ways to meet such people is by teaching English temporarily for companies likely to employ you in a non-teaching capacity. First-hand knowledge of the individual is extremely important to employers. Degrees and experience alone without personal contact rarely land outstanding positions in Japan.

Most of the inquiries I've received from readers have asked if the situation is still as promising for teaching employment as I presented it in this book. Obviously it's a subjective judgment but I honestly don't think the need for native English-speaking college grads has diminished appreciably.

But, every year, as more people find out about the work situation in Japan, more want to go over, including professional instructors who will likely be given preference in hiring. And more and more hiring is being done locally. Charles Binder, director of the afore-mentioned Tokyo Foreign Language College claims that "there seems to be an increasing number of qualified teachers willing to come to Tokyo without securing employment prior to departure, on the chance of picking something up here."

Consequently, he says, "I find that I am rarely called upon to leave Tokyo to satisfy my needs for faculty members." Bear in mind, though, that TFLC is one of the biggest and probably best of Tokyo's *hundreds* of English schools. Very few schools can afford to be especially choosy.

Remember the figures I cited earlier? One estimate puts the number of people studying conversational English (which the Japanese strongly believe can best be taught by a foreigner) at over 9 million. The Japanese government's best estimate of the number of foreigners teaching English (legally) now is 6,000. But let's say it's even 9,000. That's still a ratio of over *1,000 to 1*.

I really can't imagine that today, in 1986, with such a huge demand for native-speakers to teach English, you'd have any problem finding work. From all that I know and have heard, there really are still plenty of jobs for all and sponsorship for almost anyone who meets the minimum qualifications: native English-speaker (i.e. English is their first language) and a graduate of any four-year college program. If you aren't a graduate, best plan on going over as a student on a cultural visa. You'll still find plenty of part-time work to support yourself.

The requirement of being a "native" English speaker is an especially important one. The Japanese can readily spot someone whose English is even the least bit "unusual." That doesn't mean that if you occasionally tell your students "it's me" rather than "it is I" that you'll get booted out of the classroom. "Mistakes" like that are, in fact, a part of today's evolving colloquial American English and are perfectly OK if you explain them to your students.

Also don't worry if you've got a regional accent unless it makes your speech difficult for your own countrymen to understand. The Japanese have plenty of accents of their own and know they all are flavorful ingredients of the linguistic stew. But, just saying "sure, I speak English" isn't necessarily enough to get you a teaching job. You must be absolutely certain (especially if you are Asian) that you speak perfectly standard British or North American English.

If English was not the first language you learned, if you regularly use any "pidgin" or mix of languages or if another language is more common in your home than English, play it safe and ask an English as a Second/Foreign Language teacher locally (most colleges have at least one) to evaluate your proficiency. Or take the Test of English as a Foreign Language (TOEFL) at almost any school. The results can be confidential and they'll give you a good idea where you stand in your knowledge of the language. It's very important that you be a true native-speaker if you hope to teach English.

Another word of caution: despite growing international awareness and sensitivity, the Japanese still tend to see foreigners in terms of media stereotypes. That's fine if they see you as Paul Newman or Meryl Streep but what about seeing the black gaijin as a hustling Eddie Murphy? I'd be doing you a disservice if I didn't caution you to beware of prejudice--not a lot--just enough to require Latin and black English-speakers especially to make a little extra effort to dispel media-induced preconceptions. Orientals can expect the authenticity of their English to be questioned initially but once it's been accepted, they'll do fine.

Be cautious in accepting sponsorship. Be sure you're committing to a worthwhile employer. Talk to other sponsored teachers at the school you're considering. Don't panic and jump at the first offer of a work visa only to find you've sold your soul to a slime-dweller who came across during the interview as sweet as sugar. Check him out thoroughly and never let yourself be pressured into signing anything. And when you do sign, remember, the contract exists almost solely to satisfy the government's sponsorship requirements. Try to make sure it can be rescinded and the employer will release you if you give adequate notice. Yours is a very valuable skill in Japan, and it is worth every yen paid you by your most generous employer. Don't let yourself be taken advantage of.

Think carefully about the advantages and disadvantages of monthly or hourly salary (security vs. better pay). Just be yourself in your office, classroom and interviews and don't pretend to have more experience or training than you've had. It's usually your personality and general attitude that are being appraised, not your credentials.

Always dress professionally and conservatively. Although certainly not forbidden, men would probably do better without facial hair, women might want to avoid slacks at work. Very casual wear--such as blue jeans or tennis shoes--is definitely not appropriate classroom attire. Be especially careful about wearing traditional Japanese clothing like kimono and "geta" (the platform wooden sandals) in public. The Japanese might think you are either mocking their culture or worse, just being weird.

Try to remember that your feelings of isolation and homesickness are temporary and a phase that *every* foreigner passes through as he or she adjusts to a very different world. Your feelings will almost certainly fade in a few days when you'll once again be in love with the gentility and grace of the country. Make an effort to make friends--join one of the many clubs or organizations for people with your interests. Don't isolate yourself, especially at first. Develop a "support group" as quickly as possible.

Still, never forget that you are an "outside person"-- gaijin. The Japanese certainly will never forget it and, although they will share with you almost any aspect of their culture and help you in any way they can, you will always be slightly apart from the mainstream of the culture, regardless of how long you stay or how well you master their language. The Japanese will like you more if you maintain your own cultural identity, rather than trying to adopt theirs.

What you do with the memories and lessons learned from your stay in Nihon is, of course, up to you. You will have gained valuable insight into what may be the most dynamic economy and intriguing culture on earth. Surely your knowledge of Japanese customs and the language can benefit your career goals in some way and your savings will help you direct your life in whatever way you deem best.

I hope too that you allow the culture and the people to teach you something about yourself and human nature in general. Perhaps they will show you an altogether different way to look at and enjoy life. It's rare indeed for a person to return from Japan unaffected by the experience. This ancient nation, civilized for so many centuries more than our own, can be a valuable mentor to us, but only if we recognize that we all have many things still to learn.

Best of luck and stay in touch!

Appendix

Time Line...207
Japanese Embassies and Consulates.................220
JNTO Offices 214
Professional Organizations........................215
Employment Sources 218
Selected References 221
Japan Information Services........................223
Government Offices in Japan 225
Survival Japanese....................................227
Hospitals and Pharmacies.........................230
Accommodations 231
Japanese Language Schools.......................237
International Schools 240
Private English Schools............................243

        Tokyo.................................... 244
        Other Kanto Area 253
        Kyoto..................................... 255
        Osaka.................................... 256
        Kobe 257
        Other Kansai Area 258
        Central Honshu.......................... 258
        Nagoya................................... 259
        Fukuoka and Southern Japan 260
        Sapporo and Northern Japan 260

Map of Japan...262
Teaching Supplement Information...................263

Time Line

Many of the complications and anxiety associated with finding a job in Japan could be avoided with adequate advance planning. Because of the distances involved and the slowness of the Japanese bureaucracy, a great deal of "lead time" is necessary between the time you decide you'd like to go and when you actually leave.

By allowing plenty of preparation time, you can be sure that all arrangements have been made properly both at home and in Japan and that you will arrive at the optimum time of year for employment.

The following calendar or "time line" will allow you to gauge roughly what you should be doing and when.

FOURTEEN WEEKS BEFORE DEPARTURE

1. Contact former Japan veterans at local EFL school, military installation or "Little Tokyo" area. Discuss opportunities and living conditions.

2. Meet Japanese natives at ESL school or "Little Tokyo." Begin study of language and "katakana."

3. Obtain travel, culture and language books on Japan at "Little Tokyo" bookstore or library.

4. After consulting #1-3 above, decide in which region of Japan you'd like to live.

5. Start building savings to approximately $1,500 for temporary living and transportation expenses.

6. Select schools, companies or organizations to be contacted. Write brief letter of inquiry in simple but formal English.

7. Request general information and visa forms from nearest Japanese consulate. Specify kind of employment you are seeking.

TWELVE WEEKS BEFORE DEPARTURE

8. Request general information from nearest Japan National Tourist Organization office.

9. Continue study of language and "katakana."

10. Obtain passport or make sure it will remain valid while you're abroad.

11. Arrange for medical and dental records to be sent or hand-carried.

12. If accepting position or applying for admission to Japanese school, submit necessary papers to nearest consulate. Otherwise, consider travelling on a tourist visa.

EIGHT WEEKS BEFORE DEPARTURE

13. Begin stocking up on shoes and clothing.

14. Get Japanese magazines at "Little Tokyo" bookstore for "katakana" and numbers practice.

15. Locate discount travel agents in major coastal newspapers. Discuss fares and departure dates with several. Make confirmed reservation with best.

16. If making advance reservations for lodging, write for confirmation.

FOUR WEEKS BEFORE DEPARTURE

17. Notify banks and credit companies of your departure and estimated return date.

18. Open or replenish interest-bearing checking account. Tell bank you will provide address for checks after arrival in Japan.

19. Pack out-of-season clothing in sturdy boxes (with mothballs if necessary). Mark "sea mail" but leave address section blank. Arrange for shipment upon request.

20. Obtain international driver's license from Automobile Association or Motor Vehicle Bureau.

ONE WEEK BEFORE DEPARTURE

21. Check with airline for baggage weight restrictions (if any). Pack suitable "interview" apparel in two bags; put toiletries and reading material in "carry-on" bag. Leave space for tax-free items bought at airport.

22. Arrange transportation to international airport.

23. Party like crazy.

DEPARTURE

24. Arrive at airport two hours prior to overseas flight.

25. Check luggage, keep "carry-on" bag.

26. Convert $200 or equivalent into yen. Study bills and coins. Practice asking prices, receiving change.

27. After entering international section of airport, buy gifts at duty-free shop. Recommended: art, crafts, liquor, perfume, smoking accessories.

28. Make conversation with Japanese on board if possible. They may prove to be good connections in Japan.

ARRIVAL

29. Notify sponsoring company (if any) and embassy of your arrival.

30. Check into hotel, minshiku or ryokan.

WITHIN ONE WEEK AFTER ARRIVAL

31. Notify embassy of whereabouts in case of emergency.

32. Convert additional $300 to yen, more if yen appears to be strengthening. Best rates are obtained at large banks, worst at hotels.

33. Visit local Tourist Information Center. Obtain city and train maps.

34. Visit English-language bookstore. Buy tourist information books and local English newspapers.

35. Call companies for interviews. Do not mention tourist visa status if possible. Request escort from train or subway station to office.

36. Visit English-language coffee houses.

WITHIN FOUR WEEKS AFTER ARRIVAL

37. After determining primary work location, locate optimum neighborhood based on distance from work, mass transit connections, physical environment, rents.

38. Open ordinary savings account at local bank. Get "cash card" and forms required for bank to automatically pay utility bills.

39. Visit realtor ("fudosan-ya") and judge available accomodations on amenities (bath, type of toilet, appliances), distance from nearest mass transit stop and apparent interior sunshine and air circulation. If "tatami" and closet panels are acceptable, ask that they not be redone if realtor will reduce "key money." Sign contract and pay "key money."

40. Buy train pass ("teki") between home and primary work location. Ask employer to reimburse you for its cost.

41. Go to city hall ("shiyakusho") for alien registration, national health insurance (if employer offers none) information on municipal recreation center and location on nearest tax office ("zeimusho").

42. Visit nearest English-speaking hospital and drugstore. Notify hospital that your records will be sent shortly. Ask hospital back home to forward records.

43. Notify embassy, friends, and relations of new address and that you survived the trip with life, limbs and sanity intact.

Japanese Embassies

1. Embassy of Japan, 2520 Massachusetts Ave. N.W., Washington D.C. 20008; tel. (202) 234-2266.

2. Consulate-General of Japan, 909 W. 9th Ave. #301, Anchorage, Alaska 99501; tel. (907) 279-8428/9.

3. Consulate-General of Japan, 400 Colony Square Bldg. #1501; 1201 Peachtree St. N.E., Atlanta, Georgia 30361; tel. (404) 892-2700/6670/7845.

4. Consulate-General of Japan, Federal Reserve Plaza 14th Fl., 600 Atlantic Ave., Boston, Massachusetts 02210; tel. (617) 973-9772/3/4.

5. Consulate-General of Japan, 625 N. Michigan Ave., Chicago, Illinois 60611; tel. (312) 280-0400.

6. Consulate-General of Japan, 1742 Nuuanu Ave., Honolulu, Hawaii 96817; tel. (808) 536-2226.

7. Consulate-General of Japan, 5420 Allied Bank Plaza, 1000 Louisiana St., Houston, Texas 77002; tel. (713) 652-2977/8/9.

8. Consulate-General of Japan, Commerce Tower #2519, 911 Main St. (P.O. Box 13768), Kansas City, Missouri 64105; tel. (816) 471-0111/2/3.

9. Consulate-General of Japan, 250 E. 1st St. #1507, Los Angeles, California 90012; tel. (213) 624-8305.

10. Consulate-General of Japan, 1830 International Trade Mart Bldg., No. 2 Canal St., New Orleans, Louisiana 70130; tel. (504) 529-2101/2.

11. Consulate-General of Japan, 299 Park Ave., New York City, New York 10171; tel. (212) 371-8222.

12. Consulate-General of Japan, 2400 First Interstate Tower, 1300 S.W. 5th Ave., Portland, Oregon 97201; tel. (503) 221-1811.

13. Consulate-General of Japan, 1601 Post St., San Francisco, California 94115; tel. (415) 921-8000.

14. Consulate-General of Japan, 3110 Rainier Bank Tower, 1301 5th Ave., Seattle, Washington 98101; tel. (206) 682-9107/8/9/10.

CANADA

1. Embassy of Japan, 255 Sussex Drive, Ottawa, Ontario K1N 9E6; tel. (613) 236-8541.

2. Consulate-General of Japan, 10020 100th St., Edmunton, Alberta T5J 0N4; tel. (403) 422-3752/423-4750.

3. Consulate-General of Japan, 600 Rue de Lagauchetiere Ouest, #1785, Montreal, Quebec H3B 4L8; tel. (514) 866-3429/20.

4. Consulate-General of Japan, Toronto Dominion Center #1803 (P.O. Box 10), Toronto, Ontario M5K 1A1; tel. (416) 363-7038.

5. Consulate-General of Japan, 1210-1177 W. Hastings St., Vancouver, B.C. V6E 2K9; tel. (604) 684-5868.

6. Consulate-General of Japan, 730-215 Garry St., Credit Union Central Plaza, Winnipeg, Manitoba R3C 3P3; tel. (204) 943-5554/942-7991.

AUSTRALIA

1. Embassy of Japan, 112 Empire Circuit, Yarralumla, Canberra A.C.T. 2600; tel. 733244/733686/-733675/732272.

2. Consulate-General of Japan, Brisbane Plaza 26th Fl., 68 Queen St., Brisbane, Queensland 4000; tel. (07) 31-1430/8/9.

3. Consulate-General of Japan, Holland House 3rd Fl., 492 St. Kilda Rd., Melbourne, Victoria 3004; tel., 267-3490/3244/3255.

4. Consulate-General of Japan, CAGA Centre 36th Fl., 8-18 Bent St., Sydney N.S.W. 2000 (G.P.O. Box 4125, Sydney 2001); tel. (02) 231-3455.

NEW ZEALAND

1. Embassy of Japan, Norwich Insurance House 7 Fl., 3-11 Hunter St., Wellington 1, New Zealand. (P.O. Box 6340, Te Aro, Wellington.)

2. Consulate-General of Japan, National Mutual Center 6th Fl., Shortland St., Auckland, New Zealand.

UNITED KINGDOM

1. Embassy of Japan, 43-46 Grosvenor St., London, England W1X OBA; tel. 01-493-6030.

JNTO Offices

UNITED STATES

1. Japan National Tourist Organization (JNTO), Rockefeller Plaza, 630 Fifth Ave., New York City, NY 10111; tel. (212) 757-5640.

2. JNTO, 333 North Michigan Ave., Chicago, IL 60601; tel. (312) 332-3975.

3. JNTO, 1519 Main St. #200, Dallas, TX 75201; tel. (214) 741-4931.

4. JNTO, 360 Post St. #401, San Francisco, CA 94108; tel. (415) 989-7140.

5. JNTO, 624 S. Grand Ave. #2640, Los Angeles, CA 90017; tel. (213) 623-1952.

CANADA

1. JNTO, 165 University Ave., Toronto M5H 3B8; tel. 366-7140.

AUSTRALIA

1. JNTO, 115 Pitt St., NSW 2000, Sydney; tel. 232-4522.

UNITED KINGDOM

1. JNTO, 167 Regent St., London W1; tel. 734-9638.

Professional Organizations

1. Japan Writers Association, 2-12-15 Shibuya, Shibuya-ku, Tokyo; tel. 265-9657.

2. The Japan Pen Club, Shuwa Akasaka Residential Hotel #265, 1-7 Akasaka 9-chome, Minato-ku, Tokyo; tel. 402-1171.

3. Cambridge-Oxford Society, c/o Cornes & Co., Ltd., Maruzen Bldg., 3-10 Nihonbashi 2-chome, Chuo-ku, Tokyo; tel. 272-5771.

4. Harvard Business School Club of Japan, c/o G. Watanabe, Fine Chemical Division, Mitsui Ltd., 2-1 Otemachi 1-chome, Chiyoda-ku, Tokyo; tel. 285-5405.

5. Lions Clubs International, TOC Bldg., 22-17 Nishi Gotanda 7-chome, Shinagawa-ku, Tokyo; tel. 494-2931.

6. Rotary Club, Marunouchi Bldg., 4-1 Marunouchi 2-chome, Chiyoda-ku, Tokyo; tel. 201-3888.

7. Rotary Club, 5 Nakanoshima 3-chome, Kita-ku, Osaka; tel. 441-7930.

8. Foreign Corresponsdents Club of Japan, Yurakucho Denki Bldg., 7-1 Yurakucho 1-chome, Chiyoda-ku, Tokyo; tel. 211-3161.

9. Foreign Press Center, Nippon Press Center Bldg., 2-1 Uchisawaicho 2-chome, Chiyoda-ku, Tokyo; tel. 501-3401.

10. International Advertising Association, Kochiwa Bldg., 8-12 Ginza 4-chome, Chuo-ku, Tokyo; tel. 561-6353.

11. International Social Service of Japan, Inc., Suzufusa Bldg., 16-12 Kami Meguro 1-chome, Meguro-ku, Tokyo; tel. 711-5551.

12. Japan Medical Association, 2-5 Kanda, Surugadai, Chiyoda-ku, Tokyo; tel. 291-2121.

13. Japan Dental Association, 1-20 Kudan-kita 4-chome, Chiyoda-ku, Tokyo; tel. 262-1141.

14. Japan Pharmaceutical Association, 12-15 Shibuya 2-chome, Shibuya-ku, Tokyo; tel. 406-1171.

15. The Osaka Economic Cooperation Center, 58-7 Uchihonmachi, Hashizume-cho, Osaka; tel. 266-6405.

16. The Nagoya Economic Cooperation Center, 10-19 Sakae 2-chome, Naka-ku, Nagoya; tel. 221-7211.

17. Mensa Japan, 12-28 Roppongi 7-chome, Minato-ku, Tokyo; tel. 408-3366.

18. The American Club, 1-2 Azabudai 2-chome, Minato-ku, Tokyo; tel. 583-8381.

19. International Labor Organization, Nihon Press Center Bldg. 5F, 2-1 Uchisawaicho 2-chome, Chiyoda-ku, Tokyo; tel. 508-9217.

20. Association for International Technical Cooperation, #3 Mori Bldg., 4-10 Nishi Shinbashi 1-chome, Minato-ku, Tokyo; tel. 591-6461.

21. Japan Center for International Exchange, 9-17 Minami Azabu 4-chome, Minato-ku, Tokyo; tel. 446-7781.

22. Japan International Cooperation Agency, Shinjuku Mitsui Bldg., 1-1 Nishi Shinjuku 2-chome, Shinjuku-ku, Tokyo; tel. 346-5311.

23. United Nations Information Center, Shin Aoyama Bldg., Nishi-kan 22F, 1-1 Minami Aoyama 1-chome, Minato-ku, Tokyo; tel. 475-1611.

24. Japan Lawyers Association, 1-1-1 Kasumigaseki, Chiyoda-ku, Tokyo; tel. 581-2146.

25. Nippon Magicians Association, 2-4-16 Kita-Shinjuku, Tokyo; tel. 361-6453.

26. Japan Modern Poets Association, 7-503 Takahata-dai Danchi, Hino-shi, Tokyo; tel. (0425) 91-9458.

CHAMBERS OF COMMERCE

1. The Japan Chamber of Commerce and Industry, 3-2-2 Marunouchi, Chiyoda-ku, Tokyo 100. (Same address for Tokyo Chamber of Commerce.)

2. The Osaka Chamber of Commerce and Industry, 58-7 Uchi Homachi, hashizume-cho, Higashi-ku, Osaka 540.

3. The Kyoto Chamber of Commerce and Industry, 240 Shoshoicho Ebisugawa-Agaru, Karasumadori, Nakagyo-ku, Kyoto 604.

4.The Nagoya Chamber of Commerce and Industry, 2-10-19 Sakaie, Naka-ku, Nagoya 460.

5. The Yokohama Chamber of Commerce and Industry, 2 Yamashita-cho, Naka-ku, Yokohama 231.

6. The Sapporo Chamber of Commerce and Industry, 2-2-1 Kita Ichijo-nishi, Chuo-ku, Sapporo, Hokkaido 060.

Employment Sources

1. Japan Association of Language Teachers (JALT), c/o Kyoto Sangyo University, Department of Foreign Languages, Kamigamo Motoyama, Kita-ku, Kyoto 603. The largest TESL (Teachers of English as a Second Language) association in Japan.

2. Teachers of English to Speakers of Other Languages (TESOL), 202 D.C., Transit Bldg., Georgetown University, Washington D.C. 20057. Tel. (202) 625-4569. The largest TESL association in America.

3. Association of Foreign Teachers in Japan, St. Joseph College, 85 Yamate-cho, Naka-ku, Yokohama 231. No placement but assistance is provided.

4. The Japan-US Educational Commission, Sanno Grand Bldg. 2F, 14-2, 2-chome, Nagata-cho, Chiyoda-ku, Tokyo 100. Tel. (03) 580-3231. Administers Fulbright grants primarily. Does not offer job referral service but maintains contacts with English schools.

5. Council on International Educational Exchange, 205 E.42nd St., New York City, NY 10017. Tel. (212) 661-1414. Awards teaching assistantships to college graduates with Japan English Fellows Program (see description in text) through Asian and Professional Programs section.

6. International Internship Program, 7-5-4 Koyama, Shinagawa-ku, Tokyo 142. Tel. (03) 787-1973/784-0287.

7. English Educational Services International, 139 Massachusetts Ave., Boston, Mass. 02115. Tel. (617) 267-8063. Non-profit organization which acts a clearinghouse for information on ESL worldwide. Bi-monthly newsletter includes numerous job listings.

8. YMCA, 101 N. Wacker Dr., Chicago IL 60606.

9. US Information Agency, Washington DC 20547. Administers "Binational Centers" (BNC) program and can provide teaching positions worldwide.

10. ESOL Placement Service, Center for Applied Linguistics, 3520 Prospect St., NW, Washington DC 20007. Tel. (202) 298-9292. For teaching professionals only. No charge.

11. Register for International Service in Education, Institute of International Education, 809 UN Plaza, New York City, New York 10017. Tel. (212) 883-8224. Computer-based referral service for professional educators.

12. Department of Defense Dependent Schools, Teacher Recruitment Section, Hoffman Building I, 2461 Eisenhower Ave., Alexandria, VA 22331.

13. English Teaching Fellow Program, ICA, Washington D.C. 20547. A US government organization.

14. The Peace Corps, P-307, 806 Connecticut Ave. NW, Washington D.C. 20525.

15. Academy for International Development, 680 Fifth Ave., New York City, New York 10019.

16. American Council on Education, One Dupont Circle, Washington D.C. 20036.

17. Association for World Education, 3 Harbor Hill Drive, Huntington, NY 11743.

18. The Asia Society, 112 E. 64th St., New York City, New York 10021.

19. International Study and Research Institute, 55 W. 44th St., New York City, New York 10021.

20. United Nations International School, 24-50 E. River Drive, New York City, New York 10010.

EMPLOYMENT AGENCIES

1. Oak Associates, 5-21-5 Sendagaya, Shibuya-ku, Tokyo 151. Tel. (03) 354-9502. Often has more opportunities than applicants for certain skill requirements.

2. International Schools Services, P.O. Box 5910 (126 Alexander St.), Princeton, NJ 08540. Oldest and largest such agency. Handles job openings at international schools forming the Japan Council of Overseas Schools. Requires college degree with two years teaching experience. Charges $50 processing fee.

3. American Schools Incorporated, P.O. Box 13178, Oakland, CA 94661. Places teachers primarily in Asia, Middle East and South America.

4. Overseas Schools Services, 446 Louise St., Farmville, VA 23901.

5. Overseas Schools Services, 226 Avenue Louise, 1050 Brussels, Belgium

6. National Council of the Churches of Christ, Overseas Personnel Section, 475 Riverside Drive, New York City, New York 10027.

7. American Lutheran Church, Division of World Missions, 422 S. Fifth St., Minneapolis, Minnesota 55414.

Selected References

1. Angel, Juvenal; Looking for Employment in Foreign Countries Handbook; World Trade Academy Press, Inc., 50 E. 42nd St., NYC 10017.

2. Bajkai, Louis; Teacher's Guide to Overseas Teaching; PO Box 2748, La Jolla, CA 92038.

3. Brownell, John; A Directory of Resources for the Study of English in Japan; University Press, University of Hawaii.

4. Celce-Murcia, Marianne; Teaching English as a Second or Foreign Language; Newbury House.

5. U.S. Department of Defense; Overseas Employment Opportunities for Educators; Department of Defense, Directorate for Dependents Education, Washington D.C. 20301.

6. Department of Health, Education and Welfare; Teacher Exchange Opportunities Under the International Educational Exchange Program; Division of International Education, Office of Education, Department of Health, Education and Welfare, Washington D.C. 20202.

7. Department of Health, Education and Welfare; Opportunities Abroad for Teachers; Division of International Education, Office of Education, Department of Health, Education and Welfare, Washington D.C. 20202.

8. Department of Labor; <u>Information About Jobs Overseas</u>; Manpower Administration, US Department of Labor, Washington D.C. 20210.

9. Department of State; <u>Overseas American Elementary and Secondary Schools Assisted by the US Department of State</u>; Office of Overseas Schools, US Department of State, Washington D.C. 20520.

10. Dilts, Harold; <u>Teacher's Guide to Teaching Positions in Foreign Countries</u>; Box 514, Ames, Iowa 50010.

11. Dixson, Robert; <u>Practical Guide to Teaching English as a Foreign Language</u>; Regents.

12. Ford, Norman; <u>How to Travel and Get Paid for It</u>; Harion Publications, Greenlawn, NY 11740.

13. Gordon, Douglas: <u>Communicating in Japanese--A Tactical Approach</u>; Sci-Trans Press, PO Box 9302, Denver, CO 80209.

14. Hill International Publications; <u>Guide to Employment Abroad</u>; PO Box 79, East Islip, NY 11730.

15. Jolly, Constance and Robert; <u>When You Teach English as a Second Language</u>; Book Lab.

16. Kimizuka, Sumako; <u>Teaching English to Japanese</u>; Neptune Books.

17. Kocher, Eric; <u>International Jobs, Where They Are and How to Get Them</u>; Addison-Wesley Publishing Co., Massachusetts.

18. Leatherdale, C.; <u>So You Want to Teach English to Foreigners</u>; International School Book Service.

19. Luebke, Paul; <u>American Elementary and Secondary Schools Abroad</u>; American Association of School Administrators, 1801 N. Moore St., Arlington, VA 22209.

20. Martins, Samuel; <u>Basic Japanese Conversation Dictionary</u>; Tuttle & Co.

21. Wattenberg, Beverly; <u>A Guidebook for Teaching English as a Second Language</u>; Allyn Publishers.

22. Yamamoto, Mitsu; <u>Bridges to Fear</u>; Newbury House.

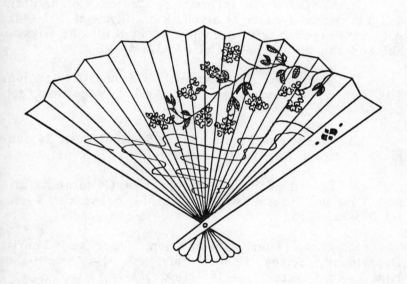

Japan Information Services

1. JNTO Tourist Information Center, Kotani Bldg. 6-6, Yurakucho 1-chome, Chiyoda-ku, Tokyo; tel. 502-1461. Also at Tokyo's Narita Airport and in Kyoto at Higashi Shiokoji-cho, Shimogyo-ku (tel. 075-371-5649).

2. Yokohama International Welcome Association, Silk Center, 1 Yamashita-cho, Naka-ku, Yokohama; tel. 045-641-5824.

3. Tourist and Foreign Trade Section, 3-1-1, San-no-maru, Naka-ku, Nagoya; tel. 052-961-1111.

4. Tourist Section, Department of Cultural Affairs and Tourism, Kyoto Kaikan, Okazaki, Sakyo-ku, Kyoto; tel. 075-752-0215.

5. Osaka Tourist Association, Trade and Tourist Department, Semba Center Bldg. #2, 1-4 Semba-sho, Higashi-ku, Osaka; tel. 06-345-2189.

6. Tourist Section, Otsu City Office, 3-1, Goryo-cho, Otsu; tel. 0775-22-3830.

7. Kobe International Tourist Association, Kobe Shoko-Boeki Center, 5-1-14 Hamabe-dori, Fukiai-ku, Kobe; tel. 078-232-1010.

8. Tourist Section, Kagoshima City Office, 11-1, Yamashita-cho, Kagoshima. tel. 0992-24-1111.

Government Offices in Japan

EMBASSIES IN JAPAN

1. United States Embassy, 10-5, Akasaka 1-chome, Minato-ku, Tokyo 107; tel. 583-7141.

2. Canadian Embassy, 3-38, Akasaka, 7-chome, Minato-ku, Tokyo 107; tel. 408-2101.

3. Australian Embassy, 1-14, Mita 2-chome, Minato-ku, Tokyo 108; tel. 453-0251/9.

4. Embassy of New Zealand, 20-40, Kamiyama-cho, Shibuya-ku, Tokyo 150; tel. 460-8711/5.

5. Embassy of the United Kingdom, 1, Ichiban-cho, Chiyoda-ku, Tokyo 102; tel. 265-5511.

MAJOR IMMIGRATION OFFICES IN JAPAN

1. Immigration Bureau, Ministry of Justice, 1-1, Kasumigaseki 1-chome, Chiyoda-ku, Tokyo; tel. 580-4111.

2. Tokyo Regional Immigration Bureau, 3-20, Konan 3-chome, Minato-ku, Tokyo; tel. 471-5111.

3. Tokyo Immigration Service Center, Sunshine City Bldg. 6F, 1-3, Higashi-Ikebukuro 3-chome, Toshima-ku, Tokyo; tel. 986-2271.

4. Osaka Regional Immigration Bureau, 31, Tani-machi 2-chome, Higashi-ku, Osaka; tel. 06-941-0771.

5. Sapporo Regional Immigration Bureau, Odori-nishi 12-chome, Chuo-ku, Sapporo; tel. 011-261-9211.

6. Nagoya Regional Immigration Bureau, 3-1, Sannomaru 4-chome, Naka-ku, Nagoya; 052-951-2391.

Survival Japanese

GREETINGS

Glad to meet you. = *Hajime mashite.*
How about it? (How are you?) = *Ikaga desuka?*
Are you well? = *Ogenki desuka?*
Good morning. = *Ohayo gozaimasu.*
Good afternoon. = *Konnichiwa.*
Good evening. = *Konban wa.*
Good night. = *Oyasumi nasai.*
Good bye. = (Try to guess this one)

PHRASES

Please. = *Onegai shimasu.*
Thank you. = *Domo arigato.*
You're welcome. = *Do itashimashite.*
Excuse me. = *Sumimasen.*
Pardon me. = *Gomen nasai.* (also *Shitsurei shimasu*)
Do you understand? = *Wakari masuka?*
Yes, I understand. = *Hai, wakari masu.*
No, I don't understand. = *Iie, wakari masen.*
Just a moment, please. = *Chotto matte kudasai.*
Can you do it? = *Dekimasuka?*
Please hurry. = *Isoide kudasai.*

Slow down please. = *Yukkuri shite kudasai.*
Please bring (give me) ---. = --- *o kudasai.*
(When beginning to eat) = *Itadakimasu.*
Thank you for your food. = *Gochisosama.*
It was delicious. = *Oishii katta.*

SHOPPING

Please show me ---. = --- *o misete kudasai.*
Please show me a cheaper one. = *Motto yasui no o misete kudasai.*
What is this? = *Kore wa nan desuka?*
How much is this? = *Ikura desuka?*
I'll take this. = *Kore o kudasai.*

GETTING AROUND

Where is ---? = --- *wa doko desuka?*
Please turn right (left). = *Migi (hidari) e magatte kudasai.*
Please go straight ahead. = *Massugu itte kudasai.*
Please stop there. = *Soko de tomatte kudasai.*
Please wait for me here. = *Koko de matte kudasai.*
How much is the fare to ---? = --- *made ikura desuka?*
Is it within walking distance? = *Aruite ikemasuka?*
How far is it? = *Kyoriwa donogurai desuka?*
I want to go here. =*Koko made ikitai no desu.*
I'm lost. = *Michi ga wakarimasen.*

Also: taxi = *takushi*; train station = *eki*; subway = *chikatetsu*; bus = *basu*; department store = *depaato*; bill = *okanjo*; post office = *yubinkyoku*; police box = *koban*; washroom = *toire* (toy-ray); restaurant = *shokudo* (also *resutoran*).

NUMBERS

1 = *ichi*; 2 = *ni*; 3 = *san*; 4 = *shi* (or *yon*); 5 = *go*; 6 = *roku*; 7 = *shichi* (or *nana*); 8 = *hachi*; 9 = *ku*; 10 = *ju*; 11 = *ju ichi*; 14 = *ju yon*; 17 = *ju nana*; 20 = *ni ju*; 40 = *yon ju*; 70 = *nana ju*; 100 = *hyaku*; 400 = *yon hyaku*; 700 = *nana hyaku*; 1000 = *sen* (or *issen*); 4000 = *yon sen*; 7000 = *nana sen*; 10,000 = *ichi man*; 11,000 = *ichi man issen*; 100,000 = *ju man*; 1,000,000 = *hyaku man*.

Hospitals And Pharmacies

All hospitals and pharmacies listed here are familiar with treating foreigners. All have large English-speaking staffs and many imported prescription and over-the-counter medications from abroad. All participate in health insurance programs, including the national "Kenko Hoken" insurance scheme.

1. Yokohama Cliff Hospital, Yokohama, tel. 0456-41-6961.

2. Tokyo Sanitarium, Ogikubo, (392-6151).

3. St. Luke's, Tsukuji, (541-5151).

4. Tokyo Medical Clinic, Shiba Koen, (436-3025).

5. Endo Clinic, Meguro, (492-6422).

6. International Catholic Hospital, Mejiro, (951-1111).

7. International Clinic, Azabudai, (582-2646).

8. American Pharmacy, Yurakucho, (271-4035).

9. Hill Pharmacy, Roppongi, (583-6044).

10. Medical Dispensary (a pharmacy), Shiba Koen, (434-5817).

Accommodations

Four general types of short-term accomodations are available in Japan: "business hotels," "minshuku," "ryokan," and youth hostels. Temples also allow paying guests but may expect them to participate in services and housekeeping and so are not recommended as lodging upon arrival to Japan. Ryokan and minshiku are highly recommended but availability in large cities may be limited. Make written reservations at least one month prior to arrival during peak travel seasons.

Business hotels ("hoteru") are western-style multistory hotels, usually located near major transportation interchanges. Rates are modest as are amenities. These clean, sometimes spartan lodgings are designed for businessmen, usually looking for a simple room while on out-of-town business. No meals are provided.

Minshuku's, traditionally, were rural farm houses in which farmers rented out rooms to travelers. Today, such true minshuku are rare, most have been constructed in urban areas as low-cost "pensions," often offering dormitory-style sleeping quarters much like youth hostels. Breakfast and dinner are often included in the modest price. Clean, safe and very reasonable, minshuku offer the foreigner comfortable accomodations and a chance to meet Japanese young people, most of whom stay in such places whenever they travel.

Ryokan's and temples are Japanese-style (i.e., "tatami" or straw mat floored) in which, like the minshuku, guests are expected to sleep on the floor and meals are usually included. Clear-cut distinctions between minshuku and ryokan have largely disappeared and some ryokan may be less expensive and more informal than certain minshuku.

Youth hostels offer the most affordable housing. Guests sleep dormitory-style with between four and eight people of the same sex per room. Membership in the International Youth Hostel organization may be required for use of the hostel. Register with IYH before leaving for Japan to allow for cheap accommodations world-wide. In Japan, hostels generally charge less than 2,000 yen per night with meals less than 1,000 yen. Obtain complete list of Japanese hostels from JNTO.

TOKYO ACCOMMODATIONS

1. Tokyo YMCA Hotel (women only), telephone, 293-5421, 1-8-11, Kanda-Surugadai, Chiyoda-ku, Tokyo.

2. Tokyo YWCA Sadohara Hotel (women and families only), tel. 268-7313/4451, 3-1-1, Ichigaya-Sadohara-cho, Shinjuku-ku, Tokyo.

3. Tokyo Yayoi Kaikan Hotel, tel. 823-0841, 2-1-14, Nezu, Benkyo-ku, Tokyo.

4. Tom Oshidori's House (dormitory), tel. 713-6064, 5-29-5, Shimo-Meguro, Meguro-ku, Tokyo.

5. Okubo House (dormitory), tel. 361-2348, 1-11-32, Hyakunin-cho, Shinjuku-ku, Tokyo.

6. Yashima Ryokan, tel. 364-2534, 1-15-5, Hyakunin-cho, Shinjuku-ku, Tokyo.

7. English House Ryokan, tel. 988-1743, 2-23-8, Nishi-Ikebukuro, Toshima-ku, Tokyo.

8. Kimi Ryokan, tel. 971-3766, 2-1034, Ikebukuro, Toshima-ku, Tokyo.

9. Shinobuashi Minshiku, tel. 712-6064, 5-29-5, Shimo-Meguro, Meguro-ku, Tokyo. 15 minutes from Meguro station.

10. Asia Center, tel. 402-6111, 8-10-32, Akasaka, Minato-ku, Tokyo.

11. Ichigaya Youth Hostel, tel. 262-5950, 1-6 Gobancho, Chiyoda-ku, Tokyo.

12. Japan YWCA (women only), tel. 264-0661, 4-8-8 Kudan Minami, Chiyoda-ku, Tokyo.

13. Shin Nakano Lodge, tel. 381-4886, 6-1-1 Honmachi, Nakano-ku, Tokyo.

14. Tokyo YMCA (men only), tel. 293-1911, 7 Mitoshiro-cho, Kanda, Chiyoda-ku, Tokyo.

15. Yoyogi Youth Hostel, tel. 467-9163, 3-1 Yoyogi Kamizono-cho, Shibuya-ku, Tokyo.

16. Hostel Kyumeikan Kendo Dojo, tel. 930-4636. No address available. Generally reserved for students of martial arts, others on space-available basis.

17. Tokyo Yoyogi Youth Hostel, tel. 467-9163, 3-1 Yoyogi Kamizono, Shibuya-ku, Tokyo 151.

OSAKA ACCOMMODATIONS

1. Hekke Club Osaka-ten Hotel, tel. 313-3171, 12-19, Togano-cho, Kita-ku, Osaka.
2. Shin-Osaka Seni City Hotel, tel. 394-3331, 2-2-17, Nishi-Miyahara, Yodogawa-ku, Osaka.
3. Ebisuso Ryokan, tel. 643-4861, 1-7-33 Nihonbashi-Nishi, Naniwa-ku, Osaka.
4. Matsunoya Ryokan, tel. 572-0665, 1-8-16, Kosei, Minato-ku, Osaka.
5. Gyokusenji Youth Hostel, tel. 0727-34-0844, 1438 Yamabe, Nose-cho, Toyono-gun, Osaka.

6. Osaka-Shiritsu Nagai Youth Hostel, tel. 699-5631, 450 Higashi-nagai-cho, Higashi-Sumiyoshi-ku, Osaka 546

KYOTO ACCOMMODATIONS

1. Kyoto Traveler's Inn, tel. 771-0226, 91 Okazaki-Enshoji-cho, Sakyo-ku, Kyoto.

2. Kyoto YWCA, tel. 431-0351, 44 Konoe-cho, Muromachi-dori, Idemizu-agaru, Kamigyo-ku, Kyoto.

3. Pension Utano, tel. 463-1118, 110-5, Narutaki-Honcho, Ukyo-ku, Kyoto. 45 minutes from Kyoto station.

4. Yuhara Ryokan, tel. 371-9583, 188 Kagiya-cho, Kiyamachi-dori, Shomenagaru, Shimogyo-ku, Kyoto.

5. Ichiume Ryokan, tel. 351-9385, Higashi-Kiyamachi, Gojo-sagaru, Shimogyo-ku, Kyoto.

6. Sanyu Ryokan, tel. 371-1968, 378 Hiraoka-cho, Kamogawasuju Shomenohashi, Nishizume-agaru, Shimogyo-ku, Kyoto.

7. Tani Guest House (dormitory), tel. 661-2391/2627, 3 Kisshoin-Inokuchi-cho, Minami-ku, Kyoto.

8. International Guest House Tani (dormitory), tel. 492-5489, 8 Murasakino-Daitokuji-cho, Kita-ku, Kyoto. 20 minutes from Kyoto station.

9. Parthenon Ozawa Ryokan (women only), tel. 371-2327, Shichijo-dori, Kawaramachi, Higashi-iru, Shimogyo-ku, Kyoto.

10. Utano Youth Hostel, tel. 462-2288, 29 Nakayama-cho, Uzumasa, Ukoyo-ku, Kyoto.

11. Otsu Youth Hostel, tel. 0775-2-8009, Yamagami-cho, Otsu City, Shiga-ken.

12. Horikawa Umermura Minshiku, tel. 441-8404, Higashi-Horikawa, Nakadachiuri-sagaru, Kamigyo-ku, Kyoto. 16 minutes from Kyoto station.

13. Sakata Minshiku (women only), tel. 541-2108, Kodaiji-Masuya-cho, Higashiyama-ku, Kyoto.

14. Arashiyama Minshiku, tel. 861-4398, 38, Saga-Kitahori-cho, Ukyo-ku, Kyoto. 40 minutes from Kyoto Station.

15. Ohara no Sato, tel. 744-2917, 41 Kusao-cho, Ohara, Sakyo-ku, Kyoto. 75 minutes from Kyoto Station.

16. Myorenji Temple, tel. 451-3527, Teranouchi Horikawa, Kamigyo-ku.

17. Jikko-in Temple (women only), tel. 744-2537, 187 Shorin Incho, Ohara, Sakyo-ku.

18. Mikawa Tsumesho Temple, tel. 351-4163, Kamijuzuya-cho, Higashihonganji-mae, Shimogyo-ku.

19. Seikanso Ryokan, tel. 0742-22-2670, 29 Higashi-Kitsuji-cho, Nara.

20. Osakaya Ryokan, tel. 0742-22-7107, 130, Nishi-Kitsuji, Jusanken-cho, Nara.

21. Shin Yakushiji Temple, tel. 0742-22-3736, 1352 Fukui-cho, Takahata, Nara.

22. Konin-ji Temple, tel. 0742-62-9303, Takashi-cho, Nara.

23, Utano Youth Hostel, tel. 075-744-2721, 29 Nakayama-cho, Uzumasa, Ukyo-ku, Kyoto 616.

24. Higashiyama Youth Hostel, tel. 075-761-8135, 112 Shirakawabashi Goken-cho, Sanjo-dori, Higashiyama-ku, Kyoto 605.

SAPPORO ACCOMMODATIONS

1. Yoshizumi Ryokan, tel. 231-3853, Nishi-9-chome, Minami-4-jo, Chuo-ku, Sapporo City.

2. Sapporo House Youth Hostel, tel. 721-4235, 3-1 Nishi 6-chome, Kita 6-jo, Kita-ku, Sapporo 001.

3. Sapporo Shiritsu Lions Youth Hostel, tel. 611-4709, 1257-2 18-chome, 1-jo, Miyano-mori, Chuo-ku, Sapporo 064.

NAGOYA ACCOMMODATIONS

1. Business Hotel Daiyaso, tel. 241-9401, 1-1-26, Shin-Sakae, Naka-ku, Nagoya.

2. Hotel Koyo, tel. 261-4401, 3-23-33, Sakae, Naka-ku, Nagoya.

3. Business Hotel Kiyoshi, tel. 321-5663, 1-3-1, Heiwa, Naka-ku, Nagoya.

4. Nagoya Plaza Hotel, tel. 951-6311, 3-8-21, Nishiki, Naka-ku, Nagoya.

5. Nagoya Youth Hostel, tel 781-9845, 1-50 Kameiri, Tashiro-cho, Chikusa-ku, Nagoya 464.

KOBE ACCOMMODATIONS

1. Kobe Plaza Hotel, tel. 332-1141, 1-13-12, Motomachi-dori, Chuo-ku, Kobe.
2. Hotel Mizukami, tel. 575-5871, 1-2-8, Mizuki-dori, Hyogo-ku, Kobe.
3. Green Hill Hotel, tel. 222-0909, 2-8-3, Kano-cho, Chuo-ku, Kobe.
4. Tsubakiso, tel. 0798-52-6161, 3-2-23, Kotoen, Nishinomiya-shi, Hyogo-ken.
5. Tarumi Kaigan Youth Hostel, tel. 707-2133, 5-58 Kaigan-dori, Tarumi-ku, Kobe 655.

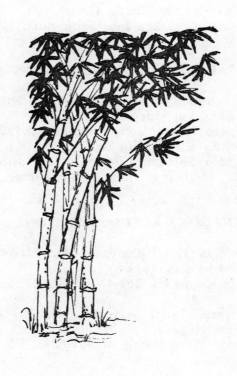

Japanese Language Schools

Japan has many language schools which offer Japanese instruction to foreigners interested in a systematic approach to language learning. Many schools also offer sponsorship for their full-time students enrolled in "intensive" classes. By law, foreign students are not allowed to work full-time in any capacity in Japan but can work part-time which nevertheless affords a livable income.

TOKYO AREA

1. International Student Institute--Japanese Language School, 3-22-7 Kita-Shinjuku, Shinjuku-ku, Tokyo 160; tel. 371-7265.

2. Asia-Africa Linguistic Institute--Dept. of Japanese Studies, 5-14-16 Shinkawa, Mitaka-shi, Tokyo 181; tel. 0422-48-5515.

3. The International Academy Japanese Language School, 4-15-1 Egota, Nakano-ku, Tokyo 165; tel. 385-2224.

4. Tokyo Kogakuin Japanese Language School, 4-5-1 Takadanobaba, Shinjuku, Tokyo 160; tel. 362-4140.

5. International Education Center--Japanese Language Institute, 1-21 Yotsuya, Shinjuku-ku, Tokyo 160; tel. 359-9621.

6. The Tokyo School of the Japanese Language (Naganuma), 16-26 Nanpeidai-machi, Shibuya-ku, Tokyo 150; tel. 463-7261.

7. Asahi Culture Center--Japanese Language Division, P.O. Box 22, Sumitomo Bldg. 2-6-1, Nishi-

Shinjuku, Shinjuku-ku, Tokyo 160-91; tel. 384-4041.
Tuition: 175,000 yen per 12-week session. No sponsorship.

8. Tokyo Japanese Language Center, 3-5-4 Shiba Park, Minato-ku, Tokyo 105; tel. 433-3378.

9. ELEC, 3-8 Kanda, Jimbocho, Chiyoda-ku, Tokyo 101; tel. 265-8911.

10. Sony Language Laboratory, 1-6-12 Nishi-Shinbashi, Minato-ku, Tokyo 105; tel. 504-1356.

11. Sendagaya Japanese Institute, 3-13-20 Sendagaya, Shibuya-ku, Tokyo 151; tel. 402-4417. Tuition: 275,000 yen per 6-month session. Sponsorship available with one session's tuition deposit.

12. Shinjuku Japanese Language School, Obori Bldg. 2F, 1-2-16 Shimo Ochiai, Shinjuku-ku, Tokyo 161; tel. 954-1317.

13. Aoyama Language Academy, Shuwa Kio-cho, TBR Bldg. 9F, 5-7 Kojimachi, Tokyo. Tuition: 145,000 yen per 11-week session. Sponsorship available.

14. Sankei College Japanese Institute, 5-9-8 Himonya, Meguro-ku, Tokyo. Tuition: 140,000 yen per quarter with 60,000 yen registration fee. Sponsorship available with 50,000 yen visa deposit.

15. International Institute of Japan, 2-11 Jingumae, 4-chome 2F, Shibuya-ku, Tokyo. Sponsorship available.

16. LIC, 15 Dogenzaka 2-chome 3F, Shibuya-ku, Tokyo. Tuition: 178,000 per quarter. Sponsorship available with one session's tuition deposit.

17. Intercult, 3-17-11 Mejiro, Toshima-ku, Tokyo 171 tel. 954-5171.

18. Intercult, 2-24-11 Nishi Gotanda, Shinagawa-ku Tokyo; tel. 492-2626.

19. Nihongo Institute, Inc., Kasuga Mansion, 1-14-4, Minami Aoyama, Minato-ku, Tokyo 107; tel. 405-7239.

20. Modern Japanese Language School, Shibuya-ku, Tokyo; tel. 461-0205.

21. Tokyo International Friendship Promotion Company; tel. 624-1759.

KYOTO AREA

1. Kyoto Japanese Language School, Ichio-dori, Muromachi Nishi, Kamigyo-ku, Kyoto 602; tel. 414-0449.

2. Kyoto English Center--Japanese Division, Sumitomo Seimie Bldg. 8F, Shijo-Karasuma, Nishi-Iru, Shimogyo-ku, Kyoto 600; tel. 221-2251.

3. Kyoto Japanese Language School, Ichijo-dori, Muromachi Nishi, Kamigyo-ku, Kyoto 602; tel. 414-0449.

4. Intercult, Kawaramachi, Takoyakushi Agaru, Nakagyo-ku, Kyoto; 223-0679.

5. Kyoto Japan Study Center, Senbon Kamichoja-machi, Higashi-iru, Kamigyo-ku, Kyoto; tel. 451-1608.

KOBE/OSAKA AREA

1. Kobe YMCA, Japanese Language Department, 2-15 Kano-cho, Ikuta-ku, Kobe 650; tel. 451-1608.

2. Kobe YWCA, Japanese Language Course, 1-1-20 Kamitsutsui, Fukiai-ku, Kobe 651; tel. 231-6201.

3. Kansai International Students Institute--Japanese Language School, 2-5-1 Ogimachi, Kita-ku, Osaka 530; tel. 361-0033.

4. Sony Language Laboratory, Umeda, Osaka; tel. 372-6777.

UNIVERSITY PROGRAMS--JAPANESE STUDIES

1. Waseda University, Institute of Language Teaching, 1-6-1 Nishi-Waseda, Shinjuku-ku, Tokyo 160; tel. 203-4141.

2. Sophia University, Japanese Language Institute, 4 Yoban-cho, Chiyoda-ku, Tokyo 102; tel. 264-7337.

3. Takushoku University, Japanese Language Center, 3-4-14 Kobinata, Bunkyo-ku, Tokyo; tel. 945-2462.

4. International Christian University, Japanese Language Program, Admission Office, 3-10-2, Osawa, Mitaka-shi, Tokyo 181; tel. 0422-33-3059.

5. Inter-University Center for Japanese Studies, Noken Bldg. 2F, 3-29 Kioi-cho, Chiyoda-ku, Tokyo 102; tel. 262-5639. Affiliated with Stanford University.

International Schools

The following schools offer instruction in English for grades Kindergarten through 9 or 12, depending on the institution. Many offer pre-school instruction in English as well.

Such "international" schools generally follow the American system of instruction and most are accredited by the Western Association of Schools and Colleges, meaning that credits earned are transferable to schools in the US. Most non-American schools will also accept such credits after a review of transcripts.

The school year begins in the middle or end of September and ends in mid-June. Most Japanese holidays are observed, as are some American.

Teachers at most schools have professional certificates from their native country (usually America) and instructional standards at the school are generally high.

In Tokyo, tuition and fees per school year at the junior and senior high school level (grades 7-12) average nearly one million yen ($4,450)--5% less for grades 1-6 and 20% less for Kindergarten. Tuition and fees of schools outside the Tokyo metropolitan area average approximately 55% of Tokyo schools'.

Enrollment is limited so parents are advised to contact schools as early as possible to obtain complete schedule and tuition information and ensure their child's enrollment.

TOKYO AREA

1. The American School in Japan, 11 Nomizu 1-chome, Chofu-shi, Tokyo 182. (Nursery-Kindergarten: 2-15-5, Aobadai, Meguro-ku, Tokyo 153).
2. The Christian Academy in Japan, 2-14 1-chome, Shinkawa-cho, Higashi Kurume-shi, Tokyo 180-03.
3. International School of the Sacred Heart, 3-1 Hiroo 4-chome, Shibuya-ku, Tokyo 150.
4. Nishimachi International School, 14-7, Moto-Azabu 2-chome, Minato-ku, Tokyo 106.
5. St. Joseph College, 85 Yamate-cho, Naka-ku, Yokohama 231.
6. St. Mary's International School for Boys, 6-19 Seta 1-chome, Setagaya-ku, Tokyo 158.
7. St. Maur International School, 83 Bluff, Naka-ku, Yokohama 231.
8. Santa Maria International School, 41 Karasawa, Minami-ku, Yokohama 232.
9. Seisen International School, 12-15 Yoga 1-chome, Setagaya-ku, Tokyo 158.
10. Yokohama International School, 258 Yamate-cho, Naka-ku, Yokohama 231.

OUTSIDE TOKYO AREA

11. Sendai American School, 1-28 Tsuchitoi 1-chome, Sendai 980.
12. Hokkaido International School, 41-8 Fukuzumi, Toyohira-ku, Sapporo, Hokkaido 062.
13. The Canadian Academy, 3-1 Nagaminedai 2-chome, Nada-ku, Kobe 657.
14. Marist Bothers International School, 2-1 Chimori-cho 1-chome, Suma-ku, Kobe 654.
15. St. Michael's International School, 5 Naka Yamatedori 3-chome, Ikuta-ku, Kobe 650.
16. Stella Maris International School, 7-3 Aotani-cho 2-chome, Nada-ku, Kobe 657.
17. Kyoto International School, Ichijodori, Muromachi Nishi-iru, Kamikyo-ku, Kyoto 602.

18. Nagoya International School, 2686 Minamihara, Nakashidami, Moriyama-ku, Nagoya 463.

19. Hiroshima International School, 2-6 Ushita-Naka 2-chome, Hiroshima 730.

20. Christ the King School, P.O. Box 14, Ginowan-shi, Okinawa 901-22.

21. Okinawa Christian School, P.O. Box 42, Urasoe-shi, Okinawa 901-22.

Private English Schools

Jobs teaching English vastly outnumber any other kind for native English-speaking foreigners and represent a good entre to other types of employment. Teaching experience or training is rarely required but may allow for somewhat higher pay and/or better working conditions. Most schools listed here teach conversational English solely, while some teach it in addition to other courses of study including other foreign languages and vocational (e.g., secretarial) skills. All employ foreigners as teachers.

The majority of conversational English students in Japan are adults; most young students of the language learn it first from Japanese English teachers. Native English-speaking instructors are used primarily to develop hearing and speaking ability among students already competent with grammar and vocabulary.

Prime hiring times are a few weeks prior to the start of the semesters, usually April and October. Teachers seeking sponsorship from overseas should send letters of inquiry no later than four months prior to the start of classes. Sponsorship usually requires a four-year college degree although those on "cultural" visas (i.e., students) without degrees may easily find teaching work but generally will not be offered sponsorship by their employers.

Processing of the working visa takes as long as three months. Teachers converting tourist or cultural visas to working visas will need to exit Japan to apply for the visa (once sponsored), then return to the same country where the application was submitted to retrieve the visa upon approval. Visa conversion cannot be done in Japan.

Schools have been divided here into major geographical regions from most populated to least. School sizes range from enrollments of 50 to 5,500 students with foreign teacher staff sizes of 1 to 150 instructors. Although an effort has been made to exclude disreputable schools, no guarantee can be given concerning individual schools. Check with instructors currently working for the school before signing any contract.

Addresses have been written in "romaji," the alphabet which the Japanese use to make their language readable by Westerners. Although usually only foreigners write addresses in romaji, postal workers are required to be familiar with it, thus ensuring delivery of overseas correspondence.

Many schools listed have English and Japanese names, usually merely translations of each other. In most cases, we have given the Japanese equivalent, written in romaji, to maximize the likelihood of your letter's being delivered by letter carriers who may know the place only by its Japanese name. If the school is known only by its foreign name, it is so listed. When writing to schools, check spelling very closely and use the three-digit postal code which appears at the beginning of most addresses.

TOKYO SCHOOLS
"03" dialing area except as noted

1. IHS; 171, Tokyo, Toyoshima-ku, Mejiro 2-34-3. tel. 989-9851. International Hospitality Society. 30 foreign teachers. Offers concentrated six-month secretarial courses, especially for executive secretaries.

2. ISS; 102, Tokyo, Chiyoda-ku, Kojimachi, 1-6 Sogo Daisan Bldg. Bekkan 5F; tel. 265-7103. Well-known business and translation school. 19 foreign teachers.

3. ILC; 101, Tokyo, Chiyoda-ku, Jinden, Jimbocho 2-1, Iwanami Jimbocho Bldg. 9F; tel. 954-5173. International Language Center. All foreign teachers (70). Home office in London. Tend to hire mostly Britons.

4. ICA; 171, Tokyo, Toyoshima-ku, Nishi Ikebukuro, 1-16-10; tel. 984-2476. Related to San Antonio College.

5. Eikaiwa Gakuin; 185, Kunitachi-shi, Higashi 1-6, Hoshino Bldg.; tel. 0425-72-3719. All American teachers (13).

6. Asahi Culture Center; 160, Tokyo, Shinjuku-ku, Nishi-Shinjuku, 2-6-1 1, Shinjuku Sumitomo Bldg.; tel. 344-941. Very large school affiliated with the Asahi publishing empire. Unlikely to sponsor but employs 22 foreign teachers.

7. Azabu Academy; 106, Tokyo, Minato-ku, Roppongi 3-14-12, Shuwa Roppongi Bldg. #701; tel. 404-841. Good location. Emphasis on accelerated courses. All foreign teachers (8).

8. Asia Center/PARC; 101, Tokyo, Chiyoda-ku, Kanda, Jimbocho 1-30, Seiko Bldg. 4F; tel. 291-5901. All foreign teachers (3).

9. Athenee Francais; 101, Tokyo, Chiyoda-ku, Kanda, 2-11 Surugadai; tel. 291-3391. One of the oldest and largest language schools in Japan. Teaches many languages. 5 foreign teachers.

10. American House Eikaiwa Center; 188, Tokyo, Tanashi-shi, Hommachi 5-4-1; tel. 0424-64-0930. Three foreign teachers.

11. Albion Gakuin; 167, Tokyo, Suginami-ku, Showan 3-26-24; tel. 333-9081. All foreign teachers (4)

12. Alec Gaigo Gakuin; 150, Tokyo, Shibuya-ku, Shibuya 1-14-13 Daini Kobayashi Bldg. 5F; tel. 400-4515. Nine foreign teachers.

13. Ishikawa Gakuin; 124, Tokyo, Katsushikaku, 3-9-12 Tateishi; tel. 697-2222. Emphasizes practical English, especially writing. 7 foreign teachers.

14. ECC; 160, Tokyo, Shinjuku-ku, Kabuki-cho 1-5-, Dairoku Arai Bldg.; tel. 209-3733. Part of a very large chain of 44 schools with 71,000 students and 200 foreign teachers. No Japanese is allowed to be spoken in the schools.

15. IF Gaigo Gakuin; 101, Tokyo, Chiyoda-ku, Kanda, Konya-cho 21-8; tel. 252-7747. 5 foreign teachers.

16. English Companion System Service; 170, Tokyo, Toyoshima-ku, Higashi Ikebukuro 3-1-4, Maison Sunshine 246; tel. 988-3611. All foreign teachers (10).

17. Inter-Tokyo; 107, Tokyo, Minato-ku, Akasaka 8--32, Akasaka Yamakatsu Bldg. 7F; tel. 479-5311. 2 foreign teachers.

18. International Institute of Japan; 150, Tokyo, Shibuya-ku, Jingumae 4-2-11, Belair Garden Bldg. 2F; tel. 05-0754. 15 foreign teachers.

19. Interlingua Club; 154, Tokyo, Meguro-ku, Yutenji 2-15-17; tel. 791-5561. 3 foreign teachers.

20. Interlang School and Service; 107, Tokyo, Minato-ku, Kita-Aoyama 2-14-6, Bell Commons 7F; tel. 497-5451. 15 foreign teachers using Interlang method.

21. Williams Academy; 150, Tokyo, Shibuya-ku, Jingumae 6-5-3, Ga-Z Bldg. 4F; tel. 486-1248. 12 foreign teachers.

22. WINS; 160, Tokyo, Shinjuku-ku, Nishi-Shinjuku 2-1-1, Mitsui Bldg. 49F; tel. 344-4882. 14 foreign teachers.

23. West Virginia Shuritsu Daigaku/Nihon Jimukyoku; 102, Tokyo, Chiyoda-ku, Gobancho 4-2, Topre Bldg.; tel. 234-0357. Students may enter West Virginia University directly upon graduation. All foreign teachers (10).

24. Eigo Semmon Kenkyujo; 110, Tokyo, Daito-ku, Higashi Ueno 6-2-2, Maruyoshi Bldg.; tel. 844-3104. 2 foreign teachers.

25. Evergreen Eigo Gakuin; 150, Tokyo, Meguro-ku, 1-21-2 Yutenji; tel. 713-4958. 7 foreign teachers.

26. ASA; 160, Tokyo, Shinjuku-ku, Nishi-Shinjuku 1-19-6, Yamate Shinjukku Bldg.; tel. 348-3333. Large school with full range of business classes. Hires only foreign teachers (150) graduated from "top-notch" American or British universities.

27. Executive Gogaku Center; 107, Tokyo, Minato-ku, Akasaka 1-9-20, Koa Dai 16 Bldg.; tel. 585-6401. Large chain of schools for businessmen. 20 foreign teachers. Comparatively poor pay.

28. SDA; 167, Tokyo, Suginami-ku, Tensho 3-17-3; tel. 392-0419. All foreign teachers (11).

29. FL Center; 150, Tokyo, Shibuya-ku, Shibuya 2-19-20, Iwasaki Bldg. 3F; tel. 400-9811. All foreign teachers (10). Experience required.

30. ELEC; 101, Tokyo, Chiyoda-ku, Kanda, 3-8 Jimbocho; tel. 265-8911. Large school with all foreign teachers (100).

31. OSCC; 101, Tokyo, Chiyoda-ku, Kanda, 2-1 Surugadai; tel. 291-1285. Emphasizes teaching English through the Bible. All foreign teachers (10).

32. GEM; 150, Tokyo, Shibuya-ku, Shibuya 1-13-5, Daikyo Bldg. 4F; tel. 406-8031. 15 foreign teachers.

33. Kanda Gijitsu Gaigo Academia, Morikyo Bldg. 1-2-9 Yoyogi, Shibuya-ku, Tokyo 151; tel. 379-1795. Uses the direct method of instruction. Offers English for Special Purposes courses.

34. Kanda Institute of Foreign Languages; 101, Tokyo, Chiyoda-ku, 2-13-13 Uchikanda; tel. 254-2731. The largest ESL school in Japan with 5,500 students and 94 foreign instructors.

35. Kilby Gakuin; 160, Tokyo, Shinjuku-ku, Nishi-Shinjuku 1-21-1, Myoho Bldg. 5F; tel. 342-6001. Features singing and dance classes. 8 foreign teachers.

36. Ginza Beikaiwa Salon; 104, Tokyo, Chuo-ku 5-9-13 Nakamura Bldg.; tel. 573-7427. All foreign teachers (19).

37. Gregg Gaigo Gakko; 152, Tokyo, Meguro-ku, 1-14-16 Jugaoka; tel. 724-0552. One of the largest schools with 102 foreign teachers.

38. Kanrisha Yosei Gakko; 150, Tokyo, Minato-ku, Nishi-Shimbashi 3-19-13, Tokyo Kensho Bldg.; tel. 433-8351. 5 foreign teachers.

39. Keishin Gaikokugo Semmon Gakko; 182, Tokyo, Chofu-shi, Senkawa-cho 1-2; tel. 300-6885. Small classes. 9 foreign teachers.

40. Kent School; 150, Tokyo, Shibuya-ku, Ebisu Minami 1-6-3; tel. 713-7046. 16 foreign teachers.

41. Cambridge English School; 160, Tokyo, Shinjuku-ku, Nishi-Shinjuku 1-13-12, Nishi-Shinjuku Showa Bldg.; tel. 348-0181. Teachers must have RSA teaching credential.

42. CLC; 103, Tokyo, Chuo-ku, Yaesu 1-9-13, Yaesu Ekimae Godo Bldg. 5F; tel. 275-0151. All foreign teachers (20).

43. Kokusai Eiken Center; 158, Tokyo, Setagaya-ku, Seda 1-19-2, Akira Mansion; tel. 709-7688. All foreign teachers (10).

44. Kokusai Kankei Gakuin; 160, Tokyo, Shinjuku-ku, 1-21 Yotsuya; tel. 359-9620. Focus on international business practices. 20 foreign teachers.

45. Kokusai Business College; 150, Tokyo, Shibuya-ku, 3-17-2 Shibuya-ku, Kaneda Bldg.; tel. 409-1981. Secretarial school. 10 foreign teachers.

46. Conan Gaigo School; 102, Tokyo, Chiyoda-ku, Ichiban-cho 4, Sagamiya Daiichi Bldg.; tel. 234-3358. 6 foreign teachers.

47. Saimaru Academy; 106, Tokyo, Minato-ku, 1-5-17 Roppongi; tel. 582-9841. 20 foreign teachers. Emphasizes simultaneous translation.

48. Sankei International College; 152, Tokyo, Meguro-ku, Hibumidani 5-9-8; tel. 794-1761. 10 foreign teachers.

49. Sunshine Gaigo Gakko; 170, Tokyo, Toyoshima-ku, Higashi Ikebukuro 3-1-1, Sunshine 60 Bldg. 9F; tel. 987-1921. 5 foreign teachers. Relatively poor pay.

50. Sunshine Business Gakko; 170, Tokyo, Toyoshima-ku, Higashi Ikebukuro 4-23-4; tel. 987-5611. 14 foreign teachers. School emphasizes business courses.

51. Sunbright Telephone Group; 105, Tokyo, Minato-ku, Shiba 3-22-7, CBC Kokusai Bldg.; tel. 451-1851. Lessons given by telephone by all-foreign staff of 34 teachers.

52. Sun Life; 160, Tokyo, Shinjuku-ku, Takadanobaba 4-11-13, Art Daiichi Bldg. 2F; tel. 367-4881. 20 foreign teachers.

53. JPS Academy; 150, Tokyo, Shibuya-ku, Shibuya Home 1308, Udagawa-cho 2-1; Shibuya-ku; tel. 464-5555. 20 foreign teachers.

54. Shibuya Gaigo Gakuin; 150, Tokyo, Shibuya-ku, Sakuragaoka-cho 15-15; tel. 461-8854. 8 foreign teachers.

55. Shimada Eikaiwa Kenkyujo; 171, Tokyo, Toyoshima-ku, Minami-Nagasaki 1-14-8; 952-0061. Specializes in voice training. 1 foreign teacher.

56. Jugaoka Language School; 152, Tokyo, Meguro-ku, Jugaoka Depato, Jugaoka 1-28-8, tel. 718-3926. 10 foreign teachers.

57. Excellence; 102, Tokyo, Chiyoda-ku, 4 Bancho 6, Palais Blanc 303. Personally recommended by a former teacher: "One of the most honest organizations I have ever dealt with."

58. Suzuki Gakuen/Salon Academy; 151, Tokyo, Shibuya-ku, Yoyogi 2-6-7, Seichi Bldg. 4F; tel. 379-5661. All foreign teachers (15).

59. Stanton School of English; 102, Tokyo, Chiyoda-ku, Rokuban-cho 7; tel. 262-3300. All British teachers (30) with TEFL license.

60. Sundai ELS Eigo Gakuin; 101, Tokyo, Chiyoda-ku, Kanda, 1-5-8 Surugadai; tel. 233-2311. Part of the world-wide English Language Service network. 9 foreign teachers.

61. Century Eigo Gakuin; 105, Tokyo, Minato-ku, Hammamatsu-cho 1-25-3; tel. 434-9484. 6 foreign teachers.

62. Sony Eigo Kyoshitsu; 160, Tokyo, Minato-ku, Shimbashi, Kurihara Bldg. 7F, 1-6-12 Nishi Shimbashi; tel. 232-0290. Affiliated with Sony Corp. 40 unionized foreign teachers. Branch locations at Shibuya, Kichijoji, Shinbashi, Yokohama, and Osaka.

63. Chuo Eigo Gakuin; 164, Tokyo, Nakano-ku, Nakano 2-23-1; tel. 380-6970. 2 foreign teachers.

64. Chuo Steno College; 160, Tokyo, Nishi-Shinjuku 7-4-7, Ota Bldg.; tel. 362-4191. 4 foreign teachers.

65. Tsuyaku Gaido Yoseijo; 171, Tokyo, Toshima-ku, Takada 3-36-1; tel. 988-6141. Emphasizes translation training. 30 foreign teachers.

66. Tsuda School of Business; 1-18-24 Sendagaya, Shibuya-ku, Tokyo 151; tel. 402-7331. Business-oriented curriculum. 14 foreign teachers.

67. TES; 103, Tokyo, Chuo-ku, Nihonbashi, Kodenba-cho 5-15; tel. 663-8771. Business school with 12 foreign teachers.

68. Tokyo Foreign Language College; 7-3-8 Nishi Shinjuku, Shinjuku-ku, Tokyo 160; tel. 367-1101. Has a large foreign teaching staff (46). See earlier description in text.

69. Tokyo Kogakuin Gaigo Semmon Gakkoo; 161, Tokyo, Shinjuku-ku, Shimo-ochiai 1-1-8; tel. 360-0341. 9 foreign teachers. Prefers British with experience.

70. Tokyo Gogaku Academy; 141, Tokyo, Shinagawa-ku, Kamiosaki 2-15-14, Takagi Bldg. 5F; tel. 440-7227. All foreign teachers (14).

71. Tokyo Suginami Eigo Semmon Gakko; 166, Tokyo, Suginami-ku, Koenji Minami 4-44-12; tel. 314-2435. 4 foreign students.

72. Tokyo School of Business; Yoyogi 1-56, Shibuya-ku, Tokyo 151; tel. 370-2222. Emphasizes all business-related ESL skills. 5 foreign teachers.

73. Tokyo Business College, Paris Saido Bldg. 1F, Hitotsubashi 1-1-1, Chiyoda-ku, Tokyo 100; tel. 213-0962. Business school training students for import/export careers. 8 foreign teachers.

74. Tokyo Business Gaigo Semmon Gakko; 152, Tokyo, Meguro-ku, Jiyugaoka 1-14-6; tel. 724-0551. Large business school with 46 foreign teachers.

75. Matsumoto Eigo Semmon Gakkoo, Shibuya 1-4-8, Shibuya-ku, Tokyo 150; tel. 400-8321. 5 foreign teachers use what is called "spartan" approach to learning.
76. Tokyo Yamanote YMCA Eigo Gakoin, 2-18-12 Nishi Waseda, Shinjuku-ku, Tokyo 160. 9 foreign teachers use "living English" with role play and conversation.

NOTE: There are many YMCA English schools throughout Japan. Pay is generally poorer than average but classes are plentiful and working conditions are usually good. Teachers may apply to individual YMCA schools in Japan or register to be notified of openings anywhere in the country by sending vita to: YMCA Overseas Service Corps (Japan), International Division, YMCA, 291 Broadway, New York City, NY 10007; tel. 374-2194 or to YMCA of the USA, Overseas Personnel Programs, 101 N. Wacker Dr., Chicago, Ill. 60606; tel. 977-0031. Assignments in other countries are also available.

77. Tokyo YMCA Eigo Semmon Gakkoo, Mitoyo-cho 7, Kanda, Chiyoda-ku, Tokyo 101; tel. 293-9471. Two-year program emphasizing culture and customs of English-speaking countries. 34 foreign teachers.
78. Tokyo YWCA Semmon Gakkoo, 1-8 Surugadai, Kanda, Chiyoda-ku, Tokyo 101; tel. 293-5421. 18 foreign teachers instruct mostly female students.
79. Toho Gakuen Semmon Gakkoo, 2-4-1 Izumi, Suginami-ku, Tokyo 168; tel. 323-8531. Affiliated with San Francisco University. Credits transferable to American universties. 4 foreign teachers.
80. TOEFL Academy, New State Mena 2F, 2-23-1 Yoyogi, Shibuya-ku, Tokyo 151; tel. 375-2307. 18 foreign teachers prepare students for the critically important Test of English as a Foreign Language (TOEFL) used for admission and hiring purposes.
81. TOEFL Seminar; 160, Tokyo, Shinjuku-ku, Takadanobaba 4-13-10; tel. 371-4391. 20 foreign teachers.
82. Travel Journal Ryokoo Semmon Gakkoo, 4-6-6 Higashi Nakano, Nakano-ku, Tokyo 164; tel. 367-8111. Travel school with 9 foreign teachers.
83. Nicholai Gakkuin, 4-1 Surugadai, Kanda, Chiyoda-ku, Tokyo 101; tel. 291-9057. Founded in 1873.

84. Nichibei Kaiwa Gakuin, Yotsuya 1-21, hinjuku-ku, Tokyo 160; tel. 359-9621. Very prestigious chool with 65 instructors teaching American English. apanese may not be spoken by students at any time in the chool. Very selective hiring.

85. Nihon Gaikokugo Kenkyujo; 160, Tokyo, hibuya-ku, Yoyogi 2-23-1, New State Manor 1172; tel. 370-454. 18 foreign teachers.

86. NASA; 160, Tokyo, Shinjuku-ku, Takadanobaba -14-5; tel. 200-9731. 5 foreign teachers.

87. Nihon Jitsumu Honyaku Gakuin; 162, Tokyo, hinjuku-ku, Agebacho 20, Daini Tobundo Bldg.; tel. 267-331. 20 foreign teachers.

88. Nihon Business School, 6-7-13 Minami Aoyoma, 4inato-ku, Tokyo 107; tel. 400-2141. Teaches secretarial nd international trading skills with 110 foreign teachers.

89. Nihon Tsuyaku Yoseijo; 152, Tokyo, Shinagawa-u, Kamiosaki 3-1-5, Meguro Eki Higashi Guchi Bldg. 8F; el. 440-4651. 8 foreign teachers for primarily translation tudents.

90. Nihon Honyaku Semmon Gakuin Tsugakubu, ohyo Kaikan 3F, 3-2-11 Surugadai, Kanda, Tokyo-to; tel. 51-4735. Translation school with small foreign teaching taff (2).

91. Berkeley House Gogaku Center, Topure Bldg. 4-, Gobancho, Chiyoda-ku, Tokyo 102; tel. 262-2711. Applicants must have TESL degree and/or certification. North American instructors only.

92. Bilingual Tokyo; 150, Tokyo, Shibuya-ku, Jtagawa-cho 39-2, Village 80 Bldg. 4F; tel. 477-1858. Large chool with 170 foreign teachers.

93. Baberu Honyaku Gakuin, NS Bldg. 2-2-3 arugaku-cho, Chiyoda-ku, Tokyo 101; tel. 295-5155. 2 oreign teachers.

94. Harajuku Gaigo Gakuin; 151, Tokyo, Shibuya-u, Jingumae 5-11-8; tel. 406-4604. 15 foreign teachers.

95. Robert Gaigo Gakuin; 151, Tokyo, Shibuya-ku, endagaya 3-61-7; tel. 401-0067. 25 foreign teachers.

96. Pan-Pacific Institute; 107, Tokyo, Chiyoda-ku, ojimachi 2-12; tel. 406-1231. 11 foreign students.

97. Hampton School of English, Daini Komatsu Bldg. 4F, 2-14-17 Shibuya, Shibuya-ku, Tokyo 150; tel. 406-

1231. Instructors must have TEFL degree or experience. British preferred. Affiliated with Cambridge University.

98. FIS; 155, Tokyo, Setagaya-ku, Kitazawa 2-10-15; tel. 468-8598. 13 foreign teachers.

99. Brittania Gaigo Gakuin; 120, Tokyo, Adachi-ku, Ayase 3-3-1, Daichi Hoshi Bldg. 3F; tel. 629-8681. All British teachers (18).

100. BEC; 160, Tokyo, Shinjuku 3-28-10; tel. 352-2958. Large school with 73 foreign teachers.

101. Berlitz School of Languages, Daini Koa Bldg. 1-11-39 Akasaka, Minato-ku, Tokyo 107; tel. 534-4211. World-wide chain in constant need of foreign instructors, due in large part to relatively poor pay and working conditions. 190 foreign teachers.

102. Horin Academia, FI Bldg. 6F, 1-26-5 Takadanobaba, Shinjuku-ku, Tokyo 160; tel. 200-7771. Large school with 60 foreign teachers.

103. Matsudo Eikaiwa, Kurokawa Bldg. 5F, 3-4 Sakuragaoka-cho, Shibuya-ku, Tokyo 150; tel. 496-0555. Has own method, stressing "mental attitude."

104. Mia American Community School; 162, Tokyo, Shinjuku-ku, Sumiyoshi-cho 108, OSK Bldg. 701; tel. 358-1475. 10 foreign teachers.

105. Miniko; Nakao Bldg. 1-29-8 Komagome, Toshima-ku, Tokyo 170. Tel. 945-1691.

106. Myosenkai Culture Center; 160, Tokyo, Shinjuku-ku, Minami Motomachi 6-2; tel. 351-0297. All foreign teachers (15).

107. Meguro Eikaiwa School, Itaki Bldg. 3F, 2-15-15 Kamiosaki, Shinagawa-ku, Tokyo 141; tel. 446-2181. Small classes for 5 foreign teachers.

108. Model Language Studio, Yasuto Bldg. 1-43-7 Yoyogi, Shibuya-ku, Tokyo 151; tel. 370-7843. Stresses "live" English with role plays, rhythm, acting exercises. 3 foreign teachers.

109. Yamate Eikaiwa School, 2-19-18 Shibuya, Shibuya-ku, Tokyo 150; tel. 400-5025. Small classes. All foreign teachers (10).

110. Uni College; 101, Tokyo, Chiyoda-ku, Kanda, Jinbocho 1-19, Narita Bldg.; tel. 291-7630. 3 foreign teachers.

111. Yotsuya Gaigo Gakuin, PL Yotsuya Bldg., Motoshio-cho 9, Shinjuku-ku, Shinjuku-ku, Tokyo 160; tel.

341-1434. Emphasizes "practical" conversational English with 20 foreign instructors.

112. Ripitomeku Eigo Kyoshitsu; 160, Tokyo, Shinjuku-ku, Shinano-cho 34, Toshin Bldg. 2F. 6 foreign instructors emphasize listening and speaking.

113. Lingua Gakuin, Yuki Bldg. 3-303, 2-19-1 Koenji Minami, Suginami-ku, Tokyo 166; tel. 312-2377. Small school with 2 foreign teachers.

114. Linguarama, Akasaka Heights #401, 9-5-26 Akasaka, Minato-ku, Tokyo 107; tel. 403-5724. All foreign teachers (9) offering wide assortment of classes. No Japanese spoken in school.

115. Lutheran Gaikoku no Gakkoo, 1-2-32 Fujimi, Chiyoda-ku, Tokyo 102; tel. 263-9835. Operated by the American Lutheran Church. 10 foreign teachers.

116. Renaissance Eigo Gakuin; 150, Tokyo, Shibuya 1-24-7, Miyashita Park Bldg.; tel. 407-8466. 5 foreign teachers.

OTHER KANTO AREA

117. East-West Gaikokugo Semmon Gakko; 281, Chiba, Inagedai-cho 18-10; tel. 0472-43-7611. 4 foreign teachers.

118. QE Eikaiwa Gakuin; 272, Chiba-ken, Ichikawa-shi, Minami Yawata 4-7-14, Yugetsu Bldg. 3F; tel. 0473-77-1143. 6 foreign teachers.

119. Chiba YMCA Eigo Gakuin, Chiba, Masago 5-20-5; tel. 0472-79-8411. 3 foreign teachers.

120. Mobara Eigo Gakuin; 297; Chiba-ken, Mobara-shi, Takashi 619-11; tel. 0475-22-4785. Very small school with 1 foreign teacher.

121. AES; 243, Kanagawa-ken, Atsugi-shi, Nakamachi 3-18-14. Tel. 0462-24-3511. All foreign teachers (20).

122. Asahi Culture Center; 220, Kanagawa-ken, Yokohama-shi, Nishi-ku, Takashima 2-16-1, Yokohama Lumine Bldg.; tel. 045-453-1122. 40 foreign teachers.

123. English House Gakuin, 4-22-1 Chiyogaoka, Kawasaki-shi 215; tel. 044-955-0809. 5 foreign teachers.

124. Gaigo Business Semmon Gakko; 210, Kanagawa-ken, Kawasaki-shi, Eki Mae Honcho 22-9; tel. 044-244-1959. 47 foreign teachers and broad curriculum.

125. Gogaku Kenshu Center; 221, Kanagawa-ken, Yokohama-shi, Kanagawa-ku, Tsuruya-cho 3-32, Academia Bldg.; tel. 045-311-5361. 35 foreign teachers.

126. Cosmos Gogaku Center; 221, Kanagawa-ken, Yokohama-shi, Kanagawa-ku, Nishi-Kanagawa 1-3-6, Coop Fuji 605; tel. 045-321-2621. 2 foreign teachers.

127. Cosmopolitan; 220, Yokohama, Nishi-ku 2-11-2, Sky Manor 405; tel. 045-453-2620. Small school with one foreign teacher.

128. JCC Academy; 223, Yokohama, Minato Kita-ku, Hiyoshi Motomachi 1867-1, Hiyoshi Center Bldg. 3F; tel. 044-63-6469. 2 foreign teachers.

129. Shonan English College, 1-2-2 Kobukurodai, Kamakura-shi, Kanagawa-ken 247; tel. 0467-46-7370. 6 foreign teachers.

130. Sony Eigo Kyoshitsu; 220, Yokohama, Kanagawa-ku, Tsuruya-cho 2-25-2, Mitsui Seimei Bldg. 4F; tel. 045-311-5803. 9 foreign teachers.

131. Designer Gakuin; 220, Yokohama, Kanagawa-ku, Daimachi 22-14; 3 foreign teachers. Emphasizes hotel and travel English.

132. Hioshi Eigo Gakuin, 1778 Hiyoshi Hommachi, Kohoku-ku, Yokohama 220; tel. 044-61-7040. 4 foreign teachers.

133. Fujisawa Gaigo Center, Hirota Bldg. 2F & 3F, Fujisawa 976, Fujisawa-shi, Kanagawa-ken; tel. 0466-26-0203. 19 foreign teachers emphasize pattern practice and speaking.

134. Berlitz School, Sky Bldg. 6F, 5-203 Motomachi, Naka-ku, Yokohama 231; tel. 045-651-2891. See description of Berlitz above.

135. Yamate Eigakuin, 1-36 Hinode-cho, Naka-ku, Yokohama-shi, Kanagawa-ken; tel. 045-231-1841. 3 foreign teachers.

136. Yokohama Academy Semmon Gakkoo, Academy Bldg., Tsuruyakucho 3-32, Kanagawa-ku, Yokohama 221; tel. 045-311-5361. Oldest secretarial school in Japan. Students primarily interested in careers with foreign corporations. 35 foreign teachers.

137. Yokohama Gaigo Business College, Yamanote-cho 45, Naka-ku, Yokohama 231; tel. 045-641-3919. Large business school, featuring "dynamic system" of practical training for office, language skills. 11 foreign teachers.

138. Yokohama YMCA Gakuin, 1-7 Joban-cho, Naka-ku, Yokohama 231; tel. 045-662-3721. 24 foreign teachers. See YMCA description above.

139. LIOJ; 250, Kanagawa-ken, Odawara-shi, Shiroyama 4-14-1, Asia Center Nai; tel. 0465-23-1667. All foreign teachers (20). Training/experience required.

KYOTO AREA
"075" dialing area, except as noted.

140. Nara Gaigo Business Typist Gakuin; 634, Nara-ken, Kashihara-shi, Uchizen-cho 5-3-31, Fuji Bldg. 7F; tel. 0744-22-7688. 3 foreign teachers.

141. Riseikan Gaikuin; 663, Hyogo-ken, Nishinomiya-shi, Kitaguchi-cho 4-25; tel. 0798-65-2011. 8 foreign teachers.

142. SEI; 520, Shiga-ken, Otsu-shi, Kyomachi 3-2-6, Eiki Bldg. 3F; tel. 0775-24-8879. 2 foreign teachers.

143. ECC; 604, Kyoto, Nakagyo-ku, Karawamachi-dori, Shijo Agaru; tel. 075-223-0196. See description of ECC in Tokyo listings.

144. Kyoto English Center, Sumitomo Seimei Bldg. 8F, Nishi Shijo Karasuma, Shimo Nyooku, Kyoto 600; tel. 075-221-2251. Emphasizes extra-curricular activities with students and foreign teachers (45).

145. Kyoto YMCA, Kado, Sanjo Yanagibajo, Nakagyo-ku, Kyoto 604; tel. 075-231-4388. Together with next listing, 50 foreign teachers.

146. Kyoto YMCA Semmon Gakkoo, Sagaru, Imadegawa Karasuma, Kamigyoku, Kyoto 602; tel. 075-432-3191. Emphasizes practical business skills. See #145.

147. Lake Gaigo Gakuin, Ikawa Hairu, Higashi Horikawa, Nakagyoku, Kyoto 604; tel. 075-221-7686. Conversation stressed for 10 foreign teachers.

148. Bi-Lingual English Conversation School; 605 Kyoto, Higashiyama-ku, Shijodori, Yamato-oji Nishi Iru, Nakanomachi 200, Kamogawa Bldg. 9F. "An expanding company" whose foreign staff manager has found <u>JOBS IN JAPAN</u> "valuable in that it has led many prospective teachers to our doorstep for interviews."

OSAKA
"06" dialing area, except as noted

149. ILC; 530, Osaka, Kita-ku, Sumida-cho 8-47, Hankyu Grand Bldg. 24F; tel. 315-8003. All foreign teachers (15) British. Main office in London.

150. ECC; 530, Osaka, Nakazaki Nishi 2-3-35; tel. 373-0144. See description of ECC earlier.

151. IF; 532, Osaka, Yodogawa-ku, Nishi Nakajima 1-9-20, Shin Nakashima Bldg. 7F; tel. 305-0721. 7 foreign teachers specialize in TOEFL and GMAT test preparation.

152. Umeda Gakuin Eigo Semmon Gakkoo, 2-30 Chayayamachi, Kita-ku, Osaka 530; tel. 376-0661. Mostly adult students for 11 foreign teachers.

153. El Business Gakko; 556, Osaka, Naniwa-ku, Nanba-naka 3-13-1; tel. 647-0011. 10 foreign teachers with hotel and tour guide classes.

154. Executive Gogaku Center; Hommachi Nomura Bldg., 4-4-1 Hommachi, Higashi-ku, Osaka 541; tel. 271-8978. 109 foreign teachers in Executive chain. See description of Executive earlier.

155. Osaka Eikaiwa Gakkoo; 530, Osaka, Kita-ku, Nakanoshima 3-6, Osaka Bldg.; tel. 441-9035. 4 foreign teachers.

156. Osaka Gaigo Semmon Gakko; 540, Osaka, Higashi-ku, Shimamachi 2-5; tel. 944-1061. 17 foreign teachers.

157. Osaka Furitsu Boeki Semmon Gakko; 543, Osaka, Tennojiku, Yuhigaoka-cho 5; tel. 942-2717. 2 foreign teachers.

158. Osaka YMCA College; 550, Osaka, Nishi-ku, Tosabori 1-5-6; tel. 441-0892. 13 foreign teachers with mostly tour guide and hotel classes.

159. YWCA Secretarial Arts School; 550, Osaka, Kita-ku, Kamiyama-cho 11-12; tel. 361-0838. 8 foreign teachers.

160. KEC; 573, Osaka-fu, Hirakata-shi, Nishi Kiino 2-4-17, Daigo Matsuba Bldg.; tel. 0720-31-0616. 2 foreign teachers.

161. Kori Gaikokugo Center; 572, Osaka-fu, Neagawa-shi, Kori Nishino-cho 12-1; tel. 0720-31-0616. 3 foreign teachers.

162. Sankei International College, Sankei Bldg. 8F, Umeda 2-4-9, Kita-ku, Osaka 530; tel. 347-0751. 8 foreign teachers. See description of Sankei earlier.

163. Semmon Gakko Tennoji Eigo Gakuin; 545; Osaka, Abeno-ku, Matsuzaki-cho 2-9-36; tel. 623-1851. 11 foreign teachers. Recommended.

164. Tomo English School; 530, Osaka, Kita-ku, Doshin 2-2-15, Sun Laurel Ogimachi 301; tel. 352-0687. 3 foreign teachers.

165. Nihon Business School, Miahara 4-4-65, Yodogawa-ku, Osaka 532; tel. 391-0061. 4 foreign teachers. See description of Nihon Business School earlier.

166. Bilingual Osaka; 520, Osaka, Kita-ku, Sonezaki Shinji 2-3-4, Ekimae Bldg.; tel. 344-1720. 170 foreign instructors in Bilingual chain.

167. Harrow Center; 532, Osaka, Yodogawa-ku, Nishi Nakajima 3-20-8, Shinwa Bldg. 5F; tel. 428-6241. All foreign teachers (10).

168. Babel Gakuin; 530, Osaka, Kita-ku, Umeda 1-11-4, Osaka Ekimae Bldg.; tel. 341-2531. 3 foreign teachers.

169. Berlitz School, Hotel Hanshin Bldg. 2F, 2-3-24 Umeda, Kita-ku, Osaka 530; tel. 341-2531. See description of Berlitz earlier.

KOBE

170. ECC, 1-1-1 Nishi Tachibanadori, Hyogo-ku, Kobe 652; tel. 078-576-7758. 4 foreign teachers. See description of ECC earlier.

171. Executive School, Kobe Shokoboeki Center Bldg. 18F, 5-1-14, Hamabedori, Chuo-ku, Kobe 651; tel. 078-251-2412. See description of Executive earlier.

172. Kokusai Business Gakuin, 5-3-5 Kotono Ocho, Chuo-ku, Kobe 651; tel. 078-242-5178. Trains students for careers in business and industry, especially import/export and secretarial. 2 foreign teachers.

173. Kobe YMCA, 2-7-15 Kanocho, Chuo-ku, Kobe 650; tel. 078-241-7201. 5 foreign teachers. See description of YMCA earlier.

174. Seinikaeru Kokusai Gakkoo, 3-17-2 Nakayamate-dori, Chuo-ku, Kobe 650; tel. 078-221-8028. Trains students to pass Cambridge University's First Certificate. 5 British instructors.

175. Berlitz, Kyowa Bldg. 4F, 5-12-7 Shimoyamate-dori,, Chuo-ku, Kobe 650; tel. 078-351-1583.

OTHER KANSAI AREA

176. Colorado Eigo Gakuin; 676, Hyogo-ken, Takasago-shi, Yoneda-cho, Yonedashin 20-3; tel. 0794-31-6507. 2 foreign teachers.

177. YMCA Gakuin; 670, Hyogo-ken, Himeji-shi, Tsuchiyama, Higashi No-cho 9-15; tel. 0792-98-5566. 2 foreign teachers.

178. Kansai Gaigo Gakuin; 640, Wakayama, Nishi Takamatsu 1-5-1; tel. 0734-36-5694. 2 foreign teachers.

179. Life Academy; 518-04, Miye-ken, Nabari-shi, Kikyogaoka 4-5-69; tel. 0595-65-0968. Features word processing training. 3 foreign teachers.

180. Ise Eigo Center; 516, Miye-ken, Iseshi, Kamihisa 1-4-11; tel. 0596-28-7629. Old but small school with only one foreign teacher on a staff of 3.

181. SDA; 730, Hiroshima, Naka-ku, Takeya-cho 4-8; tel. 082-241-2464. All foreign teachers (4).

182. Hiroshima YMCA; 730, Hiroshima, Naka-ku, Hachobori 7-11; tel. 082-228-2269. 9 foreign teachers.

SHIKOKU ISLAND

183. Anbik School; 770, Tokushima, Terashima Hon-cho, Nishi Ichome, Awa Kendo Bldg. 5F; tel. 0886-25-4291. 5 foreign teachers.

184. Takamatsu Nichibei Gakuin, 10-20 Marunouchi, Takamatsu-shi, Kagawa-ken 760; tel. 0878-21-3382. 5 foreign teachers.

185. Ehime Eigo Academy, 2-9-6 Ichiban-cho, Matsuyama-shi, Ehime-ken 790; tel. 0899-31-8686. 7 foreign teachers.

CENTRAL HONSHU

186. Niigata Business Semmon Gakko; 950, Niigata, Bandai 1-1-22; tel. 0252-41-2131. 6 foreign teachers.

187. Nagaoka Business Semmon Gakko; 940, Niigata-ken, Nagaoka-shi, Otedori 2-4-9; tel. 0258-35-1055. 2 foreign teachers.

188. Hokoku Bunka Center; 920, Ishikawa-ken, Kanazawa-shi, Hondo-cho 3-2-1, MRO Bldg.; tel. 0762-22-0101. 5 foreign teachers.

189. Yamanashi YMCA; 400, Kofu, Chuo 5-4-11; tel. 0552-35-8543. 7 foreign teachers.

190. Nakamura Eigo School; 389-22, Nagano-ken; Iyama-shi, Fukuju-cho 1138; tel. 0269-62-2835. 1 foreign teacher.

191. ILC; 500, Gifu, Nagasumi-cho 1-14; tel. 0582-63-3936. 2 foreign teachers.

192. English Center; 430, Shizuoka-ken, Hamamatsu-shi, Toshimachi 11, Kawai Bldg.; tel. 0534-56-0109. 8 foreign teachers teach full range of courses. Negative report received from former teacher. Approach with caution.

193. Nomado Gaigo Gakuin, Hattori Bldg. 3F, 3-2 Koyamachi, Shizuoka 420; tel. 0542-55-8858. All foreign teachers (5).

NAGOYA

194. Asahi Culture Center; 460, Aichi-ken, Nagoya, Naka-ku, Sakae 3-4-5, Marue Sky 10F; tel. 052-261-3866. 2 foreign teachers.

195. Nagoya Gaikokugo Semmon Gakkoo; Imaike 1-5-31, Chikusaku, Nagoya 464; tel. 741-2304. 20 foreign teachers teach mostly business classes.

196. Nagoya International School, 2686 Minamihara, Nakashidami, Moriyama-ku, Nagoya 463. Not an ESL school. Generally hires only experienced instructors with teaching credentials to teach general junior high and high school curriculum.

197. Nagoya Business Semmon Gakko, Denba 3-2-3, Atsuta-ku, Nagoya 456; tel. 052-682-7879. 3 foreign students.

198. Nihon Business School, Mei Eki Minami 1-23-17, Nakamura-ku, Nagoya 450; tel. 582-3026. 5 foreign teachers.

199. Professional English Course; 461, Aichi-ken, Nagoya, Higashi-ku, Aori 1-25-1, Nishin Bldg. 508; tel. 052-937-7339. 10 foreign teachers.

FUKUOKA AND SOUTHERN JAPAN

200. ECC Gaigo Gakuin; 810, Fukuoka, Chuo-ku, Daimyo 2-9-5; tel. 092-715-0731. See ECC description earlier.

201. Kitakyushu YMCA; 802, Fukuoka-ken, Kitakyushu-shi, Kokura Kita-ku, Kaji-cho 2-3-13; tel. 093-531-1587. 4 foreign teachers with variety of courses.

202. Caine's Eikaiwa Typing School, 1-1 Maizuru, Chuo-ku, Fukuoka 810; tel. 721-5020. 14 foreign teachers for business, vocational and general classes.

203. Sato Business School, 2-4-10 Tenjin, Chuo-ku, Fukuoka 810; tel. 771-8261. 4 foreign instructors.

204. Nihon Business School; 812, Fukuoka, Hakata Ekimae 4-18-6; tel. 092-411-6423. 3 foreign teachers, mostly vocational English classes.

205. Berlitz, Futaba Bldg. 7F, Tenjin 3-1, Chuo-ku, Fukuoka, 810; tel. 751-9888. See Berlitz description earlier.

206. Kumamoto YMCA; 860, Kumamoto, Shinmachi 1-3-8; tel. 096-353-6391. 8 foreign teachers for general classes.

207. American Center; 880, Miyazaki, Hachibana-dori Higashi 5-3, Ono Bldg. 3F; tel. 0985-53-4521. 2 foreign teachers feature role play and public speaking.

208. ELC; 880, Miyazaki, Miyata-cho 10-22, Eikaiwa Bldg. 2F; tel. 0985-25-1565. 3 foreign teachers. Many types of classes.

209. Kagoshima Foreign Language Center, Dai Ichi Seimei Bldg. Zenkan, 4-1 Oguro-cho, Kagoshima 892; tel. 0992-23-6824. 3 foreign teachers.

210. Okinawa English Center; 900, Okinawa-ken, Naha-shi, Izumizaki 1-11-12; tel. 0988-61-1487. 3 foreign instructors. Okinawa is an island about 500 miles south of the mainland with a large American military presence.

SAPPORO AND NORTHERN JAPAN

211. IAY; 060, Sapporo, Chuo-ku, Minami Ichijo 4-chome, Hinode Bldg.; tel. 011-281-5188. 19 foreign teachers. Large school with wide variety of classes.

212. English Circles/EC; 060, Sapporo, Chuo-ku, Minami Ichijo Nishi 5-chome, President Bldg. 3F; tel. 011-

221-0279. 10 foreign teachers in Sapporo's largest and oldest English school.

213. Nihon Business School; 001, Sapporo, Kita-ku, Kita Rokujo Nishi 6-chome; tel. 011-717-7751. 4 foreign teachers. Emphasis on vocational English.

214. Nihon Business Sogo Semmon Gakuin; 060, Sapporo, Chuo-ku, Odori Higashi 1, Odori Bus Center Bldg.; 011-241-8311. 5 foreign teacher. Vocational English classes mostly.

215. Berlitz, Sapporo Bldg. 9F, Nihon Seimei, 4-1-1 Nishi, Kita Sanjo, Chuo-ku, Sapporo 060; tel. 221-4701. All foreign teachers (11). See earlier description of Berlitz.

216. Hokkaido International School, 41-8 Fukuzumi, Toyohira-ku, Sapporo 062. Not an ESL school. Generally hires only experienced instructors with teaching credentials for its general junior high and high school curriculum.

217. James Eikaiwa; 980, Miyage-ken, Sendai-shi, Chuo 3-3-10, Chuo Sogo Bldg. 5F; tel. 0222-67-4911. All foreign teachers (19) for general classes.

218. Sendai American School, 1-28 Tsuchitoi 1-chome, Sendai-shi, Miagi-ken 980. Generally hires only experienced instructors with teaching credentials for its general junior high and high school curriculum.

219. Tohoku Gaikokugo Gakkoo, Chuo 4-2-25, Sendai-shi, Miagi-ken 980; tel. 0222-67-3847. 13 foreign teachers emphasizes conversation for vocational training.

220. Nihon Business School; 980, Sendai-shi, Higashi Kyuban-cho 122; tel. 0222-99-1641. 1 foreign teacher.

221. New Day School; 980, Sendai-shi, Kokubu-cho 2-15-16, Company Bldg. 5F; tel. 0222-65-4288. 16 foreign teachers specialize in children's classes.

222. Akita Eikaiwa School; 010, Akita, Nakadori 3-1-9, Kanda Bldg.; Tel. 0188-33-4843. 2 foreign teachers in small school.

223. Fukushima Eigo Gakuin, 9-29 Moriai-cho, Fukushima 960; tel. 0245-35-5670. Primarily grade school and junior high school-age students. 1 foreign teacher.

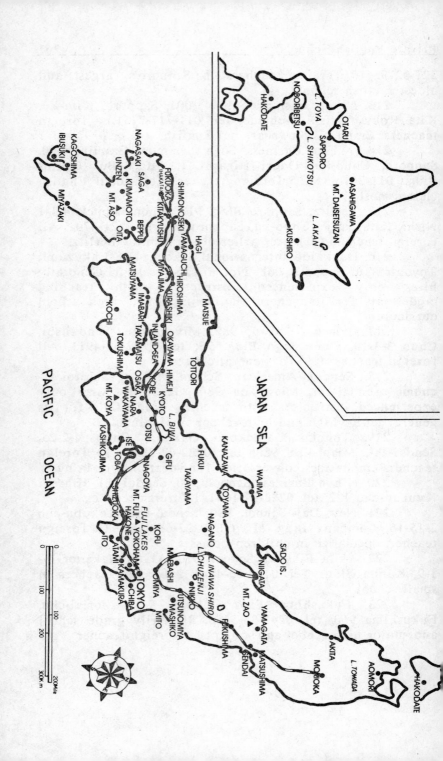

JOBS IN JAPAN
TEACHING SUPPLEMENT

If you're serious about teaching English in Japan, you'll want a copy of John Wharton's supplement to <u>JOBS IN JAPAN</u>--for teachers only!

In the <u>TEACHING SUPPLEMENT</u>, you'll learn the professionals' classroom exercises, games and strategies, guaranteed to make you a better teacher. And, you'll be given an expanded list of dozens of additional private English schools, many not listed anywhere else.

You'll be better prepared when you walk into the classroom on your first day of teaching. You'll know just what sort of students to expect, what their motives are for learning and what their reactions to you are likely to be as you teach them your language.

Intended for professional educators and newcomers to the field alike, the <u>TEACHING SUPPLEMENT</u> explains the many different types of formal English instruction while also sharing valuable tips with teachers wishing to establish their own classes and lucrative tutoring sessions.

If you're looking for a thorough overview of in Japan, order the perfect complement to <u>JOBS IN JAPAN</u>. The <u>TEACHING SUPPLEMENT</u> will give you the foundation you need in conversational English instruction to *get* and *do* the best teaching job possible! Just $4.95.

NOT AVAILABLE THROUGH BOOKSTORES!